Distant Neighbors
in the Caribbean

DISTANT NEIGHBORS
IN THE CARIBBEAN

*The Dominican Republic and Jamaica
in Comparative Perspective*

RICHARD S. HILLMAN *and*
THOMAS J. D'AGOSTINO

Foreword by HOWARD J. WIARDA

New York
Westport, Connecticut
London

Library of Congress Cataloging-in-Publication Data

Hillman, Richard S.
    Distant neighbors in the Caribbean : the Dominican Republic and
Jamaica in comparative perspective / Richard S. Hillman and Thomas
J. D'Agostino ; foreword by Howard J. Wiarda.
        p.   cm.
    Includes bibliographical references and index.
    ISBN 0-275-93927-8 (alk. paper)
    1. Dominican Republic—Politics and government. 2. Jamaica—
Politics and government. I. D'Agostino, Thomas J. II. Title.
F1938.H55   1992
972.92—dc20   91-37746

British Library Cataloguing in Publication Data is available.

Library of Congress Catalog Card Number: 91-37746
ISBN: 0-275-93927-8

First published in 1992

Praeger Publishers, One Madison Avenue, New York, NY 10010
An imprint of Greenwood Publishing Group, Inc.

Printed in the United States of America

The paper used in this book complies with the Permanent
Paper Standard issued by the National Information Standards
Organization (Z39.48—1984).

10 9 8 7 6 5 4 3 2 1

To the people of the Caribbean,

in the hope of reducing distances

Contents

Maps, Figures, and Tables

MAPS

FIGURES

TABLES

Foreword

Explaining the causes of differences between countries on the basis of their political culture, which had a long history in political science and was given renewed sophistication and an empirical methodology in the 1960s, was largely set aside in the 1970s. Under the impact of Marxian theory, dependency analysis, and the emphasis on structural factors, explanations from political culture were critiqued as tautological, static, and lacking explanatory power. But in recent years political culture has been revived as an explanatory device — particularly when used in a sophisticated way and when combined with other important factors. Among the prominent scholars leading this renaissance in political culture studies are Harry Eckstein, Samuel Huntington, Ronald Inglehart, Lucian Pye, Myron Weiner, and Aaron Wildavsky. To this distinguished list must now be added the names of Richard Hillman and Thomas D'Agostino.

The year 1992 is the quincentennial of the discovery of the Americas by Columbus. Although the debate swirling about this event is intense, no one doubts that Columbus' encounter with the New World fundamentally changed the face of the globe. The discovery and colonization of the Americas gave rise to the field of cultural anthropology, enormously expanded our horizons, marked the first large-scale encounter between the Western and the non-Western worlds, fueled the industrial revolution in Europe, and led to colonialism and imperialism among other things. Yet with all the hooplaw and controversy about the discovery, the fate of the islands Columbus discovered has never been clear. How does one study them and where do they fit in political science? That is the focus and remarkable accomplishment of this intriguing study by Hillman and D'Agostino.

Heretofore, studies and knowledge of the Hispanic Caribbean and the English-speaking Caribbean have been strictly segregated. One group studied the Hispanic Caribbean, the other the English Caribbean. There was little connection between them; their social and political processes, based on separate histories and political cultures, were assumed to be mutually exclusive. But how then can one explain the similarities in countries with diverse cultural heritages, such as the Dominican Republic and Jamaica? Can we develop an approach that, while building on cultural studies, also transcends language and historical differences, focuses on the similarities as well as differences between countries, and presents a sophisticated, multicausal explanation? That is precisely what professors Hillman and D'Agostino succeed in accomplishing in this book.

The authors begin with a discussion of the differences between the Spanish- and English-speaking Caribbean. The differences derive not just from language but from history, religion, law, sociology, and politics. But we need also to account for the remarkably similar dilemmas of development that both share. Hillman and D'Agostino seek to bridge these issues by using not only political culture but also modernization theory, corporatist theory, and dependency analysis. They seek to build bridges among these explanatory paradigms and thus to arrive at a full and complete explanation rather than a monocausal one, which is all any of these individual theories, by itself, can provide. The authors' comparison of the Dominican Republic and Jamaica is interesting not only in itself but also because it carries important theoretical implications: how divergent histories and sociopolitical traditions produce comparable developmental dilemmas and situations.

Hillman and D'Agostino have a three-part focus: the influence of political culture, the role of sociopolitical institutions and processes, and the policies these factors produce. They have an excellent analysis of the political culture variables, showing how political culture, while not determining political modalities, does influence and shape them. But they also emphasize the importance of overarching structural factors: geography, colonialism, the elimination of the indigenous populations on both islands, underdevelopment, emigration, and other factors. The authors skillfully weave these diverse strands together into an elegant, multicausal explanation of Dominican and Jamaican underdevelopment.

The book analyzes nicely the distinct aspirations, values, and attitudes that derive from the quite different colonial powers of Spain and England. It shows how past political evolution and emergent nationhood created particular patterns of legitimacy, stability, and change that shape contemporary politics in both countries. The book points out the evolving and case-specific features of each country while also emphasizing the parallels between them: the plight of small, weak, resource-poor insular countries in the modern world.

The authors advance a sophisticated analysis, based on both cultural and structural factors, of the differences between the two countries. They examine the presidential tradition of the Dominican Republic and the parliamentary or Westminster tradition of Jamaica, and suggest how and why the parliamentary tradition has been more conducive to democracy. They examine the different cultural traditions and the organizational differences of the armed forces and police in the two countries. They explore the ramifications of the Dominican Republic having a history of caudilloism and the differences with Jamaica. Religion and religious institutions have also played distinct roles in the two countries as have the law and the legal system.

The similarities, however, are at least as important as the differences. In both countries, political elites manipulate the mass populations. In both, race and class factors are clearly correlated. Both countries are cast in dependency relations vis-à-vis the outside world and particularly with regard to the United States. In both, the state plays a leading and guiding role; in neither are politics and administration strictly separated. Both countries are dominated by personalism in politics; in both clientelism and patronage provide the ingredients that grease the wheels of government. In short, Hillman and D'Agostino are concerned with showing how underlying structural similarities in an Hispanic and an Anglophone country — even with their vast cultural differences — are manifested in strong and common functional realities.

This is a very well written and analytically sophisticated book. Its overall focus is political change in transitional societies. Specifically, it wrestles with the complex issue of how and why distinct traditions have nevertheless produced similar developmental outcomes. Fortunately for thoughtful readers, professors Hillman and D'Agostino deal with these issues at the complex, multicausal level that they deserve rather than from the overly simplistic point of view of the several single causal explanations that have been advanced in the field of comparative politics in recent years.

As Hillman and D'Agostino weave these strands of multicausality together, they give the book an innovative and persuasive methodological originality, and they also articulate a larger message. The authors present a unifying vision of Caribbean politics. They recognize full well the distinct cultural influences coursing through the Caribbean, but they also detect parallel problems and, often, parallel responses. They recognize the persistence of traditional patterns in both societies, but they also see how in the Dominican Republic and Jamaica traditional and modern features are being reconciled, bridged, and fused. Even with their persistently distinct traditions, the two societies here analyzed have developed converging interests. Professors Hillman and D'Agostino see a present and future hybridization of the two cultures and a focus on common, interrelated themes.

What is nicely done in this book, therefore, is not just a methodological breakthrough and a superb analysis of two political systems, but a clear-eyed vision of the future as well.

Howard J. Wiarda
University of Massachusetts at Amherst

Preface

When Christopher Columbus landed in the West Indies, he set in motion an extraordinary chain of events in human history. Subsequent European colonization of the Caribbean, beginning with the island of Hispaniola and extending to Jamaica and other islands, literally changed the world.

In the quincentennial anniversary of the arrival of Columbus, the status of these islands is, and long into the future will continue to be, an important focus for scholars and policymakers. Although Caribbean countries have been treated in some respects as more distant from each other than from the United States, they are truly close to each other in ways that reach beyond geographic proximity. Differences separating them have tended to obscure significant similarities.

By integrating knowledge of Hispanic and Anglophone societies in the Caribbean, this comparative study of the Dominican Republic and Jamaica is intended to contribute a novel approach to a body of literature on comparative politics in which the analysis of Latin American and Commonwealth countries has been practically mutually exclusive.

Increasingly specialized scholarship has concentrated either on Spanish-speaking countries to the exclusion of the English-speaking countries and other parts of the Caribbean or on the English-speaking countries to the exclusion of the rest. This study comparing and contrasting a Caribbean state having a Spanish heritage with one having an English heritage seeks to enhance our understanding of the region in general.

The few studies that include references to the various cultures of the Caribbean do not analyze them within the context of a comprehensive definition of the region. The authors of this book define the Caribbean as a subregion of Latin America that includes every state within an area understood in geopolitical terms as the "circum-Caribbean." However, this grouping is derived less from strategic considerations than from the strong underlying similarities in countries with diverse cultural origins. Thus, certain social realities in the former British, Dutch, French, and Spanish colonies form a basis for an inclusive conception of the Caribbean. The South American and Central American states with coastal boundaries on the Caribbean Sea are as much a part of this vision of the region as are the Greater and Lesser Antilles.

Defining the region in this way emphasizes the importance of developing a comparative perspective that transcends linguistic and cultural barriers. Hopefully, such a perspective will contribute to the comprehension of, and empathy with, the political transformation taking place in the institutions, processes, and policies in the Caribbean and other developing areas and will generate insight into the most effective and mutually beneficial ways for the developed world to interact with the Third World.

The original idea for a comparative study of Hispanic and Anglophone Caribbean nations was conceived in a National Endowment for the Humanities seminar on contemporary Latin America held at the University of Washington in 1981. At the seminar, Richard Hillman presented a paper that outlined an initial comparison of Jamaican and Cuban political cultures. After eight years of intellectual gestation, the idea to study Spanish- and British-based political systems was reborn as a result of vibrant dialogue generated in a course taught by the authors on Caribbean politics.

The Dominican Republic and Jamaica are logical choices as the subjects of this study for the authors, whose interests and experiences coalesced in a study tour prior to the 1990 election in the Dominican Republic. As guests of the Iberoamerican University (UNIBE) in Santo Domingo in March 1990 for a week-long seminar on Dominican politics, the authors were able to interview major political figures and analysts. This experience and Richard Hillman's previous work, which includes interviews with principal Jamaican political leaders and scholars, provide the foundation for this collaborative effort.

Moreover, the apparent problems within the Dominican electoral process raise questions about the consolidation of democracy in the Caribbean. Jamaican parliamentary democracy appears to offer an excellent contrast that would reveal and illuminate the necessary conditions for participatory institutions in the Caribbean. But, as the following pages demonstrate, this highly complex comparison does not lend itself to facile conclusions.

Acknowledgments

This book is the product of many sources of support for which the authors are deeply grateful. Richard Hillman expresses his appreciation to the Fulbright Scholars program and to the National Endowment for the Humanities. Thomas D'Agostino acknowledges the support provided by the Maxwell School of Syracuse University. Both authors are thankful to the Iberoamerican University in Santo Domingo for providing the setting in which many important contacts were made.

While interviews with political leaders and scholars are listed in the bibliography, we also appreciate the testimony of many other citizens of the Caribbean whose commentaries provided much food for thought about island communities for which their affection is obviously profound.

The early recognition and definitive support of Praeger Publishers enhanced the publishing process in ways that made it enjoyable and fulfilling. The secretarial assistance of Lin Mocejunas facilitated production of a manuscript in half the time it would have required without her dedicated participation.

We also wish to acknowledge the participation of John Bogdal, who contributed the various maps that appear in the text, and Howard J. Wiarda, for his words of encouragement as well as his contribution of the Foreword.

The patience and understanding of our wives and families as they endured countless numbers of hours of our immersion in this project is appreciated probably more than they realize.

While the book is the result of many sources of information and support, its authors are responsible for its contents.

MAP OF THE CARIBBEAN

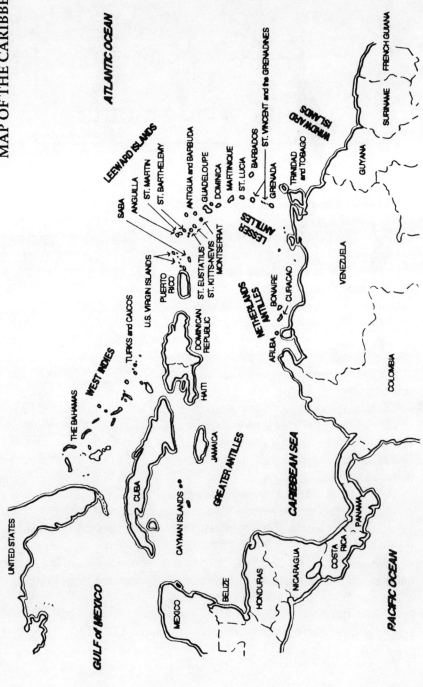

Distant Neighbors
in the Caribbean

1

Introduction:
A Comparative Approach

Thirty years ago, Kalman Silvert's exhortation to study Latin America as a distinct academic area challenged the prevailing assumption that analysis of a geographic area characterized by such a high level of social, economic, and political diversity would neither produce useful information for businessmen or policymakers nor yield meaningful generalizations for scholars (Silvert 1966).

Since Silvert's initial discussion of the utility in understanding the similarities inherent in the internal dynamics and external influences on these diverse countries in the Western hemisphere, the academic field has flourished. Scholarship on Latin America has been abundant, and the area has emerged as one of the most important in academia. Corporate planners, political analysts, and policymakers now avail themselves of the various disciplinary approaches as well as of the multidisciplinary literature on Latin America.

Over the years in which Latin America has evolved as an area of concentration within comparative political science, theories about the nature and function of political systems within the region have produced generalizations that transcend profound political and cultural differences. Nevertheless, there has been a strong tendency to segregate analysis of subregions within the Caribbean.

This segregation is clearly illustrated in the large volume of work that has been conducted on the Caribbean area. Until recently, very little mention was made regarding interrelationships or similarities between subareas of the Caribbean. Some authors include Caribbean sections in their studies but focus entirely on the Latin countries (Fitzgibbon and Fernandez 1981; Needler 1983). Others explicitly exclude chapters on the former British, French, and Dutch colonies in the area "for reasons of space" (Wiarda and Kline 1985).[1] Significantly, there are those who recognize historical linkages but do not include analyses of all the subregions (Hayes 1984).[2] One very recent text, with chapters on Cuba, Puerto Rico, and the Dominican Republic, included short paragraphs on the British Caribbean, the French Caribbean, and the Dutch Caribbean in its Caribbean section. In this context the author states that "a visit to any of the British Colonies and ex-colonies showed how distinct their politics and culture were from Latin America" (Cockcroft 1989:232).

While the Hispanic countries within the Caribbean have been considered an integral part of Latin America and are therefore included in virtually all analyses of the area as a whole, the English-speaking Caribbean countries generally have been excluded for what superficially appears to be obvious reasons. It has been argued that the Anglo-Caribbean really consists of countries whose cultural heritages are sufficiently distinct from those countries in the Hispanic Caribbean to require a fundamentally different analytical framework than that employed in the study of Latin America. For this reason, a significant book on the area asserts that most previous studies have tended to emphasize either the Hispanic or the Commonwealth sector. Indeed, Latin American scholars focus on the Latin Caribbean "often to the almost total exclusion of other areas" while Commonwealth Caribbean scholars "have usually neglected the Latin Caribbean" (Millett and Will 1979:xxi).

Reaching beyond the academic literature, "a clear dividing line has separated the English-speaking Caribbean countries from their Hispanic neighbors" (Serbin 1989:146). Another author concludes, "to a large extent, conflict in relations between the Commonwealth Caribbean and Latin America has been the result of misconceptions, misunderstanding and lack of communication ... deriving from historical, cultural, racial and linguistic differences that have also colored the mutual perceptions of both groups of countries" (Bryan 1988:41). Consequently, neither trade nor cultural and technical exchange has evolved in spite of the states' geographic proximity. However, recent studies suggest that a significant convergence of mutual economic and political interests warrants the promotion of improved relations between the diverse Caribbean states.

In the field of comparative politics, there have been few attempts to bridge the gap in the academic literature that continues to separate the English-speaking countries from the Spanish-speaking countries of the Caribbean. This book is designed to remedy that situation by comparing and contrasting the political systems of two important Caribbean nations, one with an Hispanic tradition and one with a British tradition. It is intended to contribute a vision of the Caribbean that we believe has great significance in understanding basic underlying similarities in political behavior. The groundwork for this approach is found in several inclusionary studies of the region (for example, Amburdsley and Cohen 1983; Henry and Stone 1983; Stone 1985; Lewis 1985; Domínguez 1987; Heine and Manigat 1988; and Knight 1990).

Our analysis also offers insight into the problems faced by developing nations undergoing the difficult transition toward modernity. This is particularly relevant in an era of democratization and economic integration.

Recently there has been much debate regarding the status of comparative political analysis as a subfield within the larger discipline of political science. A brief look at the evolution of comparative research reveals the mounting diversity and fragmentation many scholars have identified (for example, Apter 1965; LaPalombara 1968; Wiarda 1985a; Lange 1990; Dogan and Pelassy 1990). This lack of unity and cohesion, simultaneously lauded and lamented by various comparative practitioners, has far-reaching implications for the future direction of the discipline. Insofar as our study endeavors to compare two distinct Caribbean nations, we must recognize and come to terms with the state of comparative analysis as it exists today.

While the comparative study of politics has a long and hallowed tradition, our primary interest here lies in the profound transformations occurring in the field during the post–World War II era. Prior to the 1940s, comparative research focused almost exclusively on the developed nations of Western Europe and the United States. In addition to being essentially parochial in focus, comparative studies in this period have been criticized for their legal-formalistic approach, for being static, and for being excessively descriptive and hence, noncomparative (Wiarda 1985a).[3] World War II proved to be a watershed period in the evolution of the field because the emergence of numerous former colonies into independent nationhood turned the collective attention of comparative scholars toward these newly developing areas.

As the scope of the comparative discipline expanded to include the non-Western areas, a number of additional advances were prompted that merit discussion.[4] Greater emphasis was placed on the study of informal processes and institutions, reflecting disillusionment with the overly formalistic study of constitutions, governmental structures, and electoral systems that had traditionally dominated the field. Further, scholars became increasingly sensitive to the dynamic nature of politics, and their research sought to explain the changes visible in the developing world.

Finally, the introduction of a variety of new techniques designed to promote scientific rigor led to a heightened level of methodological sophistication within the discipline. Advanced quantitative methods and elaborate approaches to survey research reflect the movement toward making political science increasingly scientific.[5]

In light of the calamitous events that shook the world in the years preceding World War II, comparative politics in the 1950s and 1960s focused on stability and gradual, orderly change. The field was dominated by a single integrating theory, political development or modernization, and research in the non-Western areas was guided by this all-encompassing paradigm. As the United States attained its hegemonic position in the postwar global order, scholarly interests closely paralleled foreign policy objectives of promoting democratic political development throughout the Third World. These methodological advances facilitated the evaluation of the relationship between socioeconomic modernization and democracy. It was widely believed, both in academia and government, that the developing areas would follow the same stages of growth from traditional to modern as had the industrialized nations of the West. The motor propelling this transition would be rapid economic growth.[6]

The dominance of the political development–modernization perspective is clearly manifested in the comparative literature of the 1960s (Almond and Coleman 1960; Almond and Verba 1963; Apter 1965; Huntington 1968). Soon, however, works that sought to identify factors explaining the relative underdevelopment of the Third World, as well as the perceived linkages between economic expansion and democratic political development, came under intense criticism. Huntington (1968) rejected this linkage, suggesting instead that rapid socioeconomic development was destabilizing and caused political decay. Many pointed out that the concepts and categories employed in these studies were derived from experiences in the industrialized Western nations and were therefore largely inapplicable in less developed Third World societies with radically different traditions and cultures.

Moreover, the emphasis in this literature on stability and orderly change, on the need for modern institutions and processes, and on the "dysfunctional" nature of traditional institutions has been widely criticized as being ethnocentric and biased. Critics argued that Third World nations could not possibly replicate the development patterns of the early modernizers of the West because of the very different international environment they faced, as well as the timing and sequence of the problems confronting their governments (Wiarda 1985a; Klarén and

Bossert 1986). Finally, the implicit assumption in the development literature that all societies would pass through a series of universal stages along a linear continuum from traditional to modern was widely rejected. It was seen as further evidence of the inapplicability of Western social science assumptions to Third World realities.

Although the critiques of modernization theory and the political development literature abounded, it was some time before a viable alternative approach to the study of Third World nations appeared. With the decline of the field's dominant research paradigm, a process of fragmentation was initiated, and scholars pursued disparate, unintegrated efforts at general theorizing (LaPalombara 1968). In the wake of the widespread rejection of the Western development model, social scientists were forced to reexamine many of the basic assumptions and concepts in their disciplines in order to apply them to studies of the developing world.

The emergence of theories of international dependency relations in the 1970s represents, in part, the product of this retooling process. Based to a large extent on Marxist interpretations, the dependency perspective was critical of the overemphasis on endogenous factors in previous approaches in explaining the social, economic, and political development (or underdevelopment) of Third World nations. Further, in so heavily emphasizing the importance of value changes in stimulating the development process, modernization theory neglected the inherent structural constraints of economic and class relations (Klarén and Bossert 1986:307–10). Dependency theorists held that the underdevelopment of Third World nations was directly attributable to their peripheral status and role as primary commodity suppliers in the international economic order. According to this approach, dependent economic status produces a profound political impact that serves to exclude the masses through the repression of popular mobilization.

Despite its attractiveness as an alternative explanation of development patterns among Third World nations, dependency theory was not elevated to the status of an all-encompassing paradigm in the comparative field. Modernizationists were criticized for overemphasizing endogenous factors in their explanations; dependency theorists relied primarily on exogenous factors. Nonetheless, dependency theory gained a substantial following, particularly among Latin American scholars seeking answers to the perplexing state of underdevelopment in the region. The work of Frank (1967, 1969), Cordoso and Faletto (1969), dos Santos (1970), and others demonstrated how this theoretical perspective could be applied to Latin America. The popularity of the dependency approach did not insulate it from criticism in its specific application to the Latin American context. In deemphasizing internal domestic variables, dependency analysis was perceived as being insensitive to the great diversity in levels of development, cultures, and political systems within the region.

Alternative approaches to dependency theory emerged in the comparative political field as scholars sought to uncover a possible successor to modernization theory as a dominant paradigm. Both corporatism and bureaucratic-authoritarianism gained prominence as viable alternative approaches to the study of development, specifically within Latin America. The rise of these alternatives stemmed from the mounting dissatisfaction with what were broadly perceived to be inappropriate, alien models (modernization and dependency) and the realization that Latin America must be evaluated in its own indigenous terms. Indeed, many researchers suggest that it is best to engage in theorizing at the culture-area level, assuming that regional commonalities would facilitate generalizations across national boundaries (Wiarda 1985a:6–7; Dogan and Pelassy 1990). The proliferation of alternative theories of Latin American development, as evidenced by the rapidly expanding literature, demonstrates the potential value of the pursuit of regional theories. In addition, the abundance of approaches and lack of unity among Latin American scholars parallels the situation in the comparative field as a whole.

Many scholars doubt that an all-encompassing approach will ever be found. Wiarda has suggested that "we should accept the fact there is no longer a single, overarching paradigm on which all or even most students in the field can agree" (Wiarda 1985a:209; Diamond, Linz, and Lipset 1989:xiv). Opinions vary as to the implications of the increasing fragmentation, diversity, and seeming disarray within comparative politics. There are those who emphasize the negative connotations associated with these characteristics, pointing to the tendency to undermine unity among scholars. They believe the lack of consensus on a set of guiding concepts and common theories greatly inhibits the accumulation of knowledge. Quite to the contrary, some point to the diversity and proliferation of alternative theoretical approaches as a "sign of health and vigor" (LaPalombara 1968; Maisel and Cooper 1978). Beyond the dominant theories referred to above, many subtheories, offshoots, and minor theories make contributions to the literature as well. For example, the theory of competitive pluralism (modifying polyarchy) and various leadership theories (including charismatic leadership) are useful analytical constructs. In essence, the great variety of research topics and theoretical frameworks is an indication that the discipline is continuing to evolve.[7]

What implications does the current state of comparative political analysis have for the future course of the discipline? If analysts in the years following World War II were overly theoretical and subjective to the exclusion of objective analysis, in recent years they have placed a greater emphasis on empirical studies (Klarén and Bossert 1986:322). In 1968, LaPalombara sought to remedy the imbalance in comparative studies by calling for a "partial systems" or "segmented" approach to research. He envisioned studies of institutions and processes that would yield "a set of theoretical propositions relating the segment of the total system that constitutes the focus for empirical scrutiny" (LaPalombara 1968:61).

Comparative political analysts in the 1980s have similarly recommended that research concentrate on more limited and manageable topics in the hope of generating some middle range theories firmly based in empirical study. Developing linkages between existing "islands of theory" represents a viable direction for future comparative research (Wiarda 1985a). Established theoretical approaches, such as corporatism, dependency and Marxism, and modernization would guide research in subareas including political party analysis, voting behavior studies, and public policy evaluation. Such empirical work would constitute a solid foundation on which to base efforts at integrating diverse theoretical frameworks into a more cohesive whole, thereby striking a balance between empiricism and theory.

The focus of this book is on the status of comparative research on Latin America. Comparative studies of the region, while abundant, manifest the same lack of cohesiveness and clearly defined focus that characterizes the field as a whole. With no dominant theoretical orientation or guiding paradigm, comparative research in Latin America has produced a wide variety of concepts, typologies, and alternative approaches to the issue of development. These alternatives have emerged as a reaction against the imposition of Western-based models, yet they have generally been offshoots of theoretical concerns in other areas and have their intellectual origins outside the region. Latin American scholars have adapted these approaches to fit their interests. In our estimation, a solid theoretical foundation has been established that can facilitate future growth in what Wiarda has labeled a "Latin American Social Science of Development" (Wiarda 1985a:145).

In evaluating the dominant theories of change and development in Latin America, Klarén and Bossert contend that "although the different approaches have competed with one another as major means of describing and explaining the development processes, they also build on one another" and contribute to a process of "incremental growth in theory" (1986:304). Such a process would stem from efforts to synthesize and integrate existing theory in the manner in which O'Donnell (1973) developed the bureaucratic-authoritarianism model. An eclectic construct, this theory drew on the most salient aspects of previous attempts at general theorizing to explain the trend toward democratic decay and military intervention in South America during the late 1960s and early 1970s. Although some of the basic premises behind this theory have come under attack (thus prohibiting it from attaining paradigm status), this type of effort to synthesize and promote theoretical convergence could provide the basis for future advances in the field.

Similarly, major theorists in the field of comparative analysis consider the future direction for research to be eclectic combinations of earlier approaches and more recent alternatives. Comparative political analysts should strive to unite the existing islands of theory by reassessing and refining these approaches with new insights. As one author concludes, "we see such bridge building efforts as the next major step forward in comparative politics" (Wiarda 1985a:210).

A FRAMEWORK

In more ways than one, this book seeks to build bridges between diverse and heretofore separate and distinct islands. Given the variety of existing and useful theoretical approaches, it would be difficult to justify selecting one to the exclusion of other viable and worthy alternatives.[8] Therefore, in developing a framework to guide our analysis, we have evaluated several approaches and assessed their relative strengths and weaknesses.

This framework will draw on the most salient aspects of existing theories, recognizing the inherent limitations of each and making use of complementary approaches to overcome those limitations. For example, we agree with Dogan and Pelassy (1990) that functionalism is a useful theoretical framework in showing how political systems perform similar functions through different structures or use similar structures to perform different functions. However, we do not limit our analysis to structural functionalism or to any particular variant thereof.[9] Moreover, we make no claims to have produced a new revolutionary general theory. The framework employed in this book is eclectic, facilitating a descriptive and explanatory study with potential theoretical implications. It is designed to contribute to the convergence and incremental growth in theory building.

We will illustrate through comparison and contrast that the politics, policies, and problems of Jamaica and the Dominican Republic are not as dissimilar as is commonly believed. Although the comparative study of these two nations is fascinating in and of itself, there are also theoretical reasons for understanding how divergent systems have resulted in comparable situations. In addition to integrating elements from the various islands of theory into our framework, this book will provide a research bridge between two real Caribbean islands that generally have been considered too different to merit serious comparison.

In what ways do the most prominent theoretical approaches in Latin American studies lend themselves to the analysis of substantive areas? Conversely, what are their respective shortcomings? Although there is long-standing and widespread criticism of the developmentalist-modernization school for its ethnocentrism and Western bias, certain of its contributions are useful analytical devices. In discussing the impact of socioeconomic modernization in transitional societies, proponents of this theory stress the evolution of value patterns as critical to future political development. Further, the focus on the expanding middle sectors as key elements in this evolution gives insight into the effect of rapid change on values, reevaluates the question of legitimacy, and also suggests insight into the social structure, patterns of inequality, and other cleavages.[10] Many scholars attribute the almost exclusive treatment of internal factors in explaining the developmental problems of Latin American nations as a major fault in modernization theory. However, the study of the patterns of change associated with modernization (urbanization, industrialization, increased education, increased technology, and media sophistication) and their impact on social and political institutions is particularly relevant, because it has significant bearing on the question of stability.

Dependency theorists writing in the 1970s suggested that exogenous variables, including international market forces and worldwide recession, cannot be ignored in interpretations of the state of underdevelopment in the region. Although the dependency approach was derived to a large extent from Marxist class analysis, it was adapted to fit local conditions. This perspective provides insight into the social structure, class relations, prospects for economic development, generation of political outputs to meet demands, and international linkages. Whereas dependency theory offered much in terms of external explanations and analysis, it provided little in the way of discussion on endogenous factors. Although modernization theory did stress a variety of internal variables, the assumptions made explicit in the theory were routinely questioned.

Corporatist theory rejects the imposition of foreign models in the analysis of developing nations in Latin America. It represents an indigenous alternative that is firmly rooted in local culture, and it finds its origin in Iberia circa 1500. The appeal of corporatist theory lies in its sensitivity to the unique background and patterns of sociocultural evolution in Latin American nations. However, even avowed corporatist advocates are quick to note that this approach, while essential to understanding Latin American societies, is not in and of itself an exclusive explanation. It must be coupled with and supplemented by other perspectives. Moreover, its Iberian origins appear to suggest a cultural specificity inimical to our objectives in this study of culturally divergent Caribbean states.

Corporatism makes explicit the nature of the linkages between the state or governing apparatus and civil society. The term "corporatism" can be applied to "any comprehensive set of relationships in which the major interests in society have been brought into a formal, specified set of exchange relationships with the state" (Wiarda 1985a:61). It is a method of organizing society that seeks to structure represented interests hierarchically in a position subservient to the state. New social groups are integrated into the existing political culture and system structure under elite tutelage and direction, thereby perpetuating the status quo through gradual accommodation and change, as well as through the persistence of paternalistic, patron-client relationships.[11]

Corporatist theory, like modernization theory, is concerned with both values and structures. However, where modernization advocates saw traditional institutions (kinship patterns, extended family, and patron-client networks) as backward, dysfunctional, and major obstacles to development, corporatist advocates point to the flexibility, adaptability, and persistence of these traditional institutions as a sign of their viability. Such institutions are particularly important during periods of intense modernization and rapid change because they serve as a means of mediating class antagonisms and conflicts through formalized structures. Moreover, corporatist structures modify the development of class-based organizations, although they may tend to hide underlying class tensions. Rather than becoming completely overwhelmed by the impact of modernization, some traditional institutions have survived and proven to be "remarkably resilient, persistent, and long-lasting" (Wiarda 1985a:131). Most importantly, where the formation and development of modern institutions (parties, unions, and pressure groups) has been problematic, they have helped maintain some level of organization and therefore promote stability.[12]

On the basis of these theoretical considerations, we have divided the analytical framework into three major substantive areas. Given the divergent heritages of Jamaica and the Dominican Republic, we believe that cross-national comparisons are facilitated through analysis of political culture, institutions, processes, and the policies they produce. First, we will explore political culture as it derives from the set of political beliefs, feelings, and values that prevail in a nation at a given time. Political culture filters perceptions, determines attitudes, and influences modalities of participation. Analysis of colonial histories, the process of achieving independence, and the difficulties faced in nation building enhance our understanding of political culture.

The study of political culture, currently enjoying a resurgence in the comparative political analysis field, generates insight into national values, the question of legitimacy, dominant cleavage patterns, and a variety of informal aspects of politics that can often yield as much of an understanding of the political process in Third World countries as the study of formal processes and procedures (Lange 1990). It is in the study of informal aspects of politics that the theory of corporatism is useful in explaining the dynamics of traditional relationships between subgroups and the state. Similarly, the ways in which these relationships have evolved over time may be understood in terms of certain aspects of modernization theory.

As a complement to the informal setting for politics discussed under the rubric of political culture, we will include an analysis of formal procedures, such as elections and formal institutions, such as constitutions, electoral systems, political parties, executives, and legislatures. Like the study of political culture, the comparison of institutions is also returning to prominence. This type of analysis will emphasize system inputs in terms of how institutions aggregate and articulate interests and demands as well as of how the populace is integrated (if, and to what extent, it is integrated) in the political process. The nature of governmental tasks and functions will be addressed, as will an evaluation of how the political system operates in the formal sense.[13]

Because the severe economic crisis plaguing the developing areas is important, particularly in Latin America, the final section will assess public policies and political outcomes. In contrast to the focus on system inputs above, this section will look exclusively at political output production and distribution by the state.[14] In this section, dependency theory offers explanations of structural economic imbalances and asymmetrical political relationships that are useful in our analysis. Because external influence has been a crucial determining factor throughout Jamaican and Dominican history, foreign policies and international relations merit consideration. Understanding how effective government policies can be in satisfying demands, in concert with the study of values and legitimacy, is valuable in addressing the issue of regime change. Moreover, governmental responsiveness to the needs, aspirations, and demands of its citizens is an extremely important consideration in comparative analysis. As a result, the interrelated nature of political values, behavior, processes, institutions, and policies is drawn into sharp focus.

In sum, our framework incorporates selected elements of the various islands of theory and employs them in the analysis of three interrelated substantive areas — political culture, political institutions and processes, and public policies. The attention to historical experiences required in this approach has made us keenly aware of the dangers of imposing alien concepts and models that have produced ethnocentric and, in some cases, judgmental conclusions. On the contrary, it is our desire to foster greater understanding of how and why Caribbean political systems operate the way they do by comparing certain aspects of their societies and political practices. Finally, we believe that the evidence generated in this study can contribute to the process of theoretical convergence.[15]

DIVERGENCES

One observer of Caribbean culture suggested that, in terms of influence, "Caracas [is] nearer to Madrid than to Port-of-Spain and Kingston nearer to London than to Havana" (Nettleford 1978:149). Another states, "The Caribbean peoples, with their distinctive artificial societies, common history, and common problems, seem to have more in common than the Texan and the New Yorker, or the Mayan Indian and the cosmopolite of Mexico City do in their respective nations of the United States and Mexico" (Knight 1978:xi). These assertions raise interesting questions. Is Santo Domingo truly nearer in the sense implied above to, for example, Caracas than to Kingston? Which of the two capitals is closer to Washington? In what ways?

Generally perceived differences in the Caribbean have obscured underlying themes of commonality. The comparative data listed in Table 1.1 illustrate this point. Jamaica's British parliamentarian system, fostered through an era of tutelary democracy along the lines of the Westminster model, stands in stark contrast to the Hispanic authoritarian tradition of the Dominican Republic, a country that has only recently embarked on a process of transformation toward the incorporation of liberal democratic institutions. The dominant cultural heritages exemplified by divergent linguistic traditions appear to further distinguish the countries. Jamaica's smaller land area encompasses an entire island with less than half the population of the Dominican Republic. The Dominican Republic shares an island with Haiti but is over twice as large as Jamaica.

Further, the Dominican caudillo tradition with its history of military involvement in politics contrasts with the nonrevolutionary tradition of

TABLE 1.1
Comparative Data

	Dominican Republic	*Jamaica*
Geography		
Area in square miles	18,712	4,244
Capital	Santo Domingo	Kingston
Climate	maritime tropical	tropical
Population		
Total	7,253,000	2,513,000
In Capital	1,700,000	104,000
Annual growth rate	2.4 percent	1.1 percent
Rural/urban ratio	45/55	52/48
Ethnic makeup	73% mixed, 16% white, 11% black	76% black, 15% Afro-European, 3% East Indian and Afro-East Indian, 3% white, 1% Chinese and Afro-Chinese, 2% other
Health		
Life expectancy at birth	61 years	65 years
Infant mortality	28.3/1,000	16.8/1,000
Religions	95% Roman Catholic	predominantly Anglican and Baptist, other Protestant, some Roman Catholic, some spiritualistic cults
Education		
Adult literacy rate	74%	76%
Communication		
Telephones	190,000 (2.6/100)	127,000 (5.0/100)
Newspapers	9 dailies;	3 dailies

continued

TABLE 1.1 continued

Transportation

Miles of highways	10,614	11,310
Miles of railroads	1,026	230
Useable airfields	31	27

Government

Type	Republic	constitutional monarchy — recognizes Queen Elizabeth II as chief of state
Independence date	February 27, 1844	August 6, 1962
Head of state	President Joaquín Balaguer Ricardo	Prime Minister Michael Manley
Political parties	PRSC, PLD, PRD, others	PNP, JLP, WPJ
Suffrage	universal and compulsory over 18 or married, except members of armed forces and police, who cannot vote	universal at 18

Military

Number of armed forces	22,800 (1984)	3,350, plus paramilitary force of 6,000
Military expenditures (percent of central government expenditures)	10.9%	1.1%
Current hostilities	None	None

Economy

Currency ($US equivalent)	12.72 pesos = US $1 (1992)	20.61 Jamaican dollars = US $1 (1992)
Per capita income/GNP	$800/$5.5 billion	$1,160/$2.9 billion
Inflation rate	over 80% (1990)	40% (1990)
Natural resources	nickel, bauxite, gold, silver	bauxite, gypsum, limestone
Agriculture	sugar, coffee, cocoa, cacao, tobacco, rice, corn, beef	sugar, bananas, citrus fruits, coffee, allspice, coconuts
Industry	tourism, sugar refining, textiles, cement, mining	tourism, bauxite, textiles, processed foods, sugar, rum, molasses, cement, metal, chemical products

Foreign Trade

Exports	$928 million	$967 million
Imports	$2.2 billion	$1.8 billion

Source: Compiled by authors.

civilian political control in Jamaica. Whereas Jamaican political parties originated in the trade union movement of the 1930s, Dominican parties began to emerge after the demise of the Trujillo dictatorship in 1961. While Jamaica has operated under a fairly stable dominant two-party system since the early 1940s, the current multiparty system in the Dominican Republic evolved as a result of fragmentation and realignment since the early 1960s. The predominance of Anglicanism and other Protestant sects in Jamaica and Catholicism in the Dominican Republic symbolizes ideological diversity that completes the popular picture of two entirely distinct countries with very little in common.

UNITY IN DIVERSITY

Analysis in greater depth, however, reveals that beneath these differences lie important similarities. They can be seen in historical perspective, in the geopolitical and underlying sociocultural context, in their common economic experiences, and in accommodation patterns deriving from parallel pressures of remarkably congruent sociopolitical environments. Specifically, patterns are evident in the colonial legacies; in the economic, political, and military roles of foreign states; and in the evolution of modern statehood.

The Dominican Republic and Jamaica were claimed by Christopher Columbus for Spain in 1492 and 1494, respectively. In both cases of early colonization, the cultures of the Taino or Arawak Indians who had inhabited the islands were destroyed. There is not much extant evidence of these indigenous populations in either country. Interestingly, Hispaniola is geologically formed by the peaks of two undersea mountain chains, one coming from Cuba and the other from Jamaica. In fact, geography has played an important role in a variety of ways. The presence of mountain ranges, fertile lowland soil, and excellent ports in strategic locations has conditioned the economic, political, and psychological development of these societies. Both countries have traditionally relied on monocultural export economies in ways that, linked with colonization, have had profound and ongoing effects. The plantation system, primarily used to cultivate cane sugar, created a bifurcated class structure along ethnic lines that has been an integral part of virtually all aspects of life, including politics, in the Dominican Republic and Jamaica.

Eurocentric values were imposed by minority immigrant populations from Europe on majority immigrant populations from Africa. The amalgamation of these two groups continues to be an underlying theme in both countries in their respective searches for cultural identity.[16] The creolization of Caribbean life is manifested in many forms. Despite differences in Eurocentric religious, social, and political modes, the syncretic belief systems (Dominican Santería and Jamaican Obeah) represent the way in which divergent cultures were integrated through a process of coexistence and amalgamation.

At some levels, counterpoint and conflict are being resolved in an historical evolution that is manifested in blended political systems. Since the early 1960s, the incipient growth of liberal democracy grafted on a firmly implanted authoritarian tradition in the Dominican Republic has produced a presidential system that operates on the basis of personalistic leadership and patron-client relationships. After independence in 1962, Jamaican parliamentarianism experimented with varying forms of reformist programs that operate on a similar basis. Therefore, while theoretically distinct, both systems appear to converge in praxis.[17] The political parties in both systems facilitate this common praxis by providing essentially nonideological organizational vehicles for clientelism and personalistic leaders.

Moreover, both countries face very similar economic problems. Virtually all of the Dominican and Jamaican political leaders and scholars interviewed by the authors emphasized the critical dimensions of the external debt, inflation, unemployment and underemployment, trade imbalances, and other economic issues. These were perceived as political challenges in developing countries that continue to urbanize and experiment with foreign and domestic investment programs. The decline in the world market value of export commodities in both countries has forced them to seek alternative sources of income. In the absence of abundant resources, both nations have turned to the development of large tourist industries.

As a result of these economic challenges, both countries have large expatriate populations that have emigrated mainly to New York and Miami. There are approximately 2 million Jamaicans and 3 million Dominicans living outside their countries. In many ways these groups constitute an economic safety valve that alleviates economic and demographic problems and also mitigates them through the provision of large remittances to families remaining on the islands.

Both the Dominican Republic and Jamaica have struggled to create economic viability and political stability with varying degrees of success. However, in their respective struggles, their self-perceptions converge in newly emerging Caribbean identities.[18] The overpowering influences and interventions by foreign states into the internal affairs of both nations have contributed unwittingly to this convergence.

In speaking of the links between the Anglophone and Hispanic Caribbean, Nicolás Guillén summarizes the convergence theory quite succinctly when he characterizes the Caribbean archipelago as one "communal yard" due to its common heritage of slavery, imperial domination, and struggle (Guillén 1976:26). In spite of the linguistic, cultural, and formal political variations that characterize the Dominican Republic and Jamaica, common themes inherent in the colonial legacies of these two Caribbean nations point to underlying similarities in comparative perspective.

COMPARISON AND CONTRAST

Both common and divergent themes deriving from the political cultures, institutions, processes, and policies of the Dominican Republic and Jamaica are juxtaposed in the following chapters in order to facilitate analysis.

This book is divided into 3 parts. Following the introductory remarks about the nature of comparative analysis, the evolution of political culture is examined in Part I, while Part II describes and analyzes formal political institutions and processes. Part III discusses informal political influences and the kinds of policies produced in both states.

Part I is comprised of two chapters treating issues of political cultural formation. Chapter 2 compares and contrasts the political cultures of the two countries in terms of their colonial legacies. The colonial periods offer insight into the nature of socioeconomic and political variables such as land tenure patterns, social structures, attitudes and values, leadership patterns, and institutions. Chapter 3 summarizes patterns that derive from colonial legacies and are manifested in the experiences of the independence and postindependence periods. Insight into cultural and historical differences and similarities, as well as political change in evolutionary and violent forms, aids in the definition of political legitimacy and stability in the two countries. Common patterns of personalistic leadership and political clientelism in what appear to be divergent systems lead to significant questions regarding the origins and functions of the specific political institutions, processes, and problems.

Part II addresses these questions with reference to the political institutions and processes that deal with the problems facing the Dominican Republic and Jamaica. In this context, Chapter 4 studies the constitutional systems, the executive and legislative functions, and the bureaucracies of the two states. In Chapter 4 the efficacy of the presidential versus the parliamentarian system in consolidating democracy in developing countries comes under scrutiny. The discussion of the impact of these types of political systems has emerged as an important consideration for political analysis, but it has suffered from a severe paucity of scholarly research (Mainwaring 1990:157). There is little doubt, however, that the types of systems that have evolved in the Dominican Republic and Jamaica have significantly impacted the nature of executive power, the relationships between the executive and legislative branches, the role of the political parties, and the patterns of legitimacy and stability. Accordingly, the respective party and electoral systems are compared in Chapter 5.

In Part III, Chapter 6 focuses on the roles of other actors such as trade unions, pressure groups, students, business associations, the military, and peasants. Chapter 7 briefly compares and contrasts the general economic and foreign policies of the two countries. Here the consequences of the previously determined patterns of political evolution appear to converge in several ways. Both the Dominican Republic and Jamaica have been challenged to develop a legitimate framework within which very serious problems of economic, political, and social inequities can be redressed. Both nations face the complex of constraints attendant upon small insular states in the Caribbean. The ways in which each attempts to resolve these issues contributes greatly to our understanding of social development and Third World politics.

The eighth, and final, chapter reviews several theoretical considerations and general observations that derive from our comparative analysis of the Dominican Republic and Jamaica. This is followed by a short discussion of the policy implications of our findings and suggestions for further research that will contribute to a more complete vision of Caribbean political realities.

NOTES

1. A chapter on Haiti is included in the third edition of Wiarda and Kline (1990).

2. The second edition of Knight (1990), an excellent historical overview of the area, has added chapters on different cultural subregions and contains references to comparative political development.

3. The earliest and most scathing critique of the field came from Macridis in 1955. In *The Study of Comparative Government*, he presents a scheme of analysis for future comparative studies.

4. Despite being commonly labeled as Western due to the prolonged period of European colonization in the region, Latin America is sufficiently removed from and distinct from the industrialized societies of northwestern Europe and North America to

warrant non-Western status. Some writers note that while Latin America was profoundly influenced by and shaped by the European colonizers, the region is an offshoot of a unique and distant time and place — Iberia circa 1500. "Latin America may be looked on as something of a mixed case, Western and Third World at the same time" (Wiarda 1985a:139).

5. This movement is commonly referred to as the "Behavioralist Revolution." Almond and Verba's *The Civic Culture* (1963) is recognized as the first large-scale survey research work in the comparative field.

6. "Westernization, industrialization, and economic growth would generate the preconditions for the evolution of greater social equality and hence, it was assumed, the rise of stable, democratic institutions. Progress, as defined by the West, would in the end transform the underdeveloped world and propel it headlong into the twentieth century and modernity" (Klarén and Bossert 1986:11).

7. Dogan and Pelassy (1990:8, 13) take the position that "comparison is the engine of knowledge" and that "international comparison will progress by correcting a series of errors progressively revealed."

8. According to Dogan and Pelassy (1990:34), "No sociologist and no political scientist involved in comparative research can avoid becoming, at a certain point, a theorist; but both should resist becoming prisoners of grand explanations that are too encompassing not to arouse doubts."

9. We further agree with the idea that comparative analysis should illuminate "the way in which various specialized political agencies have historically crystallized — executive power, legislatures, bureaucrats, courts — and to indicate which different functions could be fulfilled by similar structures in various historic, cultural, or systemic contexts" (Dogan and Pelassy 1990:41).

10. According to modernization theory, their role aids in promoting political development and stability. More recent analysis points to the middle class as ambiguous in its role, at times favoring democratic change and at others inhibiting it.

11. The clientelistic relationship implies the dependence, reciprocity, and personalization linking of two persons or groups who control unequal resources. The social or cultural conditions favorable to clientelism occur in corporatist societies where vertical structuring is likely to take place "in a historical context that is neither modern nor traditional, but typically modernizing" (Dogan and Pelassy 1990:90).

12. Wiarda (1985a:144) concludes: "Scholars should see local indigenous institutions not necessarily as dysfunctional or doomed but frequently as viable or necessary, as filters and winnowers of the modernization process, as agencies of transition between traditional and modern, and as a means for reconciling and blending the global with the indigenous, the nationalist with the international."

13. These two areas correspond to the first two of three checklists designed to facilitate crossnational analysis in Deutsch, Domínguez, and Heclo (1981).

14. This corresponds to the third checklist in Deutsch, Domínguez, and Heclo (1981).

15. According to Dogan and Pelassy (1990:129), "One specific advantage of binary analysis is the possibility of covering political life as a whole, including institutions, structures, cultures, socialization, and recruitment processes."

16. According to Michael Manley, "In our case, you're talking about the massive assault through the system of slavery on all the cultural values and systems. So there must have been a very substantial breakdown of structures. . . . I think the

only model of which they were really aware of against this destruction of indigenous cultural impulse — would be the Westminster model as brought by imperialism. . . . I suspect you are dealing with the absence of social cohesiveness because of the nature of colonialism, all the enormous displacement of the psyche and of all the institutional relationships of a naturally evolving culture and society" (Hillman interview 1978). Juan Bosch had a similar explanation of the impact of colonialism on the Dominican Republic (Hillman and D'Agostino interview 1990).

17. Both Edward Seaga and Michael Manley spoke of the "bogus election" of 1976 (Hillman interviews 1978). Juan Bosch and José Francisco Peña Gómez referred to the 1990 election as "fraudulent" (Hillman and D'Agostino interviews 1990 and television reports). This exemplifies one way in which praxis appears to converge in both systems.

18. Interestingly, each political leader in his own subtle way implied a love/hate relationship with the developed world. Seaga said the North takes a "dim view of ability in the Third World" and Manley belies resentment by stating "Jamaicans are a very sophisticated people. It's not some grimy little dive!" (Hillman interviews 1978). Bosch and other Dominican politicians reflect this same perspective when referring to the United States as a model for democratic institutionalization (Hillman and D'Agostino interview, 1990).

I

HISTORY AND
POLITICAL CULTURE

Political processes and institutions are legitimated by underlying attitudes, values, and beliefs transmitted across generations through political socialization. Thus, ideological predisposition toward one kind of government or another is influenced by a variety of factors that collectively constitute political culture. These factors include the historical context within which a nation is created, the way in which independence is achieved, the thought and expression used to translate these experiences, and geographic and economic conditions.

Understanding the dynamics of political culture is fundamental for meaningful comparison of political systems. The reasons why certain political arrangements are considered legitimate in some countries but not in others are found in the analysis of the prevailing political culture. Failure to appreciate significant similarities or differences in the cultural heritage and foundations of political systems leads to spurious assumptions about the way it operates, its potential for change, and suitable approaches to international relations.

Our analysis of Dominican and Jamaican history reveals social, economic, and political patterns that transcend linguistic barriers and sovereign jurisdictions.

2

Legacies of the Past

The following sections summarize selected aspects of colonial and contemporary history that have contributed to the formation of political culture and institutions. Socioeconomic and political factors that derive from the strong and enduring colonial legacies of the Dominican Republic and Jamaica provide insight into how each country has attempted to develop since becoming independent. Table 2.1 lists several important events in the historical evolution of these countries.

DOMINICAN ORIGINS

From the time Europeans arrived in the New World until the present, Dominican history has been characterized by the alternation of authoritarianism, anarchy, foreign intervention and control, and short-lived democracies.

Columbus, in search of gold and silver for Spain, landed on the island he named Hispaniola in 1492. There he found the ordinarily pacific Taino or Arawak Indians who, by the time the Catholic church and the Crown accepted Bartolomé de las Casas' argument that Indians were human, were almost completely decimated by war, slavery, and European diseases.

The first Spanish colony of 39 men was established in the part of the island the Tainos called Quisqueya. When Columbus returned in 1494, he found that the colony had been destroyed by a Taino leader who resented Spanish abuses. A second colony was created in the Cibao valley, but the Tainos rebelled against continued Spanish provocation in the early sixteenth century. The rebellions were led by a courageous leader immortalized in a novel that has become a Dominican classic.[1] After defeating the Tainos, Columbus left his brother, Bartolomeo, in charge of

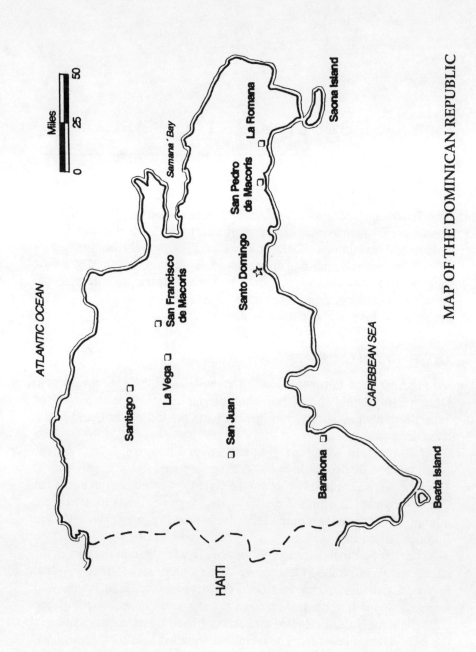

MAP OF THE DOMINICAN REPUBLIC

TABLE 2.1
Historical Evolution

Year	Dominican Republic	Jamaica
1492	Columbus	
1494		Columbus
1496	Founding of Santo Domingo (oldest European city in the Americas)	
1509		First Spanish settlement
1655		Seized by the English
1692		Port Royal destroyed by earthquake
1739		Maroons
1795	French control, slaves freed	
1802	Slavery reimposed	
1821	Independence from Spain declared	
1822	Haitian control, slavery abolished	
1834		Abolition of slavery; full freedom
1838		for former slaves
1844	Independence	
1861	Spanish protectorate by invitation	
1865		Morant Bay Rebellion, Crown Colony rule
1916	U.S. control	
1930	Trujillato	
1938		Labor unrest, unions, political parties
1944		Representative government
1958		West Indian Federation
1961	Trujillo assassinated	
1962	Political parties	Independence

Source: Compiled by authors.

the colony. He established a settlement on the south coast in 1496 that later became the capital city, Santo Domingo. Christopher Columbus' eldest son, Diego, served as governor of Hispaniola from 1509 to 1515 and as viceroy of the Indies from 1520 to 1524. With the creation of the first royal court (the Audiencia) in the New World in 1511, Santo Domingo emerged as the center of the incipient empire. This institution operated with jurisdiction over the West Indian islands and part of the mainland. The first university in the New World, founded in 1538, and the first cathedral, completed in 1544, were located in this growing city.

Santo Domingo flourished during the first half of the sixteenth century. Seeking to fully exploit the mineral and agricultural wealth of the island, the Crown introduced the *repartimiento* and *encomienda* systems to facilitate the subjugation and virtual enslavement of the Indians.[2] With the decimation of the indigenous population, the Spaniards began to import slaves from Africa as an alternative labor source to perpetuate the *latifundia* system, based on a pattern of land ownership in which large estates are owned by local gentry or absentee landlords. These owners, the *hacendados*, became an oligarchy. Their legacy has survived the transfer of wealth from early land ownership to urban, industrial elites whose power is concentrated in the modern corporate economy. The expanding slave population, along with a growing racially mixed population, eventually came to outnumber those of European descent: Hispaniola at this time was largely a plantation society with a rigidly bifurcated social structure in which the dominant, white, European minority occupied the upper levels and the mulatto and slave populations comprised the lower levels.

Ultimately, the Spaniards proved to be more interested in self-aggrandizement than colonial development. The depletion of the island's mineral wealth and source of Indian labor coupled with the discovery of massive gold and silver deposits in Mexico and South America prompted the exodus of many of the colonists. The Audiencia was moved to the mainland colonies, signalling political as well as economic decline. Once the proud symbol of Spain's Golden Age, Hispaniola was reduced to "a bedraggled way station in the Spanish colonial empire" (Wiarda 1985b:584).

Although the island had little more to offer the metropole in terms of mineral wealth, it was coveted by all of the European powers because of its strategic location. After gaining control of the western part of the island in 1697, France established a prosperous sugar-based colony called Saint-Domingue. The population of the French colony soon far outnumbered that of Spanish Santo Domingo, due primarily to the massive influx of slaves.[3] In contrast to the burgeoning western colony, Santo Domingo languished throughout the seventeenth and into the eighteenth centuries. After a mild resurgence, events in Europe compelled Spain to cede the eastern part of Hispaniola to the French in 1795.

The degradation of Santo Domingo continued because a slave rebellion against the French led by Toussaint L'Ouverture plunged the entire island into a period of great unrest. Aided by Spain, L'Ouverture's forces defeated the French, and in 1803 Haiti was established as the first independent black nation. Haitian forces subsequently invaded the eastern part of the island in an effort to seize control of all of Hispaniola. With the help of the British, Spain succeeded in reclaiming its former eastern colony in 1809. After another decade of lackluster Spanish administration, the Dominican Republic declared its independence in 1821.

This independence was short-lived, however, due to the expansionist designs of Haitian President Jean Pierre Boyer. Intent upon bringing the entire island under Haitian rule, Boyer's armies quickly subdued the Dominicans. A 22-year occupation ensued, lasting until 1844. The degradation suffered by the Spanish society at the hands of the barbaric Haitian invaders commenced a sociopsychological disposition still strongly held by Dominicans. The recurring threat of invasion from the west throughout Dominican history has been identified as a principal factor behind "a widespread desire for strong authoritative (if not authoritarian) rule" (Wiarda 1989:428–29).

In 1838, a powerful underground network of Dominican nationalists was organized by Juan Pablo Duarte. Together Duarte, Ramón Mella, and Francisco del Rosario Sánchez formed "La Trinitaria," an organization that spearheaded the movement ousting the Haitians and proclaiming independence in 1844. An attempt to establish a democratic republic, however, was thwarted by the underlying realities of Dominican society and by political opportunists seeking dictatorial control. Therefore, although de juris independence was achieved in 1844, subsequent interludes of dictatorship, Spanish protectionism by invitation, and U.S. military intervention and occupation imply a continuation of de facto dependent status. It is within this context that analysis of the Dominican historical experience proceeds through the era of Trujillo.

Despite the drafting of a constitution patterned after the U.S. model, a number of factors stultified the initial postindependence impulse for liberal-democratic government. The Dominican Republic was ill-prepared, both in terms of socioeconomic conditions and prevailing political culture for the attempted transition to democracy. The lack of institutions favoring democratic government facilitated the rise of a military style caudillo leadership. For roughly 30 years after independence from Haiti, power alternated between the rival caudillos Pedro Santana and Buenaventura Báez.[4] Both advocated protectionism and openly courted foreign powers in an effort to keep the Haitians at bay. Despite widespread public opposition, Spain annexed its former colony in 1861 and held it until mid-1865. Spain's withdrawal ushered in a period of instability and alternating leadership with Báez and Gregorio Luperón being the central political figures.

Aside from compromising Dominican sovereignty and increasing the nation's dependence upon world powers, the three decades of caudillo rule under Santana and Báez also inhibited the development of any effective political or civic institutions. As a result, an attempt to establish a reformist government from 1874–79 was largely unsuccessful, and it paved the way for the emergence of Ulises Heureaux in 1882. In the wake of economic stagnation and political chaos engendered by prolonged caudillo rule and the inability to consolidate democratic leadership, Heureaux set about establishing a modernizing dictatorship. Seeking to unify the fragmented society, Heureaux succeeded in building the nation's infrastructure, promoting economic development, and maintaining order. However, these advances did not come without cost. Over time, Heureaux's regime became increasingly repressive and autocratic, and his ambitious modernization program necessitated massive loans and other compromising agreements. This again served to compromise national sovereignty and underscored the fledgling society's dependence on external forces.

Events following the assassination of Heureaux in 1899 demonstrated the degree to which political evolution failed to keep pace with the rapid economic modernization of the late nineteenth century. Heureaux's death left a leadership vacuum that was filled by the rivalry between factions led by Horacio Vásquez and Juan Isidro Jiménez. This exacerbated the political instability and economic problems plaguing the country. A mounting external debt coupled with the desire of the U.S. government to expand its influence in the region prompted an agreement regarding the repayment of outstanding loans. Ramón Cáceres took office amidst this fragmentation in 1905, and the country enjoyed a period of relative stability, moderate reform, and some economic development until he was assassinated in 1911. The ensuing chaos and economic stagnation prompted the U.S. government to take further action to protect its interests.

The U.S. invasion and occupation of the Dominican Republic from 1916–24 can be understood in the context of the prevailing chaos and anarchy in that country, as well as the rapidly changing global environment. Economic and, subsequently, strategic interests increasingly involved the United States in Dominican affairs. At first this involvement was indirect, but when this proved untenable, it escalated to direct control of the Dominican government and the imposition of martial law by the occupying U.S. forces.

The impact of U.S. control on the Dominican Republic was profound (Calder 1984). Many of the policies, programs, and regulations implemented by the U.S. administration were clearly designed to promote strategic and business interests (Wiarda and Kryzanek 1982:33). Wiarda compares the occupation period to Heureaux's regime in terms of its "order and progress" orientation and the uninhibted use of force and repression to secure objectives. The occupation engendered an increasingly alienated population and guerrilla insurgencies, and "defensive nationalism" generated new interest and pride in Dominican culture (Black 1986:23).

Progress was achieved in terms of economic growth, infrastructural development, and the maintenance of relative stability. However, the eight-year occupation accomplished little in terms of encouraging political modernization and institution building. In essence, the United States failed to ameliorate the precise factor (the lack of established organizations and institutional processes) responsible for the anarchy and instability it sought to remedy through the occupation. Prior to the withdrawal of its forces, the United States monitored the 1924 election of Vásquez and created the Dominican National Guard. After a period of relative calm, Vásquez attempted to prolong his term, enabling Rafael Trujillo, leader of the Guard, to seize power.

For over 30 years, from 1930–61, Trujillo exercised complete and absolute control over the Dominican Republic. During this period, commonly referred to as the "Trujillato," his regime did not differ markedly from previous caudillo regimes in terms of its structure or leadership. For some time there was little evidence that it would vary from that pattern. However, political and economic power became increasingly centralized and, in consolidating its control, the regime relied more and more upon coercion, intimidation, and repression. As a result of an extensive program of economic development, the country began to transform itself from a traditional, rural agrarian society to an increasingly urban, modern one. In this sense, the Trujillato can be characterized as a transitional period in Dominican history, and the transformations initiated during this era have conditioned the subsequent evolution of the political system (Wiarda and Kryzanek 1977:422).

Trujillo's presence and charismatic leadership certainly did much to provide order and stability in a nation whose political history had been characterized by fragmentation, chaos, and intervention. Moreover, his regime initiated a protracted period of unprecedented economic growth, extensive public works, and infrastructure projects. These accomplishments account for Trujillo's immense popularity in the early stages of his reign. However, his unwillingness to accommodate the demands of an increasingly mobilized populace, particularly the newly emergent urban working class and middle sectors, ultimately contributed to his demise. The highly personalistic, authoritarian regime was no longer perceived as compatible with social and economic advances.

In the face of mounting opposition, Trujillo's response to the social and cultural changes engendered under his rule became more inflexible. In order to maintain control, the dictator chose to supplement his charismatic authority with repression designed to depoliticize Dominican society. A burgeoning, complex state apparatus and Trujillo's own Partido Dominicano (PD) served as mechanisms of control and domination. The growing opposition movement culminated with Trujillo's assassination in May 1961.

COLONIAL JAMAICA

The extenuated colonial experience (four and one-half centuries) during which Jamaica evolved from a neglected Spanish holding, to a plantocracy (a system dominated by the plantation owners) under the British empire, then to a Crown Colony, and finally to a tutelary democracy has had profound and ongoing effects on the island nation.

Columbus took possession of Jamaica during his second voyage to the New World in 1494, although the Spanish occupation did not begin until 1509. In that year, Diego Columbus, the governor general of Hispaniola, exercised his power over adjacent territory by sending Juan de Esquivel to Jamaica. As newly appointed governor, he established Sevilla Nueva on the Jamaican northern coast. Long before the arrival of the English in the seventeenth century, the Taino or Arawak Indians were brutally decimated in a manner similar to that which occurred in Hispaniola. While the island was used by Spain as a supply base, it neither prospered sufficiently nor possessed adequate precious metals to warrant special attention by the Spanish. Moreover, frequent attacks by pirates and underdeveloped settlements ultimately caused Spain to abandon Jamaica. Beyond several anglicized Spanish place names, the importation of African slaves (many of whom rebelled to form their own internal community), and the disappearance of virtually any native influence, the impact of Spanish colonial rule is nonexistent.

In 1655, an English expedition under Admiral Penn and General Venables was supposed to capture Hispaniola according to Oliver Cromwell's Western Design, a plan that involved seizing control of Caribbean islands held by the Spanish. After failing to achieve this objective in Hispaniola, the expedition sailed on and easily took Jamaica as a consolation prize by defeating the Spanish troops at Villa de la Vega. Offering very little resistance, the Spanish formally capitulated to the English in 1655, but it took another three years to expel the remaining guerrillas who held control of a fort at Rio Nuevo on the north coast. The

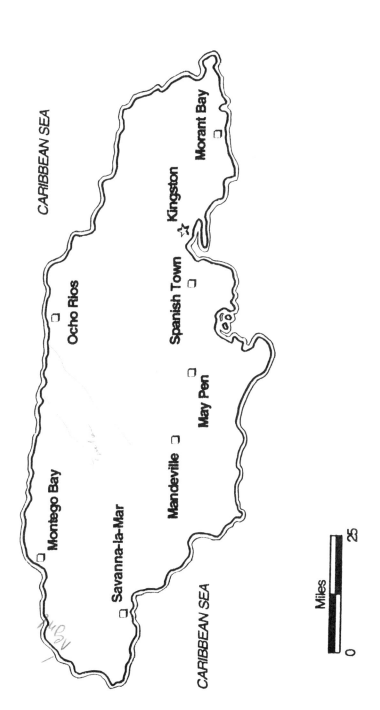

CARIBBEAN SEA

Montego Bay

Savanna-la-Mar

Ocho Rios

Mandeville

May Pen

Spanish Town

Kingston

Morant Bay

CARIBBEAN SEA

Miles

0   25

MAP OF JAMAICA

island was officially ceded to England by the Treaty of Madrid in 1670. In the interim, a group of slaves held by the Spanish fled to the hills and became known as the Maroons.[5] After an influx of British colonizers, the population spread further inland, and the Maroons began to make their presence felt. They provided refuge for slaves fleeing the new plantations and also descended from the hills at night, setting fire to the fields and stealing cattle.[6]

After an initial period of military government from 1655 until 1661, the remainder of the seventeenth century was marked by slow settlement of the island, political conflicts between the Colonial Assembly and the Home Government, buccaneer activity, and natural disasters. Colonists were granted by the king of England the rights of English citizenship, including the right to make their own laws. Under this arrangement, the governor appointed by the Crown acted with the advice of a nominated council. The legislature consisted of the governor, the council, and a representative assembly.

From 1661 until 1865, the political structure that became known as the old representative system was dominated by the governor and the council, forming an upper house appointed by the king. The lower house consisted of the elected assembly. However, the assembly represented the interests of the plantocracy and, in the nineteenth century, represented some professional and mercantile interests as well, rather than those of the general population. It is this assembly that engaged in dispute with the Home Government over financial matters.[7]

In 1728, it was determined that all English law previously used in Jamaica would continue to be "Laws of His Majesty's Island of Jamaica forever" (*Statistical Yearbook* 1986:17). Parishes similar to those used in England as local units of civil administration were transplanted in Jamaica in order to serve as a system of local government. Thus, the foundations for political participation were laid very early in Jamaican history.

Despite the prosperity brought to Jamaica as a result of buccaneer raids on Spanish territories and ships from their base in Port Royal, the growth of the English as well as the slave population was impeded by hurricanes, earthquakes, and French raids. Because large-scale plantations were able to survive these disasters, they became the most significant mode of social and economic organization by the end of the seventeenth century. The plantation in Jamaica, like the Latin American hacienda, is based on the latifundia system. Similarly, the plantocracy, like the hacendados, evolved into a landed oligarchy whose wealth was transferred to an urban industrial base.

In the early eighteenth century, Jamaica became the distribution center for Britain's newly awarded monopoly on the slave trade, and Port Royal excelled as a naval base. By the mid-eighteenth century, Jamaica's slave-based economy and society were almost entirely devoted to the production of sugar. Large plantations were owned mostly by absentee landlords or a small group of island born creoles, and Jamaica, considered England's most valuable possession, was viewed as a place to make an investment rather than as a community in which to establish ongoing social institutions.

The slave rebellions and insurrections in Hispaniola created great concern in Jamaica. The unsuccessful British intervention in 1793 in support of the French against Toussaint L'Ouverture and the difficulties with the Maroons contributed to a fear of slave revolts among the British and creole populations that were diminishing in relation to the growing numbers of slaves from West Africa.[8]

The aforementioned political problems and anxieties of the plantocracy left Jamaica prone to the machinations of the Maroons, whose initial provision of assistance to the English in defeating the Spanish was rewarded with small land grants. Later, as runaway slaves fortified the Maroon groups living in the Blue Mountains and the practically impenetrable Cockpit Country (an area in the northwest with miles of limestone caves and cavities), they increased their forays into the spreading plantations. This provoked a costly irregular war to be waged by British troops unaccustomed to the tropical environment. Although the assembly was prepared to continue the battle, the Crown authorized a treaty of peace in 1737 in which the Maroons were guaranteed full freedom, 1,500 acres with hunting rights, and a measure of sovereign jurisdiction over their own affairs. The Maroons, in return, agreed to cease hostilities and receive no more runaway slaves. Over two centuries later, small Maroon settlements in the Cockpit Country continue to maintain their state within a state. Their largely symbolic impact on Jamaican political culture resides in the fact that an honorable disposition of this conflict was reached.

The sugar economy began a precipitous decline toward the end of the eighteenth century. Coincidentally, as a result of a humanitarian movement in Europe, the British parliament began to debate the legitimacy of slavery in colonies such as Jamaica. Thus, in 1807 the parliament, despite the opposition of the plantocracy, abolished the slave trade between Africa and Jamaica. Slavery itself was abolished in 1834 and complete freedom for former slaves was declared in 1838.

As Jamaica's wealth continued to decline in the early nineteenth century, so did its importance to the metropole. Differences between the plantocracy and the home government sharpened after emancipation and grew increasingly bitter as the financial condition of the colony worsened. In the 1840s and 1850s, Indian and Chinese laborers began to arrive on the island, adding to the predominantly black and mulatto working classes. Despite the existence of a local government and legal system, landowners and their political allies abused power, and legislation was unresponsive to the demands of the workers.

This provoked disputes, reminiscent of the days of slavery, between the laborers and the plantocracy, to which the governor reacted by issuing harsh penalties against the workers. Wendell Bell states that from emancipation in 1834 until the Morant Bay Rebellion in 1865, "the Jamaican Assembly stubbornly refused to accept the new conditions, and failed to pass any legislation necessary to ameliorate the conditions of the mass of the people, the lower socio-economic-racial groups" (Bell 1964:15). These groups lived under an unrepresentative, repressive system that did not provide an effective transition for those whose legal status was changed from property to free. Thus, they perceived the manner in which they were treated by the government and the governor's harsh and unfair punishments in response to minor demands and infractions as not unlike their previous treatment as slaves.

One local dispute between the estate owners and the workers occurred in Morant Bay in 1865 when Paul Bogle, supported by George William Gordon, led a protest against a magistrate's unjust decision. The protest escalated into a riot in which Bogle was killed, and Gordon was subsequently tried and executed (both became national heroes). As a result of this rebellion in Morant Bay, the old representative system and its constitution were replaced by a Crown Colony government in which the governor was granted almost despotic power.

In 1884 a change was made permitting the election of unofficial members of the legislative council, although the electorate was still restricted by financial qualifications. This move toward the reestablishment of representative government was attempted during the governorship of Henry Morgan (1883–89). He called for the election of nine members of the legislative council, along with the five official and five nominated members. However, the governor retained his dominant authority, and the elected councilmen constituted a largely ineffectual opposition. From 1884 to 1944 very few changes occurred, although women were allowed to vote on a restricted basis in 1919.

The Crown Colony system did not encourage political activity. However, events in the 1930s introduced concerns and an emergent self-consciousness in Jamaica that led to the development of incipient nationalism. Marcus Garvey became known as a spokesman for racial pride. A worldwide economic depression caused a slump in sugar prices. Discontent over widespread poverty and workplace grievances caused a series of protests, disturbances, and riots in 1937 and 1938. Stimulated by anti-imperialist ideology, Jamaicans began to consider the potential for self-government. Changes in the value systems and conditions, not only in Jamaica, but also in England and other Western societies, contributed to the emergence of the new nationalism.

Movement toward the unionization of labor provided a vehicle for the organization of public opinion and political expression in Jamaica. Thus, trade union development served to reinforce incipient nationalism. One of the leaders of the demonstrations was Alexander Bustamante, who formed the Bustamante Industrial Trade Union in 1938 and captured the imagination of the Jamaican masses. Norman Manley, a former Rhodes scholar and a leading barrister who argued the Jamaican case for independence, formed the People's National Party (PNP) in the same year. In 1942, Bustamante created the Jamaica Labor Party (JLP), and the PNP organized its trade union affiliate, the National Workers' Union. Although there was some potential for the unification of the two groups, their division and subsequent competition provided the basis for the dominant two-party system that has functioned since 1944.[9]

For over 20 years, Bustamante and Norman Manley dominated Jamaican politics. The former's identification with the workers and latter's focus on nationalist ideology and political democracy differentiated the two leaders in every way except their personal charisma. Each became known by one group or another as the father of Jamaican independence.

With Britain's resolve depleted by many factors and with increasing assertiveness in Jamaica, a new constitution was proclaimed in 1944, under which the island regained representative government.[10] The new system included an elected house of representatives, a legislative council (partly ex officio and partly nominated by the governor), and an executive council of ten members (five chosen by the house and five by the governor). In 1953 the executive council was reconstituted providing for eight ministers selected by the house. Further progress toward self-government was made with amendments in 1955, 1956, and 1957. Jamaica became a member territory of the West Indies Federation in 1958, but withdrew as a result of a referendum held on the island in

1961, deciding to seek independence in 1962. Norman Manley's political aspirations were damaged by his support of the federation. Bustamante capitalized on his own opposition to an idea that was either misunderstood by, or unpopular with, the masses. When Jamaica achieved independence in 1962, the new constitution was modeled on the British parliamentary system.

The period between 1944 and 1962 of tutelary democratic incrementalism was facilitated by the emergence of a tourist industry, the development of the bauxite industry, the establishment of the University College of the West Indies, and the further acceptance by the international community. However, the multifaceted impact of over three centuries of colonialism still remained. Jamaican social scientists, like Trevor Munroe and Carl Stone, as well as Michael Manley in his writings, suggest that elite identification with British social and political forms and Anglomania were inevitable consequences of colonialism. Lindsay expands this argument by suggesting that Jamaicans feel cheated by a history in which they were deprived psychologically of an heroic (revolutionary) episode. According to this logic, the transition to independence was so orderly that it provided the newly privileged classes with the adopted culture of their former rulers while denying the vast majority an indigenous alternative.

TRANSITIONAL DOMINICAN REPUBLIC

Throughout its independent history, the Dominican Republic has been plagued by the inability to attain even a moderate level of organizational development and political institutionalization. Nowhere was this problem more apparent than in the immediate post-Trujillo era. As a result of Trujillo's absolute control and dominating charismatic presence, the country was left "without an alternative method" of governance upon his death (Kryzanek and Wiarda 1988:41). Attesting to the lack of institutional development during the Trujillato, one observer suggests "the country was only slightly more advanced in 1961, when Trujillo was assassinated, than in 1844, when independent life began" (Wiarda 1989:434).

Rapid modernization in the post-Trujillo era continued to alter the composition and structure of Dominican society, as well as the aspirations, expectations, and values of the populace. Given the enormous institutional and leadership void that existed, the nation's primary tasks were to integrate the newly emergent and mobilized groups into the political process and to avoid the instability typically associated with the influx of such groups into the system.[11]

It is at this point that one sees the emergence of the first truly viable Dominican political party.[12] The Partido Revolucionario Dominicano (PRD), founded by Juan Bosch while in exile in 1939, formally reemerged to present Bosch as a candidate for the 1962 presidential election. Bosch and the PRD were overwhelming victors in the nation's first competitive, democratic election. Despite this electoral success, affirming the desire of the popular sectors for a more participatory, representative system, the PRD's democratic experiment faced serious obstacles.

The greatest barrier confronting the fledgling democratic government was the intransigence of the political and economic elite. The vast majority of Bosch's electoral support came from the masses, a result of the PRD's highly successful campaign to mobilize the emerging modern classes and the lower classes traditionally excluded from the political arena. The elite, while opposed to the excesses of Trujillo, did not share the PRD's enthusiasm for widespread reform.

Whereas the PRD's electoral victory in 1962 appeared to promise an opening of the political system to accommodate the newly emergent classes, Bosch's ouster after only seven months in office underscored the lack of national consensus regarding the future direction of Dominican politics. The suppression of the PRD, the nation's most advanced democratic institution, following the coup did not bode well for the maintenance of stability. The potential for mass discontent and violence, which ultimately erupted in April 1965, was exacerbated by the increasing imbalance between the number of those seeking access to the political system and the availability of viable institutional channels to direct their participation (Lowenthal 1969:48).

Following the U.S. intervention and subsequent defeat of the pro-Bosch constitutionalist forces in the civil war, Dominicans returned to the polls in 1966. Joaquín Balaguer, candidate of the Partido Reformista (PR), easily defeated Bosch and the PRD. Having served as president during the latter stages of the Trujillato, Balaguer developed close ties to Trujillo that enabled him to inherit the dictator's enormous rural support base. Further, his conservative stance endeared him to the Dominican elites, the international business community, and particularly to the U.S. government.

Few people contest the validity of the outcome of the election itself, yet questions abound as to the legitimacy and fairness of the entire electoral process (Brea Franco 1984). The campaign period was tainted by threats and violence directed against Bosch and his supporters. Some view the 1966 contest as a "demonstration election" in light of the U.S.

military presence and the Johnson administration's unquestionable support of Balaguer.[13]

The literature on the Dominican Republic is replete with references to the parallels between the 12-year Balaguer regime (1966–78) and earlier authoritarian periods.[14] In particular, attention is focused on the continuity between Balaguer and his mentor, Trujillo. In both regimes, political power was highly personalized and centralized, with the leaders completely dominating the decision-making process. All forms of political organization, including their respective political parties and the national legislature, were subordinated to the leaders' personal power. The PD under Trujillo and the PR under Balaguer were created for specific purposes: the PD as a device for mobilization and control, the PR as an electoral vehicle and dispenser of patronage. Both provided a democratic facade, as did the ineffective and impotent legislatures. Elections, while regularly held, were not competitive and were held exclusively to legitimize the regimes and add credibility to the democratic process.

Both Trujillo and Balaguer relied to a great degree on the material benefits derived from economic revitalization programs to build support for their regimes. Bolstered by fortuitous international circumstances, these programs led to periods of sustained economic growth. In this manner, Trujillo and Balaguer were able to mollify the internal and international business communities, as well as to co-opt and effectively buy off the expanding middle classes. Moreover, investment in large-scale public works projects with high visibility proved to be an effective strategy to gain the overwhelming support of the rural populace. Thus, the longevity of both regimes derived from their success in promoting national development because it was parlayed into widespread support from a variety of sources.

The eventual demise of both Trujillo and Balaguer can be attributed to the similar responses of their regimes to rapid socioeconomic development. Rather than promote some degree of political modernization to parallel the societal transformations, both leaders practiced a politics of exclusion by restricting participation to the elite. Moreover, they each initiated a systematic campaign to demobilize and depoliticize the populace in an effort to minimize the threat of upheaval and instability (Kryzanek 1977b; Brea 1987:200–2). The use of these tactics contributed to the delegitimization of the respective leaders.

Despite the continuities that have been identified linking Balaguer to the Trujillo dictatorship and to other authoritarian periods of the past, one cannot overlook some significant differences. Unlike Trujillo, Balaguer chose to adapt his leadership style somewhat to the changing times. While the late 1960s and early 1970s were characterized by a high level of anti-opposition repression, it did not exceed what Dominican society considered reasonable bounds (Wiarda 1989:436). Moreover, the regime became more flexible and lenient over time, allowing some degree of organizational development and reducing the constraints imposed on the opposition. Whereas those seeking to oust Trujillo had no recourse but to act through extraconstitutional channels, Balaguer's opponents were able to operate within an established electoral framework to change the government.

Balaguer has been variously referred to as a "civilian" or "modern" caudillo.[15] During his 12 years in office, one begins to see the blending of democratic elements with the strong authoritarian tradition. Clearly the impetus for the introduction of such reform lies in Balaguer's realization that the evolving social context of the late 1960s and early 1970s made certain modifications necessary. Nevertheless, Balaguer's leadership style became anachronistic in the increasingly complex, transitional Dominican society.

Many scholars contend that 1978 marks the true beginning of competitive electoral politics in the Dominican Republic. After defeating Bosch in 1966, Balaguer faced minimal opposition in his bid for reelection in 1970 and again in 1974. A variety of factors prompted the PRD, which had boycotted the contests in 1970 and 1974, to resume electoral politics in 1978. As already mentioned, Balaguer became more tolerant of opposition activity, permitting greater latitude in organizational development and institution building. Most importantly, the resolution of the PRD's internal conflict regarding the party's role in the political system, culminating in the departure of Bosch, brought to the forefront those leaders advocating electoral participation (Kryzanek 1977a). With the PRD committed to electoral politics, the 1978 contest saw the conservative authoritarian leadership of Balaguer once again challenged by the forces advocating reform and participatory, representative democracy.

In an effort to appeal to a broad cross section of voters, the PRD selected the moderate Antonio Guzmán as its candidate. His overwhelming victory over Balaguer can be attributed to support drawn from the middle and upper classes attracted by his moderate positions as well as to the success of the party organization in mobilizing its traditional urban support base.[16] Aside from the immediate post-Trujillo era, the campaign period prior to the 1978 election saw the most intensive efforts to aggregate and integrate the popular classes in the nation's history. If

1962 marked the emergence of the masses on the political scene, 1978 clearly represented their reemergence.

Other factors contributed to the PRD victory. The party successfully utilized the theme of "continuismo" against Balaguer, who was seeking a fourth consecutive term. The PRD also attacked the government's human rights record and turned charges of high level corruption in Balaguer's government into a main campaign issue. Demographic trends during the 1970s, particularly massive rural-urban migration, appeared to favor Guzmán. Finally, the expansion of the middle class and the private business sector generated demands for decentralized decision making and more active participation. (F. Espinal 1987:239). With Balaguer unwilling to effect such changes, the people turned to Guzmán and the PRD.

For the first time in Dominican history, a constitutionally elected government peacefully turned over power to another. Although the PRD victory has been widely characterized as a democratic opening, the election was not without incident. Wary of the PRD's reformist orientation, the military interrupted the vote count by sequestering ballot boxes. Only after intense international pressure, mainly from the Carter administration, did the military relent. Nonetheless, Guzmán's victory was tainted by the highly conspicuous decision of the electoral commission, the Junta Central Electoral (JCE), to award five congressional seats (four Senate and one Chamber) won by the PRD to the PR. Known as the fallo histórico, this decision was clearly a compromise to make Guzmán's government palatable to the military because it gave Senate control (and the concomitant prerogatives) to Balaguer's party.

Aside from the difficulty in placating the military and domestic elite, the transition to more democratic rule under the PRD faced other obstacles. The economic crisis that plagued Balaguer at the end of his term deepened, exacerbated by the second world oil shock and low international market prices for sugar and other export commodities. The lack of adequate financial resources made it difficult for Guzmán to carry out the economic reforms sought by PRD supporters.

Moreover, the tension within the PRD's own collegiate leadership, which first manifested itself during the 1977 party convention, erupted into bitter factional rivalry between the *tendencias* headed by Guzmán and Salvador Jorge Blanco (R. Espinal 1987b:296). Jorge Blanco at times led efforts to block government initiatives in Congress. Thus, Guzmán was not only faced with an artificially imposed PR majority in the Senate, but also with members of his own party who adopted the role of opposition in the Chamber. These various factors, some internal and others external, combined to undermine Guzmán's efforts to implement policy and accommodate the demands of his diverse constituency.

In the 1982 election, the PRD sought to overcome the inherent obstacles associated with incumbency. Jorge Blanco was nominated as the party's candidate, advocating more extensive and ambitious reform programs. He also promised to extend the progress made by his predecessor in the area of human rights. With Balaguer once again the candidate of the PR, this election offered an even greater contrast between conservatives and reformists than in 1978.

Although the PRD's credibility was called into question by Guzmán's lackluster performance and charges of high-level corruption within his government, Jorge Blanco was able to defeat Balaguer. This victory affirmed the Dominican people's desire for liberal-democratic government and reflected the continued shift in values and attitudes. Yet soon after taking office, it was apparent the Jorge Blanco government would fare no better than its predecessor in implementing its desired programs. Although the PRD won a majority in both houses, Jorge Blanco faced the obstructionist tactics of a faction led by Jacobo Majluta, Guzmán's heir apparent. The resulting immobilization, coupled with a mounting debt and rapid economic decline, forced Jorge Blanco to negotiate with the International Monetary Fund (IMF) for the imposition of an economic stabilization program. The accord, calling for a reduction of the bloated state bureaucracy, new taxes, wage freezes, and price increases, sparked immediate unrest and protests. More extensive civil violence that erupted in April 1984 was quickly crushed by government forces.

The Jorge Blanco regime, which portrayed itself as the protector of human rights and purveyor of socioeconomic reform, lost credibility on both counts. Faced with excessive internal and external obstacles, the government became increasingly reliant on clientelism and corruption to maintain its support. As a result of the bitter internal disputes, the party became less democratic and more dominated by the party elite. Many scholars identify the 1985 PRD convention as the most visible sign of the party's fragmentation and deterioration (R. Espinal 1987b; Hartlyn 1987:14, 33; Oviedo 1989:49–56).

With the poor showing of the successive PRD administrations, Balaguer was able to regain power in 1986 as the candidate of his newly reconstituted Partido Reformista Social Cristiano (PRSC).[17] After a period of prolonged economic stagnation, many saw in Balaguer the opportunity to return to the days of relative prosperity known as the Dominican Miracle. Ironically, Balaguer's victory can be attributed to the resurgence of Bosch who, as the candidate of the Partido de la Liberación

Dominicana (PLD), drew a good deal of support away from the PRD's Majluta. This victory, however, should be interpreted more as a result of fortuitous circumstances than as a signal of increasing conservatism among the electorate (Penn 1986:8).

Various scholars identify this period as one of recomposition and realignment of the party system. The rise of the PLD substantiates this claim, and its emergence as a viable third alternative indicates a shift from a bipolar to a multipolar configuration. The appearance of several minor parties with the potential to gain permanence adds further credibility to this view. The party system exhibited a certain vibrancy, making the 1986 election critically important in determining the future course of Dominican politics.

Balaguer's continued popularity and Bosch's reemergence attest to the emphasis on strong, authoritative leadership in the Dominican political system.[18] While in some ways their presence has added a degree of stability to party politics, it also has tended to inhibit the emergence of alternative leadership.

Once in office, Balaguer initiated a massive infrastructure and public works program in an effort to rebuild the country. Despite insufficient financial resources, the program continued because it provided the government with support and reinforced Balaguer's clientelistic links with the rural, and increasingly, the urban masses. A sense of economic revitalization pervaded the country, based largely on a false vision of progress and prosperity engendered by new construction projects.

The most recent election, held May 16, 1990, saw the continuation of several trends emerging since 1978. First, preelection polls reaffirmed the trend toward multipolarity. Majluta's official split from the PRD to form the Partido Revolucionario Independiente (PRI) reflects further realignment of the party system. The polls also indicated the contest would be extremely close, continuing a pattern in which each election since 1978 has been increasingly competitive.

Campaigns prior to the election focused on the Balaguer government's policy of massive public spending while disregarding inflation. The political opposition attacked Balaguer for offering palliatives that have exacerbated the country's severe economic crisis. While the development of free trade zones and the tourist industry have attracted foreign investment and provided a number of low-level jobs, they have not offset the impact of indiscriminate inflationary spending. Undaunted, Balaguer vowed to continue rebuilding and characterized his candidacy as a path with no danger.

Polls indicated that the highly visible infighting between PRD factions was interpreted by the electorate as a sign of weakness and deterioration. As a result Bosch, running on a moderated platform advocating privatization and fiscal discipline to combat spiralling inflation, emerged as the primary challenger to Balaguer.[19] Majluta and José Francisco Peña Gómez, while attracting substantial support as candidates of the PRI and PRD, respectively, did not appear capable of overtaking the front runners. Peña Gómez was hindered to some degree by the racial implications of his alleged Haitian ancestry, although he remained immensely popular among the urban masses.

As in previous elections, the 1990 contest provided some indications of institutional progress and a growing sentiment for liberal democracy. The electoral process allowed for a high level of political competition within a relatively stable framework. Election-related violence was minimal. Campaigning became increasingly sophisticated through more extensive media coverage, generating a high level of awareness. A new type of ballot, the Triple Rayado, was introduced and could allow for greater representation and thereby strengthen the legislature.[20]

Finally, the emergence of several smaller parties and organizations offers potential for the continued evolution of the political system. Roberto Saladín, candidate of a coalition of small parties, Marino "Vincho" Castillo, candidate of the Fuerza Nacional Progresista, and other minor party officials indicate that their current function is to educate, aggregate popular interests, and build support for the future. They recognize as their fundamental challenges overcoming the mystique of personalistic politics and positioning themselves for future elections.[21]

Notwithstanding these positive steps, the post-election period has once again demonstrated the difficulties faced by developing nations while they attempt to consolidate democracy. The JCE, amidst charges of fraud, suspended a final proclamation during a month-long recount. Despite Bosch and Peña Gómez questioning the JCE's handling of the situation, Balaguer was eventually declared the victor by a margin of 24,845 votes. Widespread protests in the wake of the announcement, along with the threat of Peña Gómez to obstruct the presidential inauguration, indicate that the electoral dilemma has yet to be resolved.

Unlike the three previous elections in which voter participation was fairly high, the 1990 election saw a comparatively low turnout. The JCE reported the registration of only one-fourth of the potential new voters. Analysts, who attribute the low registration to alienation among the youth, see this not as a rejection of party politics but as a perceived lack of viable alternatives in this election.[22] The politics of this new generation could have a dramatic impact on the future.

JAMAICA SINCE INDEPENDENCE

Beginning in 1944 during the transitional phase of tutelary democracy and continuing after independence in 1962, the Jamaica Labor Party (JLP) and the People's National Party (PNP) have alternated roles as majority and opposition in parliament. This has been accomplished in four competitive elections prior to independence and seven since independence. While the incumbent party has been unable to sustain sufficient electoral support for more than two terms, the system has never been commandeered by alternative parties, vested interests, or the military.[23] It appears that Jamaica has become a genuinely functioning democracy, clearly distinguishable from most other Caribbean states. However, contemporary developments in Jamaica require some qualification.

Those scholars who argue that Jamaica's image as a model democracy is misleading emphasize the role of entrenched elite interests in co-opting leaders who are adept at manipulating the blind partisan loyalties of the masses in order to consolidate their influence over public policy (Edie 1991). According to Edie,

> The myth is that there is a symbiosis between the formal institutions of democracy and democratic practice. The existence of political parties, frequent elections, and representative bodies does not guarantee representative government. Indeed, Jamaican democracy has been undermined because the formal democratic organizations have been transformed into an instrument of regimentation (Edie 1991:47–48).

The electoral process can be understood as a catharsis; its sense of efficacy generates a psychic value in the electorate that belies its disproportionate representation of wealth and power. Others contend that Jamaican cultural identity is problematical. According to this view, the masses were deprived (by virtue of the peaceful transfer of sovereignty) of a nationalist revolution that they believe would have fostered the creation of uniquely indigenous institutions and a less ambiguous sense of self-identity.[24]

There has also been violence (especially prior to parliamentary elections) associated with political gangs organized to defend their supporters' access to government patronage. Both parties have gerrymandered constituency boundaries, some military officers have attempted unsuccessfully to plan a coup, and "Jamaican politics, indeed Jamaican society, is both elitist and authoritarian in its fundamental values" (Payne 1988:4). Further, it is argued that the parties, rather than aggregators of mass interests, are truly vehicles for elite control and patronage. Thus, by the time of independence "both parties were basically non-ideological, multi-class, clientelistic political machines" (Biddle and Stephens 1989:416). This system is embedded in a personalistic tradition reflected in the flamboyant rhetorical style of virtually every leading Jamaican politician.[25]

In the 1950s and into the 1960s, Jamaica's industrialization by invitation policies generated economic growth based on foreign investment. Tourism expanded and bauxite production fueled an increase in the gross domestic product. However, rapid population growth, high unemployment, and continued emigration contributed to the progressive polarization of the population according to traditional racial and class distinctions. It is in this context that the Rastafarian movement reacted to conditions of poverty and alienation among African-Americans.[26]

Many of the issues in modern Jamaican politics may be traced to origins in colonial society. Racial and class divisions, problems of the workplace, and distributive justice seem omnipresent under political regimes that have experimented with a variety of development strategies in their attempts to maintain order and stability. In the early 1960s, this was not a difficult task because independence created no abrupt alterations in a political culture defined by great continuity with the past. A republican form of government was rejected in favor of maintaining an apolitical governor general as representative of the monarchy. In fact, the same British civil servant who had served as governor general prior to independence was retained in office after 1962. This demonstrates how political legitimacy was fostered through integrative mechanisms developed over time and the cooperation of the local power structure with the imperial power.

The preeminence of two personalistic trade union leaders is directly responsible for the dominant two-party system in Jamaica. It was Bustamante, a union organizer with a powerful messianic personality, and Norman Manley, a renowned intellectual, whose leaderships of the JLP and the PNP, respectively, offered Jamaicans their initial electoral choice. Both became folk heroes. Bustamante was seen as the charismatic champion of the barefoot man, yet his appeal within the context of the existing economic system gained the support of conservatives as well.

Norman Manley, by eloquently espousing Fabian socialism, appealed primarily to middle-class liberals. In the first general elections of 1944 and 1949, the JLP and Bustamante defeated the PNP and Manley; but the PNP won in 1955 and 1959. The steady decrease in the percentage of votes cast for independent candidates and parties other than the JLP and PNP clearly demonstrated the emergence of the dominant two-party system.[27]

The dominance of the two-party structure was institutionalized in the 1962 Independence Constitution, which recognizes one leader of the opposition. Despite problems with bogus voting, gerrymandering, violence, intimidation, and victimization, elections have resulted in JLP governments in 1962 and 1967, PNP governments in 1972 and 1976, JLP governments in 1981 and 1983, and a PNP government in 1989. The PNP and the JLP formed the opposition during the terms in which they did not form the government except from 1983–88 when the PNP refused to participate, claiming that the JLP called an early election prior to the preparation of voter registration.

National identity and economic development problems have continued to challenge Jamaican society. The conflicts engendered by these issues have evoked both well-articulated intellectual responses and violent protests. In either case, a common reference was to "a history of slavery and colonialism that has inculcated habits of dependence and a sense of inferiority" (Kaplan et al. 1976:210).

Government and political patterns in Jamaica are clearly products of its past. Prior to and in the years since Jamaica was a Crown Colony, participatory institutions actively included only a small percentage of the population, excluding the vast majority from the inner circles of power. The ideological perspectives of the masses, developed through parties that were linked to unions, fostered a tendency to evaluate politics in economic terms. Their nationalism was seen largely in terms of the ability of one or the other political party to provide employment or improve the general standard of living.

Protests in the late 1960s against government policies that appeared to benefit only the elite have been understood by some scholars as part of an historical pattern in which the elite groups have refused to democratize decision-making structures (Stone and Brown 1977:12; Lacey 1977). According to this theory, these protests, the labor disturbances of 1938, and the Morant Bay Rebellion of 1865 illustrate the continuation of frustration with the inequities of a largely dual class society in which the distance between the rich and the poor has not been sufficiently narrowed.[28]

The PNP's call for change and social equity was inspired by Norman Manley, whose dynamic personality and intellect provided a real alternative to Bustamante's demagogic and authoritarian conception of leadership. Bustamante refused to define an ideological position for the JLP (his appeal was to both populist and business-oriented interests), while the PNP attempted to integrate Manley's lofty vision of social democracy.[29] When Norman Manley retired in 1969, the PNP chose his son Michael to lead the party. By then economic problems had worsened, and various groups began calling for more radical change. For example, the Abeng, a group of radical intellectuals and advocates of black power, attacked the PNP and the JLP alike for neglecting the black masses.

In the 1972 campaign, Michael Manley symbolically appealed to the Rastafarians as well as to the masses to bring an end to a decade of JLP government. Manley carried an ornamental cane reputedly given to him by Haile Selassie (to whom the Rastafarians referred as their spiritual leader), wore informal Caribbean attire in public, and used reggae music in his campaign. He thus cultivated a personalistic image geared to a society undergoing rapid change. Despite mounting economic problems, his administration was not without some successes, and Manley was reelected in 1976.[30]

Like other Third World leaders, Manley's "politics of change" articulated a strong desire for autonomy in political as well as in economic affairs. However, the government's attempted application of democratic socialist principles met with severe criticism from the right as well as from the left. Conservatives generally claimed that Manley had "gone too far" while radicals believed that he had "not gone far enough" (Hillman 1979b:396). Although Manley was twice elected on platforms that promised change, objective indices showed that progressive change in Jamaica during the 1970s was very slow and severely constrained (Duncan 1978:33; Kuper 1976:16, 34). Led by Edward Seaga, an advocate of capitalism and strong ties with the United States, the JLP was hindered by a reduction in its members of parliament. Nevertheless, Seaga's vocal opposition to socialism and attribution of Jamaica's pressing problems to economic mismanagement effectively challenged the politics of change.

In retrospect, Manley's administration based on democratic socialism failed to produce visible short-term improvements in the living standard. Despite legitimate historical antecedents, the imposition of a dynamic conception of political development on a static social order that was premised on a traditional class system was disruptive. Manley was perceived by Jamaicans as being correct in his historical interpretation of the need for change yet incorrect in his assessment of party loyalty and the time frame within which the goals of his programs could be realized (Hillman 1979b:405). However, the nature of politics in Jamaica, its development problems, and Manley's reelection indicated the need for a long-term evaluation of the politics of change. A detailed evaluation of Michael Manley's policies of democratic socialist reform suggests that despite unfavorable conditions, there were many achievements that will be long-lasting (Stephens and Stephens 1986).

Manley's PNP government from 1972–80 was one of charismatic imagery, rhetorical eloquence, and the much debated policies of democratic socialism. Seaga's JLP government from 1980–89 was based on the technocratic theme of fiscal management competence that appeared to be an explicit rejection of democratic socialism. In fact, the 1980 election was heralded by the Western press as a victory for capitalism. Manley's break with the IMF and his insistence on an independent foreign policy were replaced by Seaga's cooperation with the IMF and severance of the strong Cuban-Jamaican relationship initiated by Manley.

The development strategies of Manley and Seaga varied more in style and emphasis than in political ideology and substance. To claim, as many observers did, that their competition has been a struggle between capitalism and communism is simplistic and misleading. Seaga's approach was a blend of conservative modernism and traditional development theory that stressed monetary stability. Manley's approach may be termed progressive modernization because it emphasized reforms and called for a New International Economic Order. Manley adhered to a mixed economy, repudiated the radical wing of the PNP, and accepted electoral defeat. Manley did lead a PNP boycott of the 1983 election on the grounds that the snap election precluded sufficient time for preparation. However, far from a disruption of the system, this action can be understood as part of an overall political strategy through which Manley was reelected in 1989. Seaga remained amenable to government intervention throughout his terms in office. This is not surprising given Seaga's involvement in welfare state programs earlier in his career. Seaga was adamant on this point: "To say that the Labor Party is conservative is PNP propaganda. . . . There has been more social reform under JLP than PNP governments" (Hillman 1979a:30–31). According to Seaga, the national insurance scheme, schools, Tivoli and the Waterfront developments are examples of Labor Party reforms.

Both leaders have tried to reduce government indebtedness, reduce imports, increase exports, stabilize the Jamaican dollar, enhance the average standard of living, and make Jamaica a showcase of Caribbean development. Manley's leadership in the Non-Aligned Movement, his conspicuous role in the Socialist International, and his endorsement of democratic socialism were attempts to demonstrate independence from both capitalist and communist philosophies. Seaga attempted to make Jamaica a showcase through the Caribbean Basin Initiative and the Caribbean Democratic Union. While Manley's appeal to the masses also captured the imagination of a small segment of the intelligentsia, Seaga's appeal was directed toward the middle class. Both formulas for development, indeed both governments, were judged in terms of their perceived ability to deliver on their promises to improve the plight of the average Jamaican.

According to Edie, one explanation for the perception of government failure derives from a system in which "clientelism as political currency became more important than economic development in the larger society" (Edie 1991:77). Clearly, progress in socioeconomic development has defied governmental initiatives and is constrained by historical, structural, and natural obstacles. Manley's first term may have set in motion the "psychological and political transformation" of which he speaks. Such a transformation may have even fostered changes in social attitudes that could have a long-term impact on Jamaican society. Nevertheless, immediate economic problems appear to hold great political currency for those whose daily lives are so adversely affected (Hillman 1979b). The vicissitudes of the international economy also contribute to domestic conditions that impact directly on the Jamaican people who want immediate improvements in their daily lives. These economic realities include fluctuating commodity prices, a negative balance of trade, high public spending in nonproductive areas, minimal private productivity, currency devaluation, and the devastation caused by natural disasters.

Such conditions have resulted in a series of economic restraints under both PNP and JLP governments. While Manley attempted to glorify suffering in order to make progress, Seaga spoke of austerity. In 1985, a 20 percent increase in gasoline prices as stipulated by the IMF was met with protests and violence. The Jamaican dollar has continually been devalued, the minimum wage has been decreased to around US$11 per week, the government debt has quadrupled since the 1970s, inflation has exceeded 25 percent per year, and unemployment hovers at around 26 percent. New fiscal policies to generate revenue have been controversial. Higher taxes, particularly on luxury items, have produced verbal protests and intense lobbying. Other problems include pilfering on the farms, graft in some areas of the civil service, and cynical disillusionment regarding the illegal drug trade.[31] Jamaican life has been transformed by the magnitude of these problems, and most Jamaicans decry the erosion of the standard of living. One author notes that a "desperation and grim viciousness has crept into Jamaican politics in recent years" (Bell 1985:34).

Manley and the PNP regained the government in 1989 in a much less violent election than that of 1980, when around 800 people were killed. In 1989, the middle class abandoned its support for Seaga, and the lower classes rallied in favor of another chance for democratic socialism.[32] While Seaga's approach to development initially elicited a sympathetic response, a lack of perceived progress threatened the continuity of his government just as it had in Manley's prior regime. Manley was given two terms to deliver results, then Seaga was allowed the same. Edie concludes that the scarcity of resources for patronage that fosters such shifts in power could lead to the collapse of clientelism. This would have a destabilizing effect on the democratic system (Edie 1991:150).

Ironically, Manley's personalistic appeal was not damaged by his softened positions that facilitated yet another opportunity to govern. He deemphasized his independent foreign policy which had in the past flaunted ties with Cuba. He also indicated a predisposition to work with the IMF and multinational corporations, and sought strong ties with the United States. Manley acknowledges his own transformation and attributes it to the lessons of the 1970s.

The absence of sufficient progress in ameliorating economic and social problems convinced voters that the JLP had not initiated a viable long-term development program. Moreover, the PNP captured 10 of 13 parish councils in the 1986 local elections. These results clearly presaged the subsequent defeat of the JLP in the 1989 national election.

The promotion of patience, either through suffering or economic austerity, among people who require change in the short term is a political paradox. In Jamaica, even if the resources were available, the system may transfer power before any program has had sufficient time to produce results. As a result, the alternating images of democratic socialism and IMF capitalism promoted by individual leaders have left the creation of a viable development program an elusive problem for Jamaica.[33] While significant elements of parliamentarian democracy have deeply ingrained legitimacy in the Jamaican political culture, personalistic and clientelistic politics as well as certain attitudes traceable to the colonial past have demonstrated great tenacity. This has further exacerbated the problem of adapting the political system to the needs and aspirations of this developing nation.

The attitudes, values, and aspirations that derive from the colonial period, from past political evolution, and from emergent nationhood in both the Dominican Republic and Jamaica have created particular patterns of legitimacy, stability, and change that have shaped contemporary politics in each country. These patterns of accommodation to geopolitical and socioeconomic forces are constantly evolving.

Many patterns are specific to the precise situation in which they develop. For example, the incremental nature of the development of participatory institutions and practices in Jamaica stands in stark contrast to the alternation of authoritarianism, anarchy, and foreign control that preceded the emergence of an embryonic democracy in the Dominican Republic. However, some patterns of accommodation are similar. In what Knight (1990:58) describes as coexistent settlement and exploitation societies, "the overlapping political and economic aims of the various states were handled by a series of institutions that did not reveal fundamental differences across imperial boundaries." Later on, the employment of clientelistic politics and personalistic leadership in both cases demonstrates a kind of functional convergence, despite the obvious structural divergences inherent in emergent presidential and parliamentarian systems.

The Caribbean may be perceived as a whole, "despite the linguistic differences, the region forms one variegated culture area, no more internally diverse than India, West Africa, the British Isles, Europe, Iberia, or the United States" (Knight 1990:86). Obviously, this does not mean that there are no important differences. But, as Knight (1990:87) concludes, "it does indicate a pervasive commonality throughout the region, a commonality imposed by the long experience with the twin yokes of European imperialism and African slavery."

Chapter 3 explores the nature of social, economic, and political patterns that derive from the legacies of the past and continue to affect contemporary politics in the Dominican Republic and Jamaica.

NOTES

1. Manuel de Jesús Galván wrote *Enriquillo* in 1882.
2. The repartimiento (from the Spanish verb repartir) system permitted colonists to divide up the Indians for forced labor. The encomienda (from the Spanish verb encomendar) system, a legal device adopted in 1503, was conceived by the Spaniards to "civilize" the Indians by entrusting them to plantation owners for their labor in exchange for their spiritual salvation. It did little to mitigate the brutality of the repartimiento.

3. According to Wiarda and Kryzanek (1982:27), in 1790 the population of the French colony on Hispaniola was roughly 520,000, while the larger Spanish colony contained less than 100,000. Williams (1938:376) cites an 1824 census that claimed a population of 54,000 Spanish Dominicans, while the number of Haitians exceeded 660,000.

4. Wiarda and Kryzanek refer to this period as "The Era of the Dual Caudillos"; various Dominican writers use the term "bipartidismo caudillista." Cedeño (1986:17) cites Juan Isidro Jimenes Grullón, *Sociología Política Dominicana, 1844–1966* (vol. I, p. 31) as a source of this term.

5. "Maroon" is a word derived from the Spanish *cimarron* (wild or untamed one). The Maroon towns in the English colonies had their counterparts in *palenques* in the Spanish colonies. Knight (1990) distinguishes between *petit marronnage* (personal conflicts between masters and slaves) and *gran marronnage* (attempts to form autonomous communities of former slaves).

6. "The offer made in 1663 of land and full freedom to every Maroon who surrendered was ignored" (Black 1965:75).

7. "Local and imperial interests clashed almost without intermission" during this period (Bell 1964:13).

8. The slave population of Jamaica is estimated at roughly 40,000 at the beginning of the eighteenth century, 130,000 by 1754, and 300,000 by 1800. The European population is estimated at 9,000 in 1677, 7,000–18,000 in 1734, and 25,000 in 1787 (Kaplan et al. 1976:50).

9. There appears to be an implicit "tradition" of alternating power between the PNP and the JLP after two terms in office. However, in response to Richard Hillman's question about this historical "coincidence," Orlando Patterson, a Jamaican sociologist, flatly denied that such a tradition exists. The exchange took place at the Wilson Center in Washington, D.C., on November 30, 1983.

10. As a reaction to the labor disturbances of 1938, the Moyne Report, based on an investigation conducted by a royal commission, recommended reforms but not self-government. Its findings, however, reaffirmed the need for social and economic change. The political implications of this need became apparent in the following tutelary period.

11. See Huntington (1968) for a discussion of the problems faced by modernizing societies lacking the institutional apparatus to accommodate rapidly expanding participatory populations. With regard to the Dominican Republic, Oviedo (1986:56) notes that the period 1961–65 reflected an "intense pressure toward democratization" due to the emergence of the modern classes into the political arena.

12. Reference to "Red" and "Blue" parties of the mid-nineteenth century is misleading. These groupings were little more than the loosely organized retinues of rival caudillos competing for power.

13. For an overview of the extraordinary circumstances surrounding the 1966 election, see Herman and Brodhead (1984).

14. A number of writers contend that Balaguer's victory in 1966 began a process of authoritarian restructuring (Oviedo 1987:57, 219, 223; Brea 1987:198; Catrain 1987:272). Brea Franco (1984:22) notes that, with his electoral victory in 1966, Balaguer "reconstructed the Trujillista political model with slight modifications." Wiarda and Kryzanek (1977:428) state that "In effect Balaguer has sought to resurrect the ancient caudillistic system of the past."

15.　See Wiarda and Kryzanek (1982:48, 100; 1977:427); and Kryzanek (1977b: 103). Many others refer to Balaguer's leadership style as caudillistic.

16.　The economic stagnation which followed the boom years of Balaguer's "Dominican Miracle" caused a great deal of discontent among the lower and middle classes. The exodus of middle-class support has been identified as a principal factor behind Balaguer's defeat.

17.　In 1984, Balaguer merged his Partido Reformista (PR) with the smaller Partido Revolucionario Social Cristiano (PRSC) to form the Partido Reformista Social Cristiano (also PRSC). The merger provided Balaguer with a badly needed organizational apparatus, a well-defined set of programs, financial support, and visibility through international linkages with other Social Christian groups.

18.　Although neither Balaguer nor Bosch can be labeled a charismatic leader in the strict Weberian sense, they are referred to with a deference that attests to their exalted status.

19.　Bosch spelled out his platform to the authors in a seminar on Dominican politics held at the Iberoamerican University (UNIBE) in Santo Domingo on March 12–16, 1990.

20.　Unlike previous election procedures, the Triple Rayado allows voters to select members of different parties to fill offices at the national, provincial, and municipal levels. In separate interviews with Thomas D'Agostino, Julio Brea Franco and Flavio Darío Espinal suggested that the real impact of the Triple Rayado would not be seen until future elections. Despite governmental efforts to educate the electorate on the use of the new ballot, both analysts felt most voters would not take advantage of the opportunity to "split the ticket" in this election. However, they did recognize the potential impact of the ballot. Roberto Saladín told the authors that the new ballot would greatly benefit smaller parties by enabling them to gain representation in the national legislature. He noted that his coalition had promoted the use of the ballot and felt that their educational activities would produce immediate results in this election.

21.　These opinions were expressed in a seminar on Dominican politics held at UNIBE in Santo Domingo, March 12–16, 1990.

22.　Flavio Darío Espinal offered this view in an interview with Thomas D'Agostino on March 16, 1990.

23.　The most recent examples of failed challenges by third parties are the Communist Worker's Party of Jamaica (1978) led by Trevor Munroe and the Jamaica/America Party (1986) led by James Chisholm.

24.　Munroe (1971) and Lindsay (1975) argue that the process of decolonization led to the creation of an internal colony and the myth of independence. Analyses of the blending process within which Eurocentric and Afrocentric values and images have contended with each other in the formation of the Jamaican identity include Bell and Robinson (1979) and Nettleford (1978).

25.　This point is made in most analyses of Jamaican politics, and is very clear in Nettleford (1971) and Hillman (1979a:54).

26.　Rastafarianism, based on an emergent consciousness of the African heritage in Jamaica, symbolically repudiates a culture in which the traits of the vast majority are not considered desirable symbols of the national identity. Adherents, who maintain an antisocial appearance and remain outside the mainstream, believe the creole ideal suggested in the Jamaican motto "out of many, one people" has been vitiated by the predominance of English values.

27. The percentage of votes cast for parties other than the PNP or JLP decreased from 35.1 percent in 1944, to 13.8 percent in 1949, to 10.5 percent in 1955, to 0.9 percent in 1959. The trend has continued since independence.

28. Michael Manley characterized the Jamaican worker "as part of an economic entity that could be traced back to slavery" and the workplace as one affected by the attitudes derived from that earlier period (Hillman 1979a). Many Jamaicans' disdain for manual labor is based on their association of this type of work with slavery.

29. In reality, the parties have remained nonideological with the masses unable to understand PNP platforms and the JLP becoming increasingly pragmatic.

30. Even Edward Seaga recognized Manley's successful renegotiation of the bauxite taxes. Seaga stated, "I must give credit for the renegotiated bauxite levies." Manley pointed to changes in consciousness as an example of his success, stating that "the real transformation has to be a psychological and political transformation first . . . of that I have no doubt whatsoever . . . and we have paid a certain economic price for embarking upon that road of transformation . . . but I think we've made alot of progress" (Hillman 1979a:55).

31. The prolific work of Carl Stone includes public opinion surveys that have illuminated Jamaican responses to economic and social problems. Hillman (1979b) provides a ranking of selected problems revealing that in 1978 the single most important problem in Jamaica was perceived to be the domestic eocnomy.

32. Several of Carl Stone's surveys revealed diminishing support for Seaga in the mid-1980s. Stone Poll #12 (*Gleaner*, January 23, 1986) shows Seaga's performance as prime minister dropped from 18 percent "good" and 39 percent "poor" in March 1983 to 10 percent "good" and 50 percent "poor" in December 1985. Stone Poll #13 (*Gleaner*, January 24, 1986) shows that if an election were held then, the PNP would receive 48 percent and the JLP 27 percent as opposed to 37 percent PNP and 50 percent JLP in October 1980.

33. According to a prominent Jamaican businessperson, "Michael [Manley] is obviously debilitated by illness, and after his medical operation in England this month [August 1990] it is widely believed that he will not resume as Prime Minister. Moreover, if he resigns, P. J. Patterson would not be able to manage the government. So we [Jamaicans] really think we may see the PNP in power for only one term!" Jonathan Hartlyn's commentary on Dominican politics offers an interesting comparison. Regarding the prospects of Balaguer's candidacy in 1986, he states, "It is another indicator of the country's low level of institutionalization that so much can depend upon the health and intentions of one individual" (Hartlyn 1987:35).

3

Socioeconomic and Political Patterns

The divergent experiences outlined in Chapter 2 show how political evolution in both Jamaica and the Dominican Republic manifests an inherent tension between political cultures deeply rooted in colonial experiences and the patterns of change associated with modernization. Comparative analysis sheds light on the way this tension has shaped politics in the Caribbean.

The enduring legacy of Spanish colonial rule is visible in many facets of Dominican society. The all-encompassing impact of the colonization of Hispaniola entailed the transfer of a set of values based on absolutism, authoritarianism, and a rigid social hierarchy in which authority and decision making flowed from the top down. Accordingly, "the Spanish colonial system represented a whole way of life — political, social, military, religious, legal, and intellectual, as well as economic" (Wiarda 1989:426). These patterns reflect the corporatist nature of Spanish colonial life.

Just as Spanish values were transplanted in the Dominican Republic, British values that laid the attitudinal basis for ensuring political relationships in Jamaica permeated a colonial model. Although this system was not based on Hispanic corporatism, it produced some effects similar to those in the Dominican Republic. For example, elite domination of decision-making institutions in Jamaica derives from

Social stratification [that] can be seen in terms of three classes — usually designated upper, middle, and lower — characterized by distinctive institutional systems. Historically, they correspond to the color categorizations of white, brown and black. This has been the order of their traditional dominance and is the exact reverse of their relative numerical strength (Kaplan et al. 1976:103).

The hierarchical nature of power relationships is reflected even in the most humble Jamaican rum bars where there is invariably an area designated for important members of the local community. A high correlation between race and class is observable in this context. As pointed out by Carl Stone, the hierarchies of power, status, and wealth derive primarily from combinations of property, occupational position, and skin color (Stone 1974). Also, while the interests of the landed aristocracy were represented in dealings with the Crown (thereby mitigating the absolutism of the monarch), the vast majority of the population remained alienated from the political system until the final suspension of the Crown Colonial government.

Subsequent developments in both nations have challenged these colonial legacies, causing conflict and change. However, the initial interposition of European institutions in the Caribbean by means of the distribution and use of the land provided the fundamental basis for the creation of many enduring aspects of colonial society.

LAND TENURE AND SOCIETY

Control of the land in Latin America and the Caribbean typically translated into political power. In the early stages of nationhood, social status and wealth derived directly from the organization of agrarian economic systems. The large landed estates of the latifundia established a structure of relationships between the elites and the masses that has had continued impact. Moreover, there has been a strong tendency toward the perpetuation of racial attitudes that had their origins on the plantations.

The colonial legacy in Hispaniola is grounded in the system of land tenure established by the Spaniards. Early settlers were drawn to the island in search of mineral wealth, although many subsequently engaged in various agricultural pursuits (Hill, Silva, and de Hill 1965:211). The indigenous population was exploited as a source of cheap labor by means of the encomienda and repartimiento systems. The decimation of the Indians, who were unaccustomed to the extreme labor and vulnerable to the diseases brought by the Europeans, prompted the importation of African slaves beginning in 1503. This shift, however, did not alter the colony's rigid dual class social structure since the black slaves merely replaced the native Indians in the lower levels of colonial society. There was an unmistakable correlation between race and class, and the structure of colonial society "was reinforced by racial criteria, so that the class barriers to social advancement became virtually impossible to overcome" (Wiarda 1989:427).

With the rapid decline in the Indian population of Hispaniola, Spanish colonists became increasingly interested in land ownership. It has been suggested that "for Spaniards land became the symbol of wealth that encomienda had formerly been," creating "a new colonial aristocracy not related to the earlier conquistadores and *encomenderos*" (Gibson 1966:152). The rise of the hacienda as the primary form of land ownership perpetuated the stratification of society between white European owners and native or black African laborers. Moreover, it established land ownership as the principal source of power and prestige in the colony. The later implications of this pattern of land tenancy can be seen in the persistence of patron-client relations.

Jamaican racial and ethnic composition was similarly established through the importation of African slaves by Europeans who obtained land through the Crown.[1] In this case, the Europeans were English. But the coexistence of these two immigrant groups established, through various patterns of minority white dominance over the black majority, the basic underpinnings for the stratified class system that has subsequently manifested an extremely high correlation between race and class.[2] Despite exceptions, the social structure generally has been comprised of black lower classes, brown middle classes, and white (or very fair complexioned) upper classes.

This color or class stratification, far from disappearing with emancipation in 1838, has been the cause of ongoing alienation and protest. For example, the Morant Bay Rebellion in 1865, to which the Crown responded with the imposition of an authoritarian regime, was precipitated by the discontent with which mulattoes and blacks viewed the administration of justice by their previous masters. In fact, 100 years after emancipation, the concept of workers' rights became a basic tenet of Jamaica's democratic revolution, which was to a large extent a response to attitudes and conditions traceable to colonialism and slavery (Bell 1967). The privileged plantocracy created by colonialism was transformed into an oligarchic elite emulated by the brown middle sectors. In this way, the hierarchical pattern of society was perpetuated, albeit by different groups (Edie 1991).

The race and class correlates of the social institutions generated by the plantation systems in both countries, as well as in most of the Caribbean, are powerful indicators of attitudes and values. In the Dominican Republic and in Jamaica, the Caribbean was perceived by the Europeans as a place for the acquisition of wealth. The Spaniards and the British believed in their inherent superiority over the Indians and Africans, and thus created in the social dynamic a Eurocentricity that predominated Indo- or Afrocentric forces (Bell and Robinson 1979:249).

Much of the subsequent history of the Caribbean involves the interaction between and resolution of these conflictual forces. The extent to which this history produced an amalgamation of cultures and ethnic groups is demonstrated in various ways, always including the idea of something new or different from its constituent elements. This process of fusion has resulted in the Caribbean variant of the *raza* with its combinations and permutations in Spanish-speaking ethnic, social, and cultural forms and the counterpart Caribbean creole version in the English-speaking societies.[3] While local nationalisms within the region have inhibited political and economic integration, an affinity among Caribbean peoples is observable in the expatriate communities and may offer potential for future expression in regional affairs.

Both Jamaicans and Dominicans articulate a disdain for manual labor, reflecting a self-concept that has its origins in the colonial legacy. Elitist refusal and inability to work the plantations, along with the pejorative association of physical labor with slavery, yielded an ethos based on race, class, feelings of inferiority, and resentment of dependent status. The massive influx of Haitian laborers who cut the sugar cane that Dominicans refuse to cut, Commonwealth islanders who seek menial labor in Jamaica, and the migration of island labor in general are, in large part, products of these value structures. Coexisting with these feelings, however, is the sense of national pride that each country has developed along creole ethnic and cultural lines.

Jamaicans and Dominicans celebrate their individuality while disparaging the conditions of their states. This is apparent in the tendency toward political cynicism that has its origins in colonial societies.[4] A negative disposition evolved toward political institutions that produced policies perceived to be antagonistic to local interests. This phenomenon was characteristic of the Spanish as well as the British crowns.[5] The residual effects of such perceptions helped to reinforce greater confidence in informal political channels and personality-based politics than in the official institutional structures.[6] A heightened awareness of the limited options available to those seeking upward mobility in rapidly urbanizing societies has also resulted in alienation and cynicism.

In both Jamaica and the Dominican Republic, the traditional social structures have been altered due to the impact of rapid modernization. The emergence and growth of the middle sectors coupled with increasing urbanization and social mobilization have engendered pressures for democratization in both countries. These changes have modified class structures and transferred the locus of power from rural to urban areas, raising questions about political legitimacy.

LEGITIMACY AND CHANGE

How have the enduring legacies of colonialism that were initiated through patterns of land tenancy been challenged by the achievement of independence in the Dominican Republic and Jamaica? Have patterns of self-identification, confidence in governing institutions, and conceptions of political acceptability been transformed by the forces of modernization in the Caribbean?

In transitional societies such as those under review, attitudes and values reflecting rapidly changing socioeconomic conditions often come into conflict with traditional concepts of political legitimacy.[7] However, traditional institutions may provide a sense of stability, especially in the early stages of social transformation. Moreover, ideological change is an arduous process that requires emotional alteration as well as objective consideration of power and interest.

The manners in which political independence were attained in the Dominican Republic and Jamaica led to distinct conceptions of appropriate authority. In both countries, the late emergence of middle and urban working classes, their mobilization, and their subsequent pressure for integration into the political systems, created new forces with which the old systems could not adequately deal. In the Caribbean and elsewhere in the Third World, the effects of modernization require traditional systems to adapt to new realities. One common response to rapid change has been the blending of the old with the new, producing the hybridization of political systems (Malloy and Seligson 1987). In the cases under review, the imposition or adjustment of foreign models played important roles in the formation and evolution of political systems and beliefs.

Although the Dominican Republic and Jamaica followed very different paths in gaining independence, both paths were fraught with obstacles to the development of distinctively indigenous political institutions. While Jamaican independence in 1962 followed 79 years of authoritarianism under the Crown and 18 years of guided incremental transition, Dominican independence in 1844 was followed by 116 years of alternating subjugation to external control, internal dictatorship, and short-lived democratic experiments.

The process in which the Dominican Republic achieved this form of independence provides insight into the various obstacles that have typically confronted the nation. Although independence from Spain was declared in 1821, the Dominicans were subjected to over two decades of occupation by neighboring Haiti. This period was characterized by intense animosity because the Haitians deprecated Dominican society, the economy, and particularly the white former ruling class. The occupation has been identified as "the initial cause of the racial, social, and political antagonism that even today separates Dominicans from Haitians" (Wiarda and Kryzanek 1982:27).

The inability of Duarte and his compatriots to establish a form of democratic government after the Haitians were ousted in 1844 can be attributed to a variety of factors. First, the landholding system and social class structure militated against the establishment of democratic institutions and processes. According to one author, "a liberal constitutional framework had been superimposed on a social structure that was still cast in authoritarian molds" (Wiarda 1989:430).

Second, while a relatively strong impulse for a liberal-democratic government did exist among certain segments of the population, by no means was there a universal consensus in support of this movement. On the contrary, many felt that democracy, while an ideal to be strived for, was patently inappropriate in the post-independence Dominican context. The country had absolutely no experience in democratic self-government. It lacked strong civil institutions; and those traditional institutions that did exist (the church and the oligarchy) clearly did not advocate democratic reform, seeking rather to maintain the status quo.

With no clear precedence in Dominican history, liberal-democratic government was not considered a viable, legitimate alternative. Imbued with a strongly authoritarian political culture derived from the Iberian tradition, Dominicans favored strong, centralized leadership supported by the military. In light of the massive institutional void following the expulsion of the Spaniards and Haitians, this type of leadership was not only preferred, but perhaps necessary. This preference was reinforced by the perceived threat of further Haitian incursions and by the widespread desire to replicate the Golden Age of Hispaniola, a period characterized by a rigid class hierarchy, authoritarian leadership, and a centralized, state-dominated economy. These features were associated with a period of glory and prosperity and hence were highly valued by many Dominicans.

The inability to promote democracy early in the nation's history has had profound implications for the evolution of the political system. Those Latin American nations with the greatest success in establishing relatively stable democratic systems are those that were able "to develop and institutionalize some kind of partial, oligarchical democracy in the nineteenth century" (Diamond, Linz, and Lipset 1989:8). In the post-colonial era, most countries in the region saw the rise of a powerful alliance uniting a small landed aristocracy, the hierarchy of the Roman Catholic church, and a national military organization. With the support of the military and the church, the oligarchy was able to monopolize political and economic power. This experience seems to have paved the way for subsequent democratic evolution in some Latin American nations.

However, a tripartite alliance never materialized in the Dominican Republic because historical factors inhibited the consolidation of both a national military institution and a strong, cohesive oligarchy. Further, the church was weakened substantially prior to independence and has not attained the stature it enjoys elsewhere in Latin America. These circumstances produced a leadership void "which was filled by the continuous, virtually unchecked struggle of caudillos and their adherents" (Lowenthal 1969:53). Therefore, conditions in the Dominican Republic differed markedly from those found elsewhere throughout Latin America and did not prove conducive to intraelite competition.

In Jamaica, after an atypically early experience (for a Caribbean colony) with limited participation in government, political activity on the island was discouraged by the imposition of the Crown Colony system. However, the existence of a representative assembly that was engaged in a dispute over revenues with the home government for the first 65 years of its existence fostered a strong sense of legitimacy in participatory institutions. In this context, the transplantation of the English parish system allowed for the performance of limited social services. Despite the imposition of martial law on several occasions (usually during times of anxiety caused by the perceived potential of slave insurrection), the foundation for participatory government had been created, at least in the minds of the elite. This was not the case in the Dominican Republic.

While Jamaican elites engaged in institutionalized political processes designed to resolve the issues of the day, Dominican politics during the nineteenth century became the exclusive domain of rival military leaders. During these periods of "bipartidismo caudillista," political competition revolved around charismatic figures and their loosely organized followers (Cedeño 1986:17). These groupings are sometimes referred to as political parties, although they bear little resemblance to the traditional Liberal and Conservative parties that contributed to the institutionalization of political competition in a democratic framework found in other Latin American countries.

The limited political competition that the British parliament permitted prior to Morant Bay was suspended by those who interpreted the rebellion as a full-scale revolution. Crown Colonial status, according to a large majority in parliament, would return Jamaica to the control of a responsible authority that could prevent any repetition of the events of 1865. Far from the caudillistic authoritarianism of the Dominican Republic, Crown Colonial status in Jamaica nevertheless introduced a protracted period during which the incipient growth of limited democracy was stultified.

The former monopoly of political influence enjoyed by the plantocracy, which was now subject to the Crown, was modified further by the new demands for participation in the political processes of the island by emerging intermediary classes. From 1865–1944 the Crown suspended mechanisms through which Jamaicans could express themselves directly. During this period, changes in Jamaica produced demands for wider political participation than had been permitted under traditional elitist structures. Neither the Crown nor earlier mechanisms for political representation would be considered sufficient for the newly mobilized middle and working classes. As a result of social evolution and discontent, the new Jamaica required a different forum for political expression.

Thus, the "imperialist ideology of constructive paternalism" would be challenged by economic, social, and external forces that would lead to the labor disturbances of the 1930s (Kaplan et al. 1976). By the early twentieth century, the Jamaican economy experienced a large increase in the number of small farms, in the consolidation and amalgamation of the large sugar estates, in the growth of the banana and tourist industries, and in more external investment. Global economic depression and the threat of war limited the capacity of the political and economic systems to satisfy the heightened aspirations of the population. The resulting sense of restiveness and frustration challenged the status quo on the island.

In direct response to the labor disturbances of 1938, the British government created a royal commission to investigate conditions in the British Caribbean and make recommendations for their amelioration.[8] No such response was available in an independent Dominican Republic where external control alternated with internal cycles of authoritarian leadership and ephemeral attempts at democratic governance.

This propensity for Dominican leadership to alternate between political orientations has left the country with two conflicting constitutional traditions — authoritarianism and democracy. Despite the tendency to look to authoritarian leadership in times of crisis or instability, the democratic current has persisted and gained acceptance as part of the Dominican political culture.

Just as transformations over time in Jamaican society created the need for new political configurations, the Dominican Republic faced similar pressures for political change. The failure of the first U.S. intervention and occupation from 1916–24 to address the nation's persistent lack of viable institutions paved the way for the emergence of Rafael Trujillo. During the 30-year dictatorship, rapid economic modernization encouraged the development of intermediary classes. Trujillo's unwillingness to modify his highly personalistic style of leadership in light of such major social changes coupled with mounting demands on the system precipitated his eventual downfall. Despite the election of reformist Juan Bosch in 1962, significant political modernization was delayed by the second U.S. intervention in 1965 and by the subsequent rise to power of Joaquín Balaguer in 1966. Balaguer's electoral defeat in 1978 renewed hope for the continued evolution of democratic institutions.

As the demise of authoritarian governments in both the Dominican Republic and Jamaica illustrates, rapid socioeconomic development can have destabilizing effects. Earlier theoretical assumptions that economic growth would fuel the same transition from traditional to modern institutions that had occurred in the industrialized Western nations cannot account for the political and social dislocations within these former colonies. However, as wealth declined during various periods in the histories of both the Dominican Republic and Jamaica, their importance to their respective metropoles declined. Thus, their peripheral economic status translated into concomitant peripheral political status.

More recently, economic programs have been used to produce political support in both countries. The production of conspicuous public works as part of a patronage linkage to the masses has perpetuated control by the elite. As Caribbean economies have declined, political leadership has continued to be judged on its ability to provide visible amelioration of endemic problems. In this context, ideology and, to some extent, charisma are becoming less important than performance. From a systemic perspective, this can be understood as part of a feedback cycle that assesses the government's responsiveness to societal needs and aspirations (Easton 1966). The very legitimacy of a regime may be subject to this assessment.

In our estimation, the perception of the populace regarding the performance of a government is more important than ideology in transitional societies. While ideology may have some relevance to certain segments of the population, the masses are more concerned with everyday government performance than with an abstract belief system. The masses view performance in terms of their access to resources allocated through clientelism (Edie 1991). Similarly, while charismatic leadership is clearly an important point of reference in transitional societies, charisma is ultimately dependent upon performance.[9]

In the case of the Dominican Republic, the persistence of personalistic leadership has become a constraint to institutional development. The presence of this form of leadership is paradoxical, for while it has provided stability in the past amidst the lack of strong civil institutions, it simultaneously has created the potential for instability by inhibiting the emergence and maturation of viable institutions.[10] Similarly, elite manipulation of partisan loyalties within Jamaica's two-party system has obstructed the ability of the system to arbitrate and aggregate mass interests. Moreover, such manipulation serves to divide the masses. Despite their divergent appearances, the Dominican and Jamaican political systems have been essentially elite-dominated and exclusionary. For these reasons, the perception of elections as a democratic facade has become increasingly popular in the Caribbean.

The elite domination and clientelistic relationships that support this corporatist social and political structure, not only in the Dominican Republic, but also in Jamaica, are based on foundations laid early in history.

> The level of political legitimacy has deep roots. The rigid system of stratification, the narrow spread of mass education, and the widespread lack of group confidence among the population all combined to promote an elite leadership of Jamaican society, deriving from the educated middle classes and based on their ability to deal with the colonial masters and get things done on behalf of the masses (Edie 1991:42).

However, it is the absence of an external stabilizing agent in the Dominican Republic that led to the exertion of caudillistic power, and it is the presence of the stabilizing influence of the British Crown that led to the institutionalization of representative government in Jamaica. At the current stage of political evolution, both systems have integrated elements that derive from traditional and transitional forces. The alternation between authoritarian and democratic leadership in the Dominican Republic has given way to leadership exhibiting characteristics of both political currents; while, in Jamaica, the transition from the old representative system, through the Crown Colony phase, to independent parliamentarian government also has produced a blended political system. The hybridization of the Jamaican and Dominican political systems reflects a process of convergence that can be attributed to the societal transformations engendered through modernization.

The styles of leadership and political interaction, which derive in large part from the patterns of evolution outlined above, exhibit this convergence. The incorporation of modified aspects of caudillismo and democracy in the Dominican Republic parallels the accommodation of parliamentarianism to local conditions and transitional forces in Jamaica. In both cases political processes and behavior are innovative responses to evolving conceptions of political legitimacy. Significantly, despite differing cultural influences, these nations were propelled into the contemporary period by personalistic charismatic leaders who have, in some ways, impeded and, in other ways, accelerated the development of viable institutions.

POLITICAL LEADERSHIP

The socioeconomic patterns characterizing the early colonial period, most notably the hacienda or plantation land tenure system and the bifurcated social class structure bore major implications for the development of political leadership and institutions.

The hacienda system in Latin America was a primary factor behind the proliferation of regional caciques.[11] Typically, local plantation owners would band together for purposes of defense and the protection of their interests. One leader would emerge in control of a given area, and the local population would offer him their loyalty and support. The power of the regional caciques was potentially destabilizing because it "was very great and beyond the effective control of the central government" (Tannenbaum 1965:32).

The impact of caciquismo was profound since the lack of effective national control over the regional leaders impeded the process of national consolidation, compromised the legitimacy of the central leadership, and encouraged fragmentation. The chaos and anarchy that came to characterize Dominican society ultimately engendered national caudillo figures, particularly Heureaux and Trujillo, who sought to unify the country through strong, centralized leadership.

The pattern of local leadership in Jamaica derived, not from Hispanic caudillismo, but from a wealthy English plantocracy that felt under increasing pressure. Their shrinking numbers in proportion to the total black and mixed population and the diminishing military support supplied by a British parliament preoccupied with European conflicts contributed to this pressure. This sense of isolation on the part of rich landowners gave rise to both informal and, in some cases, formal planters' organizations in which there was a natural ascendency of leaders. These leaders gained great influence over the strategies and political positions taken by owners of plantations in various locations throughout Jamaica. They were even able to manipulate the governor, who often felt caught between the Crown and the plantocracy. After emancipation, the planters often voted "no confidence" to governors' attempts to stabilize local disputes through democratization. Most disputes were between owners and workers who were formerly masters and slaves. The territorial power of these planters' groups was similar to that of caciques.

The local leadership in Jamaica, however, was able to elicit a degree of responsiveness on the part of the British Crown that was never forthcoming from Spain in the Dominican Republic. The Dominican Republic's earlier separation from the mother country had diminished the possibility of benevolent intervention. Because the plantation owners were able to run things basically in their own way, Jamaica did not experience the political fragmentation and chaos characteristic of Dominican history. Although remnants of the plantocracy retained positions of economic and political importance, the plantation system was modified by the termination of slavery and the emergence of international competition.[12] Social and political power then shifted from the country to the city. The significance of the transformation of wealth from a land base to an urban, industrial, or commercial base resides in the ability of the traditional elite groups to perpetuate themselves. Certainly other entrepreneurial elements were added to their ranks. Nevertheless, there remain palpable distinctions between old and new money. This had both formal and informal political consequences.

Formal or legal institutional channels are subject to informal political behavior, linkages between leaders and society, and mass mobilization patterns. In developing countries, these patterns are often determined by individuals whose special abilities to communicate, relate to the aspirations of the masses, and capture the national imagination distinguish them from ordinary citizens. The capacity to mobilize public opinion is particularly significant in societies whose institutions remain in the formative stages. Similarly, the roles of myth and symbolic politics are also influential in the functioning of these systems. Caribbean political leaders are well aware of these considerations. Illiteracy is prevalent among the masses whose imagination is captured by personalistic appeals rather than by ideology or abstract theory.

Consequently, twentieth-century leadership patterns in both the Dominican Republic and Jamaica have been shaped by the conflicting influences of past traditions and new directions, the legacy of old myths and symbols, and the emergence of new alternatives, as well as by the persistence of linkages between the elites and the masses. In both countries, the predominance of several luminaries illustrates the impact of the person on national politics.[13] Attempts on the part of some contemporary politicians to create charismatic images also exemplify this impact. As Knight (1990:315) observes,

The appeal of the caudillo throughout the region should not be surprising. The colonial experience carried with it strong elements of authoritarian rule invested in governors, governors-general, and captains-general. The representative assemblies of the British territories until the middle of the twentieth century were oligarchic and, as far as the majority of the people were concerned, never truly represented their interests. The new nationalist politicians established their legitimacy by popular acceptance.

Such acceptance was contingent on the creation of personal charisma, in contrast to ideological values.

In the Dominican Republic, traditional caudillismo has been moderated by civilian leaders who have become increasingly reliant on the support of political parties. In Jamaica, the Crown Colony gave way to the emergence of charismatic leaders who institutionalized their followings in a dominant two-party system. But in each case, the personalistic leaders employed clientelistic relationships with their followers. There has been a clear tendency toward patron-client relationships in which political leaders are linked to the masses in a system that distributes employment, favors, and protection in exchange for labor, support, and loyalty. This political configuration has served to consolidate the power of elites through the use of political patronage.

The national heroes of these two Caribbean states are individuals who symbolize the struggle for independence, democracy, and social equity. Dominicans Duarte, Mella, and Sánchez formed La Trinitaria in order to promote equality and justice under a democratic regime. Jamaicans Gordon and Bogle fought for the same ideals. Garvey attempted to promote racial justice. Norman Manley and Bustamante became folk heroes in their quest for Jamaican national independence, and so did Juan Bosch in promoting democracy in the post-Trujillo era in the Dominican

Republic. In each case, the charismatic figures were able to focus authority, mobilize mass support, and preside over social change. Significantly, they emerged in transitional political cultures as champions of values that challenged traditional institutions.

Modern caudillismo in Dominican politics has been challenged by the growth of new political parties designed to offer an alternative to the patron-client system. The transfer of clientelistic loyalties from charismatic leaders to the political parties in Jamaica illustrates a similar process of transition. The difficulties experienced by contemporary politicians who have attempted to generate charisma in both countries are due, in part, to changes in the particular social conditions in which charismatic leadership emerged spontaneously in the past. Such conditions are under increasing suspicion in political cultures attempting to move toward new ideals.

Juan Bosch and Joaquín Balaguer have played major roles in the evolution of Dominican politics, and Norman Manley and Alexander Bustamante have played similar roles in Jamaican politics. More recent leaders include José Francisco Peña Gómez and Jorge Blanco in the Dominican Republic, and Michael Manley and Edward Seaga in Jamaica. It is important to recognize, however, that the commonly applied characterizations of el profesor Bosch and el doctor Balaguer as caudillos and Busta and Norman Manley as charismatic leaders — each individual to be followed by a new crop of caudillos or charismatics — require further clarification.

There is much debate on whether contemporary Dominican politicians can be truly defined as caudillos. Aside from Balaguer and Bosch, who have been variously referred to as modern or civilian caudillos because of their personalistic styles of leadership and tight control over their respective party organizations, no other current political leaders may legitimately be labeled caudillos.[14] Furthermore, none of the current Jamaican leaders truly qualifies as a charismatic leader according to the classic Weberian model.[15] But they do conform to certain aspects of these categories, and their leadership patterns represent a blending of the traditional and the modern in transitional societies. They have each risen to power and exercised authority based on a personalistic appeal and a clientelistic relationship with their supporters in political cultures characterized by the persistence of these methods.

It may be that personalism and clientelistic politics "symbolize the debilitating heritage of the Trujillo era," and the caudillistic leadership of Bosch and Balaguer represents the "basic cleavage in the Dominican polity, a cleavage based less on class than on traditional versus modern and rural versus urban orientations" (Black 1986:147). But the pattern also signals the continuing importance of the presidential office in the Dominican Republic and the persistence of authoritarian and paternalistic (as opposed to bureaucratic and institutionalized) leadership. The fanaticism of the political followers and their expectation of visible material rewards, such as massive public works and construction projects, reinforces this pattern.[16]

Michael Manley's use of symbols such as the "rod of correction," the Kareba, the appellation "Joshua," and reggae music in the early 1970s helped to create the image of one who was in touch with the changing times. However, such tactics were unable to recapitulate the heroic stature attained by earlier leaders. Bustamante, for example, was regarded by large segments of the population as a heaven-sent savior of the nation who possessed magical qualities. He was a messianic folk hero who inspired fanatical loyalty and devotion.[17] Flamboyant Michael Manley's defeat in 1980 by Edward Seaga, who was perceived as a technocrat, demonstrated Jamaicans' overwhelming desire for improvement in living conditions. Their judgment was made on the basis of perceptions of objective conditions rather than on blind allegiance.

However, in both Caribbean nations, earlier personalistic and clientelistic politics encouraged the emergence of larger-than-life heroes, the proverbial "men on horseback" who could assume responsibility for the amelioration of practical problems and the achievement of results on behalf of alienated and dependent populations. This tendency to identify with and rely on strong leaders to ensure governmental responsiveness also resulted in the perpetuation of patron-client relationships as a mechanism to institutionalize the power structure.

Unlike purely charismatic or military leadership, the clientelistic pattern does not rest entirely on the personal qualities of the ruler or the threat of coercion. In clientelistic politics, the patron acts as a broker for clients seeking material rewards. Such relationships, while providing access to the system, nonetheless reinforce the existing social hierarchy. In both the Dominican Republic and Jamaica, clientelism has evolved from its original rural agricultural base, in which the patron was the landowner, to the urban industrial base, where employers and governmental agents provide jobs and opportunities for loyal, dependent employees and followers. While allegiances to charismatic leaders have been transferred to political parties founded by the early leaders in Jamaica, a similar transformation has just begun in the Dominican Republic. Does this mean that the patronage function will be performed exclusively by political parties in the futures of both of these Caribbean states? The answer to this question may lie in the ability of clientelism to effectively respond to ongoing challenges.

ENDEMIC PROBLEMS

The socioeconomic and political patterns that have been identified in the divergent histories of the Dominican Republic and Jamaica are manifested in five general problem areas that continue to challenge the respective governmental institutions of each nation (Dogan and Pelassy 1990:107). These areas may be summarized as follows: racism and classism, poverty and economic inequity, frustration and violence, inefficiency and corruption, and external influences.

Racism and Classism

The vast majority of the populations of both the Dominican Republic and Jamaica is either African or an Afro-European admixture. Classification varies due to divergent social conceptions of race (Mörner 1970; Harris and Wagley 1958). Jamaica is generally represented as 76 percent black, 15 percent Afro-European, 4 percent Afro-Asian, 3 percent white, and 2 percent other (referring to the Chinese and East Indian descendants of the indentured workers). The Dominican Republic is generally classified as 73 percent mixed (or mulatto), 16 percent white, and 11 percent black.[18]

After the decimation of the indigenous populations early in the sixteenth century, plantation systems were organized around a foundation of African slaves in both countries. The extremely close correlation between race and class that developed as concomitants of the rigidly structured plantations continues to impact society. After the decline of the plantation economies, the European elements continued to constitute the dominant elites, the mixed groups formed the minuscule middle sectors, and blacks were relegated to the working and lower classes.

Many Jamaicans and Dominicans deny that a subtle form of racial discrimination operates in their countries. The Jamaican national motto, "Out of Many, One People," is cited as evidence that their ideal is racial harmony. Similarly, Dominicans disclaim charges of racism with references to their membership in the raza and the fact that both Heureaux and Trujillo were mulattoes.[19] Nevertheless, the correlation between social class, economic position, and race is clear in both cases; and limited access to private secondary schools and higher education for the wealthy lighter-colored population ensures its perpetuation. Privilege and access are reserved with few exceptions to those who qualify by virtue of these tradition-based criteria.

Despite the Black Power movement that impacted both Jamaica and the Dominican Republic to some extent, the degree to which feelings of superiority and inferiority have been inculcated according to racial characteristics has been profound. The Dominican animosity toward Haitians, so deep and inseparable from the racial theme that many believe it has impaired the political career of Peña Gómez, and the Rastafarian rejection of Anglo-Jamaican values are poignant examples of how racism and classism have affected Caribbean life. But it is in the daily routine and in the profound inequalities of life that one observes the debilitating effects of race and class divisions and social cleavages.

Poverty and Economic Inequity

The social structures of both states show a distribution of wealth that reflects a "have/have not" dichotomy.[20] In 1986, the per capita incomes of the Dominican Republic and Jamaica were $858 and $820, respectively. Unemployment in 1989 ranged from 20 percent to 30 percent, while underemployment was much higher. Inflation has continued to increase to between 40 percent and 60 percent. Mounting external debts, negative balances of trade, and falling commodity prices have continued to plague both countries as well. Degradation of the environment continues unabated. Garbage is strewn in the streets of Santo Domingo, and a caustic material produced as a by-product of bauxite extraction continues to be dumped in the "mud holes" of Jamaica.[21]

Poverty in the Dominican Republic and Jamaica is highly visible in urban areas. Extensive shantytowns and barrios surround and permeate Kingston and Santo Domingo. Although less apparent to tourists and businessmen, the rural areas of each country are plagued by even more profound poverty and inequality. Health and education indicators reveal the endemic nature of inequities engendered by the class dichotomy.[22] At the same time, a small group of wealthy aristocrats has continued to prosper.

Frustration and Violence

Frustration and violence are not surprising responses to economic inequality in societies dominated by elites.[23] While conflict in Jamaica has never reached the level of civil war that broke out in the Dominican Republic, campaigns and elections in both countries have been accompanied by violence. However, Jamaica has not experienced the coups that have punctuated Dominican history, and its tradition of peaceful transfer of power from one elected government to another dates back to 1944. The first peaceful transfer of an elected Dominican government did not occur until 1978.

During the late 1960s and into the 1970s, protests at the University of the West Indies in Mona, Kingston and at the Autonomous University in Santo Domingo signaled frustration with declining economies, unfulfilled political promises, and external interference. Small-scale riots and civil disorders continue to erupt intermittently into the 1990s in response to electoral fraudulence, police brutality, and austerity measures implemented by the governments of both states.[24] Studies have been conducted that document the dimensions of violence and its sociopolitical context.[25] Much of the violence has occurred in isolated incidents, although the root causes appear to be ingrained in the social and political cultures of both countries. The ubiquitous iron gratings in the windows and around the patios of Dominican and Jamaican homes are a reflection of a deep-seated insecurity generated by increasingly widespread crime. The activities of political gangs in Kingston and gun-carrying civilians guarding restaurants and businesses in Santo Domingo are other manifestations of societal malaise.

The larger scale of violence that erupted during the attempt in 1965 to reinstall the first democratically elected regime in the Dominican Republic has not led to ongoing class warfare. This is due to the magnitude of power demonstrated in the solidarity between U.S. and Dominican elites as well as to the primacy of economic development programs provided through clientelistic relationships with authoritarian leaders.

A similar proclivity toward patronage solutions to economic problems is manifested in the Jamaican penchant for rhetorical and physical violence as a demonstration of support for candidates or political parties during elections. Therefore, the disruptions and violence associated with recent elections in the Dominican Republic and Jamaica may be understood as expressions of frustration with unsatisfactory results of economic and social policies rather than as indictments of the political systems.[26]

Inefficiency and Corruption

Jamaica's civil service, while based to a limited extent on the British model, has been subject to political manipulation and inefficiency (Nunes 1974:344). The Dominican civil service, for all intents and purposes, is nonexistent. Dominicans' lack of respect for public bureaucracy is clearly reflected in the popular reference to government employees as botellas (bottles) who work in el huacal (a box for collecting empty bottles).

Public administration has been a more significant domain of political patronage in the Dominican Republic than in Jamaica.[27] However, both states suffer from bureaucratic inertia in rapidly changing societies. Political leaders have used public works programs to construct projects with high visibility in order to deliver on their promises to ameliorate problems. Balaguer has expended massive funds on public housing and projects such as El Faro, a monument to Columbus in honor of the quincentennial anniversary of the discovery of the Americas. Critics claim these policies have exacerbated inflation and serve only the interests of partisan supporters.[28] The construction of housing projects like Tivoli Gardens and Rema under the Jamaica Labor Party government and Duhaney Park, Independence City, and Arnett Gardens under the People's National Party government have created virtual partisan territories within which rival political gangs are dominant.[29]

Charges of fraud and corruption have accompanied recent elections in both countries. Manley propounds an intricate explanation of the reasons for irregular electoral procedures (Hillman 1979a). On July 16–17, 1990, there were massive disturbances and riots in Santo Domingo when, after a recount, the Junta Central Electoral (JCE) declared Balaguer the winner over Bosch by 24,845 votes. Strikes and demonstrations against government economic policies in early August 1990 erupted in sporadic violence and paralyzed the national economy. Both Bosch and Peña Gómez have challenged the results of the 1990 Dominican presidential contest on the grounds that the JCE miscounted the votes in a deal with the incumbent party. Such charges serve to reinforce the frustration and alienation felt by the masses.

External Influences

Due to the geographic location of the Dominican Republic and Jamaica in the Caribbean, the influence of the United States has been predominant in the affairs of both states. Since the Monroe Doctrine (1823), U.S. suzerainty over the Dominican Republic has been manifested in the establishment of customs receiverships, marine occupations, dollar diplomacy, and interventions. In Jamaica, U.S. hegemony has been less blatant; yet the exercise of U.S. power throughout the Caribbean has created resentment and suspicion. The United States appears to have filled a power vacuum created in the decolonization process.

Occupations by Haitian as well as U.S. forces have left a legacy of insecurity in the Dominican Republic. Thus, Dominican leaders have forfeited independence for security on several occasions. The result of their first truly democratic election in 1962 was treated by U.S. policymakers as a threat to Dominican stability and U.S. hegemony in the area. U.S. intervention in opposition to the attempt to restore a democratically elected Bosch government served to preserve the traditional order and frustrate those who sought change. A subsequent U.S. administration championed the cause of democracy by leveraging respect for the results of the 1978 election; this also demonstrated the extent to which U.S. leaders could determine political outcomes in the Dominican Republic. Whereas strategic interests motivated past interventions and manipulations, U.S. business and trade interests constitute powerful influences as well.

Similarly, the U.S. presence in Jamaican affairs has been notable since 1962. Although U.S. military troops did not occupy Jamaica, financial assistance was provided to the Jamaican Defense Forces and the Jamaican Constabulary Forces under the Military Assistance Program and the Agency for International Development Public Safety Program (Lacey 1977). Defense pacts and military treaties were also signed in the 1960s. However, the overwhelming influence of trade patterns and U.S. foreign investments on the island had the effect of creating an asymmetry in U.S.-Jamaican relations that is similar to that in the rest of the Caribbean. Given this setting, Michael Manley's claim that the United States was destabilizing his regime in the mid-1970s through a series of covert actions, obvious reductions of credit and assistance, and propaganda in the international press did not appear unfounded (Manley 1982).

It remains to be seen whether or not U.S. policy will begin to take into account the needs and aspirations of Dominicans and Jamaicans in their quests to develop mechanisms that would address indigenous problems in a changing international political environment. Meanwhile, the sovereignty of both the Dominican Republic and Jamaica continues to be compromised by increasing external debt and reliance on international mechanisms like the International Monetary Fund. Edie's (1991) dual clientelism thesis holds that external dependency fuels the domestic patronage system through the provision of resources and thereby contributes to underdevelopment.

It is clear that in neither country are representative institutions (notwithstanding their relatively different degrees of evolution) perceived as sufficiently responsive to endemic problems and changing attitudes. Therefore, subsequent sections of this book analyze the nature and function of formal and informal political institutions in the two Caribbean states.

NOTES

1.   In the seventeenth and eighteenth centuries, the foundations of the plantation production and social systems were created. A small number of planters held large acreages either by allotment or by purchase. By the eighteenth century, as wealthier planters returned to England and ran their estates as absentee landlords, it was estimated that blacks outnumbered whites in Jamaica by at least five to one (Kaplan et al. 1976:43).

2.   "Four white families — the Ashenheims, Henriques, Issas and Matalons — owned or had major interests in 107 companies" (Lacey 1977:15). Jamaicans still speak of the "21 families" that are reputed to have owned most of the land on the island since its earliest distribution by the Crown.

3.   José Vasconcelos' idea of la raza cósmica, a new cosmic racial admixture created in the New World, was conceived as an ideological alternative to operative conceptions of elite superiority and political dominance. The general use of la raza, however, refers to the similar way in which Latinos perceive themselves as a distinct ethnic group. Despite great variations in racial mixture between Europeans, Indians, Africans, and their creole progeny, the fusion itself provides a common point of reference. This level of affinity between Caribbean peoples, notwithstanding antagonisms on other levels, is highly observable in their interactions. We suggest that the affinity transcends cultural origins when, for example, Dominicans and Jamaicans identify with each other as natives of the Caribbean.

4.   See Hillman and Ekstrom (1990:71). The Hispanic saying, "la política es el asco de la vida" (politics is the most loathsome aspect of life) and the Jamaican proverbial "soon come" in its political application, exemplify a certain negative disposition toward governmental solutions to social problems.

5.   "Obedezco pero no cumplo" (I obey but I cannot comply) became a refrain within the audiencia in response to Royal edicts that could not be carried out even by loyal subjects. The ability of Jamaican governors was similarly constrained by the pressure of planters loyal to the Crown but motivated by self-interest.

6.   "Elections and parliamentary maneuvers often do not really resolve key issues of power and distribution. And they seldom produce viable parliamentary-based coalitions to support the government, especially regarding innovative programs. In the end, intrabureaucratic and patrimonially focused factional politics are often more important than electoral, parliamentary, or programmatic politics" (Malloy and Seligson 1987:242).

7.   Appropriate or rightful authority that is compatible with predominant attitudes and values is determined by political culture.

8.   The Moyne Commission published its report in 1940. It concluded that the problems were based on socioeconomic, not political, conditions. However, the report became the basis for the argument that political change was required for social improvement.

9.   "If he is for long unsuccessful, above all if his leadership fails to benefit his followers, it is likely that his charismatic authority will disappear" (Weber 1968:49–50).

10. According to McDonald and Ruhl (1989:343–44), "personalism and charismatic leadership are functional substitutes for party institutions. That is, they perform the same functions as institutions, albeit in different ways, and for short periods of time they can perform them relatively well." However, they also recognize that charisma and personalism "impede the growth of institutional parties."

11. "Caciquismo — or caudillismo in the larger theater — is the natural form of Spanish political association. Under such a system the caudillo or cacique (jefe político in Spanish America) is the political chieftain or boss of the community, as the patron is in other relationships. The tie between him and the local citizenry is a personal one, with well-understood responsibilities on both sides. It is not democracy, but it does help to give some order to the normally inchoate structure of Spanish politics" (Schurz 1964:94; Gibson 1966).

12. "The number of plantations in Jamaica [was reduced] from five hundred in 1846 to seventy by 1910 and about twenty very large latifundia estates by 1960" (Lacey 1977:22).

13. We define personalism as the dominance of the individual in politics. Personalistic leaders, rather than institutions or ideals, tend to gain the allegiance and loyalty of the people.

14. Peña Gómez has stated that he cannot be a caudillo because neither is he a military leader, nor can he command the absolute loyalty of his supporters (Rosenberg 1980:10–11, 44–46).

15. Here charisma refers to "a certain quality of an individual personality by virtue of which he is set apart from ordinary men and treated as endowed with supernatural, superhuman, or at least specifically exceptional powers or qualities" (Weber 1947:358).

16. Balaguer's 1986 campaign slogans "Esto lo hizo Balaguer" (This was done by Balaguer) and "Juntos con Balaguer Vamos a Rehacer el País" (Together with Balaguer we are going to reconstruct the country) exemplify this point (Bonnelly Ricart 1986:8).

17. His followers often sang "Bustamante is a good man, Bustamante never did wrong, We will follow Bustamante till we die."

18. A wide variation in statistics on racial composition in Latin America and the Caribbean reflects the subjective criteria used in classification. These composite data are drawn from a variety of sources.

19. This may be attributed to the fact that one of the few sources of upward mobility in Dominican society has been the military. Despite this, "prejudice does exist with regard to darker-skinned persons, and Dominicans are very conscious of racial backgrounds and features" (Wiarda 1989:443).

20. In the Dominican Republic, 50 percent of the population receives 13 percent of the national income while 6 percent receives 43 percent; roughly 80 percent "remain in a situation of undernourishment and malnutrition" (Wiarda and Kryzanek 1982:52). Jamaica "in the mid-1960s had the highest rate of income inequality in the world, the upper 5% receiving 30% of the national income and the lowest 20% receiving 2% of the total" (Kaplan et al. 1976:105).

21. Ironically, in both countries the consequences of ecological destruction hold potentially disastrous consequences for tourist industries based on environmental beauty. The Alcan, Reynolds, and other "mud holes" in Jamaica are repositories for

caustic bauxite wastes that are beginning to pollute the subsoil water table throughout the island.

22. In the Dominican Republic, unemployment in the rural areas has been estimated at over 50 percent, illiteracy at 80 percent, life expectancy at around 51 years, and incomes at levels far below those in urban areas (Wiarda and Kryzanek 1982). These conditions have prompted a massive exodus from rural areas that has exacerbated the problems of rapid urbanization.

23. Huntington (1968:58–59) argues that "economic development increases economic inequality at the same time that social mobilization decreases the legitimacy of that inequality. Both aspects of modernization combine to produce political instability."

24. Both the Dominican Republic and Jamaica experienced violent anti-government rioting when, in collaboration with the International Monetary Fund, the prices for gasoline and other basic commodities were increased in the mid-1980s.

25. For information on political violence in Jamaica, see Lacey (1977). For a discussion of political violence in the Dominican Republic, see Kryzanek (1977b). Herman and Brodhead (1984) also treat the topic of governmental repression. These sources focus on the activities of La Banda, a death squad linked to the Dominican military and police that terrorized the opposition in the late 1960s and 1970s.

26. This form of anomie helps to explain the low voter registration in the 1990 Dominican elections.

27. Despite campaign rhetoric attacking the bloated state bureaucracy, the PRD governments of Guzmán and Jorge Blanco actually expanded public sector employment from 120,000 in 1978 to 250,000 in 1985 (Black 1986:141).

28. According to Fernando Periche, former government advisor and official, the Faro costs three times the national education budget.

29. It is unsafe for known supporters of a rival party to even set foot inside the boundaries of these turfs.

II

POLITICAL INSTITUTIONS AND PROCESSES

The attitudes and beliefs that derive from political culture do not exist in a vacuum. They are given expression in the formal and informal mechanisms of government. Comparative analysis of these mechanisms reveals the extent to which either formal or informal political institutions and processes are employed in resolving conflicts and allocating values.

Early legal-formalistic approaches to comparative politics have been criticized for being static and excessively descriptive, especially in cases characterized by a high degree of divergence between formal structures and observable political behavior. Analysis of informal processes and behavioral studies subsequently emerged as an alternative to the study of constitutions, governmental structures, and electoral systems. Such analysis has made it clear that political systems may perform similar functions through different structures or may use similar structures to perform different functions. However, it would be an error to conclude that formal institutional analysis is irrelevant. In fact, the degree to which political behavior is institutionalized is a central consideration in the comparison of patterns of legitimacy.

The fundamental questions for comparative analysis are whether or not citizens have confidence that their governments operate according to well-defined principles that are consonant with their cultural values and with their best interests. In order to respond to these questions, the relationship between formal and informal political institutions and processes must be understood.

The evolution of the presidential system in the Dominican Republic and the parliamentary system in Jamaica has significantly impacted the nature of executive power, the relationship between the executive and the legislative branches, the role of the political parties, and the patterns of legitimacy and stability. Despite the divergent institutions in each state, their impact has resulted in several common patterns. Elite tutelage and direction of social groups into political structures and the consequent difficulties in applying those structures to the resolution of development problems have characterized both systems. Thus, understanding the nature and function of the institutions and processes that deal with these problems provides insight into the efficacy of presidential versus parliamentary regimes in particular settings. Such understanding also reveals the reasons why these institutions and processes are not widely perceived as sufficiently responsive to endemic problems and changing attitudes.

4

Governmental Structures and Administration

The fundamental legal framework that defines the rules by which power is supposed to be distributed in a state is found in its constitution. Written constitutions are widely regarded as vehicles for the expression of a framework for authoritative institutional relationships. They attempt to accomplish this by making explicit principles that derive from political culture.

The degree to which formal power diverges from actual power is determined by how effectively the constitutional principles reflect, rather than create, patterns of legitimacy. Accordingly, the "legitimacy of a system is not established by the constitutional instrument but through active politics within the context of political culture" (Maingot 1986:120). The constitutional system may be understood as an expression of societal intentions and as the embodiment of aspirations.

As a statement of governmental goals, constitutions attempt to define the major functions of politics. They outline how laws are proposed, determined, and implemented; how leaders and positions are chosen; what can be done in emergencies; and what are acceptable procedures for changing the aforementioned functions. They spell out citizens' rights, place limitations on the government, and delineate the general aims of the state.

The following survey of major constitutional principles that are articulated in the written documents of the Dominican Republic and Jamaica focuses on a comparison of the separation or fusion of power between the executive and legislative branches, the division or centralization of power between the national and local levels, and an analysis of the presidential and parliamentary models.

THE CONSTITUTIONS

The Dominican Republic has had 25 different constitutions since independence in 1844. Jamaica has had only five variations since 1655, including the current one adopted when the country became independent in 1962.

Constitutional instability in the Dominican Republic underscores the difficulties the nation has encountered in reconciling its dual political traditions. Further, it reflects a turbulent history characterized by the alternation of authoritarian and democratic regimes. The large number of constitutions reflects a practice wherein a new basic law is promulgated each time there is an amendment or even a modest change in procedure. Throughout the nation's history, particular constitutions have been interpreted as symbols of particular leaders. In fact, Dominican leaders in the past typically rewrote the constitution upon assuming power in order to prescribe a distinctive philosophical program that would identify the new regime.

Each Dominican constitution has guaranteed human rights, proclaimed the separation of executive, legislative, and judicial power and provided for popular sovereignty. The current document, promulgated in 1966, describes the government as "essentially civil, republican, democratic, and representative."[1] While this particular constitution represented an effort to incorporate both the authoritarian and liberal traditions, in reality "none of these documents effectively protected civil liberties, established the independence of the legislature and judicial branches of government from the executive, or made public officials significantly responsible to the people" (Weil et al. 1985:131).

The Dominican political system has traditionally been characterized by a high degree of formalism, exhibiting a divergence between legal procedures and political practices. Although the nation's numerous constitutions have articulated lofty ideals and principles, the fact remains that these precepts have been routinely neglected by national leaders. It has been suggested that

Dominican politics rests almost exclusively on the quality of personal leadership. . . . The country has been shaped not so much by formal constitutional and institutional arrangements, but rather by the talents, personalism, charisma, strength, and machismo of the individuals who occupied the national palace (Wiarda and Kryzanek 1982:97).

Nonetheless, democratic values have begun to take root, and recent experiences have served to reaffirm the basic principles outlined in the constitution.

In dramatic contrast to Dominican history, principles of parliamentary democracy, administrative responsibility, and the rule of law were transferred from Britain to Jamaica in varying degrees over long periods of time. However, Manley argues that the Westminster model "as brought by imperialism" displaced a constitutional system that could have derived from an indigenous cultural movement (Hillman 1979a:54). As early as the end of the seventeenth century, a form of representative government operated in the colony. This old representative system, which benefitted the plantocracy, was replaced by Crown Colony government after the Morant Bay Rebellion in 1865. Representative government was reintroduced in small increments starting at the end of the nineteenth century. After the 1938 labor disturbances, a new constitution was adopted in 1944 in order to provide the framework for a transition to full internal autonomy. This constitution was amended several times. For example, in 1953 the powers of the house were expanded, and the elected members of the governor's council were made accountable to the legislature.

Jamaica received full internal autonomy as a member of the West Indian Federation in 1959. After leaving the short-lived federation in 1961, Jamaica ratified an independence constitution in 1962. Although that document is still in effect, questions have been raised about the extent to which civil liberties and rights guaranteed in Chapter 3 of the constitution have been enforced without reference to individuals' social, economic, and political status (Payne 1988:4). Nevertheless, the Jamaican constitution has allowed for the relatively peaceful transfer of power through elections of civil administrations seven times since independence. Political leaders and citizens of all classes were committed to the Westminster model because each group perceived it as a means to achieve their interests through political empowerment (Edie 1991:40).

Discrepancies between constitutional procedures and political realities in both countries derive, in part, from the interposition of foreign legal systems. While there is a higher degree of formalism in the Dominican Republic than in Jamaica, both countries demonstrate the problems associated with the development of legitimate institutions in transitional societies. The Dominican constitution of 1966 and the Jamaican constitution of 1962 are based on code law and common law, respectively. The Dominican constitution, consisting of 124 articles in 14 titles, is unique among Latin American republics in its incorporation of the Napoleonic Code. The Spanish legal system was replaced by French law based on the Napoleonic Code during the Haitian occupation. The Dominican National Congress adopted the Napoleonic Code in 1844. Officially translated into Spanish in 1884, it became the basis of the modern legal system.

Nevertheless, a cynical conception of legal authority, as opposed to personalistic authority, can be traced to the colonial era. The Hispanic tradition "obedezco pero no cumplo" (I obey but I cannot comply) and the centralization of power have imbued the constitutional government with a type of legalism that emphasizes government control rather than limitation. Such a conception has, in effect, denigrated the rule of law as a widely perceived guarantee of justice.[2] With respect to the period 1966–78, a prominent Dominican scholar characterizes the constitutional system by paraphrasing Balaguer's assertion that the constitution is "really a piece of paper" (F. Espinal 1987:237).

The Jamaican constitution, drafted in England with Jamaican input, consists of 138 articles in 10 chapters. The tradition of English common law in Jamaica has yielded a highly litigious society. However, insufficient legal aid for the poor in a system based on adversary proceedings has resulted in a low level of mass confidence in the legal system. The Poor Persons Law of 1941 theoretically provides for legal aid in civil cases brought before the Supreme Court; but in reality it is not used, and assistance can be sought only by virtual paupers. The Poor Prisoners Defense Law of 1961 provides for legal aid only in capital crimes and other serious offenses (Kaplan et al. 1976:209).

Code law in the Dominican Republic is premised on the interpretation of statutes by appointed judges and thus reaffirms the authority of the state; in Jamaica the practice of common law in a dual class society reinforces the authority of the elite. Therefore, while divergent legal traditions produce different methods of jurisprudence, they both result in reinforcement of the power structures. Similar constitutional provisions regarding civil rights, methods of amendment, passage of laws and governmental policymaking must be understood in light of these interpretations and practices.

Neither the Dominican municipalities nor the Jamaican parish councils have much power. Their inability to provide services in the areas of their limited responsibilities have made the local governments increasingly dependent on assistance from the central governments.[3] Dominican municipal councils are responsible for street maintenance, garbage collection, provision of water, and fire protection. Jamaican parish councils are responsible for roads, street lighting, relief for the poor, public health, and water supplies. In both cases, clientelistic linkages between the national parties and the local elites have reinforced "authoritarian paternalistic" relations between those elites and the impoverished masses (Edie 1991:56; Kaplan et al. 1976:207).

THE EXECUTIVES

The nature of executive power as defined in their respective constitutions is considerably different in the Dominican Republic and Jamaica.[4] It is in this area that the dissimilarity in Hispanic and British traditions is most profoundly manifested. The influence of Spain's legacy of centralized executive authority based on personalistic leadership and active military support is apparent in the Dominican presidential system (see Figure 4.1). There has been much speculation on why the successful U.S. presidential system has not been transferred easily to Latin American republics. The failure of democracy in countries like the Dominican Republic is often attributed to indigenous political, economic, and social factors. This focus has obscured the inherent limitations of the presidential system, particularly in its cross-cultural application.

In contrast, the Westminster model of parliamentary politics with civilian dominance and military subservience has been firmly implanted in Jamaica. The only major departure from the British tradition was to produce a written constitution. But, while the main features of the Westminster tradition are present, "the political violence of the 1960s was illustrative of the credibility gap between constitutional theory and political practice" (Lacey 1977:46).

While in the Dominican Republic the president is elected to a four-year term by a direct vote and may succeed himself in office, in Jamaica the governor general (a ceremonial head of state) is appointed by the queen, the nominal head of the Commonwealth of Nations.[5] The governor general may only perform his ceremonial functions on the advice of the prime minister or in concert with the leader of the opposition. In practice it is the prime minister and his cabinet that "constitute the principal instrument of policy."[6] Parliamentary elections in Jamaica must be conducted at least every five years.

Although the Dominican president is constitutionally constrained by several procedures that require legislative approval, executive supremacy over the legislative and judicial branches of government has been the historical reality. The Dominican constitution empowers Congress, or the president himself when Congress is not in session, to declare a state of siege or a national emergency. During this time, the president's special

FIGURE 4.1
The Government of the Dominican Republic

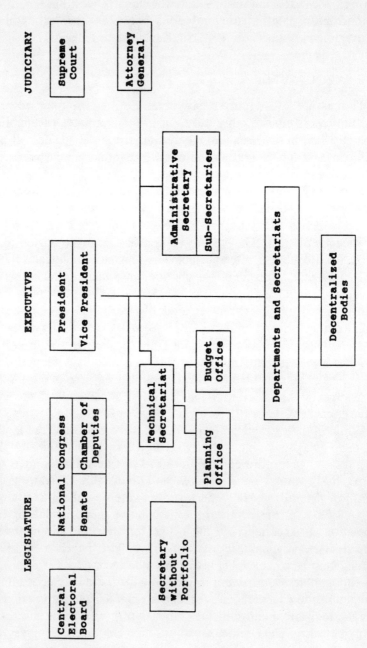

Source: Compiled by authors.

emergency powers authorize both all actions necessary to defend the nation and the suspension of all personal rights other than inviolability of life.[7]

As leader of the majority party and in concert with the cabinet, the prime minister of Jamaica is charged with the general direction and control of government (see Figure 4.2). The prime minister and the cabinet are collectively responsible to the House of Representatives. This fusion of executive and legislative authority in parliamentary systems contrasts with systems characterized by a weak legislature dominated by a strong executive. Nevertheless, the prime minister has been able to assert strong control over policy directions through the selection of a cabinet comprised of politically amenable ministers.[8]

As chief executive and head of state, the Dominican president possesses broader powers than the prime minister of Jamaica. The excessive centralization characteristic of the Dominican political system has compromised the legislative and judicial powers, which at times have been "subordinated unilaterally to executive authority" (F. Espinal 1987: 237). As head of public administration, the president appoints and removes cabinet ministers, provincial governors, and other public officials. Moreover, although there have been attempts to establish a career civil service in the Dominican Republic, it is not included in the constitution and an elaborate system of clientelism has prevailed. "Reality exhibits a strong executive preponderance. The President of the Republic is, in conclusion, a kind of elected monarch. He can control all the resources and leverages of power" (Brea Franco 1989:74–75). Accordingly, major turnovers of personnel occur from one administration to another.

In contrast, the Jamaican constitution provides for a public service commission to preside over a career civil service organized into administrative, professional, technical, executive, clerical, and manual categories. There have been tensions between the bureaucratic and political arms of the executive branch, and several reforms of the system have been implemented. As a result, patronage has been reduced in the civil service allowing for the formation of a bipartisan cadre of administrators in Jamaica. Nevertheless, Manley argues that the most talented people are not attracted to the civil service and that "no developing country can hope to overtake its priorities in a strategy of change with the bureaucracy that it inherits from colonialism nor with the kind of bureaucracy that it can hope to evolve in the short-run of independence" (Manley 1974:188).

It is clear that formal executive authority is more concentrated in the presidential system than it is in the parliamentary system. It is, therefore,

FIGURE 4.2
The Government of Jamaica

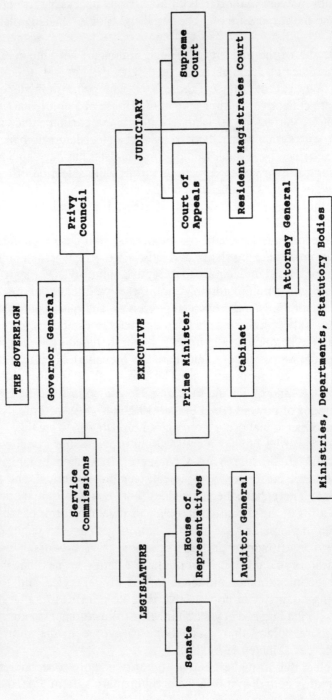

Source: Compiled by authors.

consonant with the divergent historical experiences of these two Caribbean states. However, the relative ability of each type of executive system to implement development programs or consolidate democracy has been determined less by structural factors than by cultural and socioeconomic ones.

THE LEGISLATURES

The bicameral Dominican Congress, based on the U.S. model, is theoretically empowered to legislate on all matters that are not assigned to another branch of government. Its explicit powers include the "power of the purse," the determination of local boundaries and jurisdictions, the approval or rejection of treaties, the initiation and authorization of legislation, and the amendment of bills that become law (over a presidential veto when passed by a two-thirds majority in each chamber). In practice the legislature has been unable to fulfill its powers completely as an effective check on the presidency because it lacks the technical and economic resources and the interest required to do so.[9] Moreover, until the introduction of the Triple Rayado in the 1990 election, representatives were insulated from responsibility to the electorate.

Jamaica's bicameral parliament, based on the British model, consists of the House of Representatives and the Senate. While the house has primary responsibility over fiscal matters, other bills are introduced in either house of the legislature. Because standing committees have relatively little investigative power, it is the cabinet that exercises legislative initiative. Because members of the cabinet are chosen and led by the prime minister from his own majority party, it is the tradition of the loyal partisan opposition rather than of the bipartisan legislature that provides a check on the executive. Manley argues that the "uncritical transplanting of the Westminster model" has, in limiting ministerial appointments to elected representatives, constrained the capacity of the prime minister to form a cabinet based on the best available talent and expertise. He further asserts, "ministerial duties can only be performed at the expense of constituency representation, and hence the maintenance of communication between the people and the government" (Manley 1974:189).

The Dominican Chamber of Deputies is comprised of 120 members elected for four-year terms in apportioned districts by the people of the 29 provinces and the National District. With a vote of three-fourths of its total membership, the Chamber may present impeachments of public officials before the Senate. The senate consists of one elected official from each of the provinces and the national district. Among its exclusive powers are the election of judges to the Supreme Court of Justice and all lower courts, the election of the president and members of the Central Electoral Board, the approval or rejection of diplomatic appointments, and the trial of impeachment cases. While the president may not leave the country for more than 15 days without the permission of both houses of Congress, the extraordinary powers granted by Article 55 of the constitution serve to underscore the effective predominance of the executive branch in the Dominican Republic.

The Jamaican House of Representatives consists of 60 members elected by universal suffrage, and the Senate is a body of 21 persons appointed by the governor general, 13 on the advice of the prime minister and 8 on the advice of the leader of the opposition. The Senate may be overridden if a majority in the House passes bills delayed by the Senate three times in succession. Constitutional amendments, however, require Senate concurrence. Appointment to the Senate provides an important vehicle for the enhancement of political party patronage (Edie 1991; Manley 1974).

Despite the constitutional principle of bicameralism, neither the Dominican nor the Jamaican senate has been able to effectively protect the integrity of local governmental operations from central government encroachments. Moreover, Dominican presidential powers have not been limited in practice by the legislature. Our interviews in the Dominican Republic confirmed the idea that the legislature has not been perceived as an effective check on executive power. While the Jamaican prime minister is subject to minority party opposition, central control can be exercised through his cabinet as long as government policies receive majority support in the legislature.

Although limited decentralization of authority has occurred in Jamaica, federalism is traditionally very weak in Latin America. It is not surprising that the executive branch in the Dominican Republic has not conformed to the distribution of power as stated in the constitution.

The prime minister in a parliamentary system, such as that of Jamaica, is accountable to the legislature in different ways than the chief executive is in a presidential system such as that of the Dominican Republic. This fact has become the focus of an interesting debate concerning the efficacy of the two distinct systems in developing countries. While the type of governmental structures in Jamaica would appear to offer the potential for the reduction of the excessive personalism and clientelism characteristic of Dominican politics, it is not clear that the functioning of formal structures can be understood in an extracultural context.[10] Nowhere is this as pronounced as it is in the state system for the implementation of public policies.

BUREAUCRACY

The state plays an active role in the lives of citizens through the effectiveness of its public bureaucracy in developing the economy and building the nation. In the Dominican Republic, this has occurred within the context of a military-authoritarian tradition with a highly personalistic and paternalistic orientation. In Jamaica this has occurred as a concomitant of the social democratic movement. It is significant that in neither system are politics and administration divided.

Conceptual theories of development administration based upon a dichotomy between politics and administration provide little information about how these bureaucracies really operate. Do public administrators participate in decision making or do they merely execute policy? Are they subject to external forces? What levels of expertise are available to them? Are the institutions specialized? How are they composed? What are the true goals of the bureaucracy?

Structural-functional analysis is helpful in focusing on how state systems maintain and adapt themselves through political recruitment and socialization and on how systemic performance is evaluated within a particular cultural environment. When applied to Caribbean bureaucracies, this type of analysis reveals a low level of competence in operating programs designed to extract or distribute resources.[11] Excessive bureaucratic power combined with inefficiency lead to confusion in distinguishing between ritual and rational technologies. For these reasons, according to Carl Stone (who included both the Dominican Republic and Jamaica in his study), an area of extreme weakness in the liberal-democratic systems of the Caribbean is "the high-handed, nonbargaining, nonconsultative, and nonresponsive tradition of decision-making and policy formulation inherited from the colonial civil service system" (Stone 1985:24). Stone argues that state institutions in the Caribbean are a product of Western European institutions grafted on a subculture of authoritarian colonial administration. This has resulted in weakness and tension in public administration that has allowed subversion and manipulation of state programs.

With regard to the Jamaican case, "ruling groups have been able to anesthetize popular discontent by a politics of clientelism, keeping the masses quiet by a politics of *jobs for the boys* at every social level" (Lewis 1985:227). It is apparent through discussions with a number of observers that political patronage operates in much the same way in the Dominican Republic.

As indicated in previous sections of this study, public administration in both the Dominican Republic and Jamaica has been constrained by the legacies of colonialism, elite domination or manipulation, corruption, and inefficiency. As an apparatus for responding to the problems of development, neither administrative system has demonstrated the ability to deliver innovative solutions. Thus although based on different bureaucratic models, the state systems of both counties are widely perceived as obstructions to, rather than vehicles for, the amelioration of social and economic conditions (Hillman and D'Agostino interviews 1990).

Of course, politicians have viewed the respective state bureaucracies as structures for the distribution of patronage. For example, Wiarda and Kryzanek (1982:94) characterize Dominican politics as a "zero-sum game" in which winners have monopolized the administration. Similarly, the neutral bureaucratic model derived from the British system has "clashed with Jamaican reality" as politicians have often used partisan criteria to "bypass civil servants with the delegation of functions to semi-autonomous state agencies or the appointment of special advisors" (Stephens and Stephens 1986:41; Nunes 1976). Attempts by leadership in both countries to upgrade their public administrative capacities have been stultified by the combination of private demands, rising socioeconomic pressures, political uncertainty, and an indigenous cultural context in which central control has been exercised through clientelistic practices supportive of elite interests.[12]

It is not surprising that Dominican public works programs generally benefitted the wealthy rather than the poor. In fact, Vincho Castillo's defection from Balaguer's government was due to the "violence and corruption that accompanied the implementation of agrarian programs" (Black 1986:44; Hillman and D'Agostino interview 1990). Castillo resigned in 1972 when laws requiring some land redistribution to peasants were resisted by landowners and poorly enforced by the government.

Given the nature of the Jamaican system, it is not surprising that "the state's capacity to promote and direct economic and social development in the interest of the mass of the people was severely hampered by the close link of both parties to members of the private sector" (Stephens and Stephens 1986:41). For example, when private, middle-class interests determined that the People's National Party (PNP) program of democratic socialism was unable to satisfy their interests, "the allegiance of the security forces and the bureaucracy shifted" abandoning the Manley government and thereby contributing to its demise (Stephens and Stephens 1986:323).

With these observations in mind, it is important to recognize that the very concept of a career civil service is a recent development in the Dominican Republic. In the early 1970s, the United Nations provided assistance in the creation of the National Office of Administration and Personnel (ONAP). ONAP was to be responsible for studying government administration, training public employees, and preparing the regulations for the establishment of a career civil service (Weil et al. 1985:140). While some progress has been made toward these goals, centralized executive authority combined with a strong tradition of power brokerage through clientelism has made a truly modern public administration quite elusive in the Dominican Republic.[13]

The career civil service in Jamaica has been riddled with tensions between the bureaucratic and political arms of the executive branch (Kaplan et al. 1976:205). The Public Service Commission, responsible for personnel management, entered into controversy when the general secretary of a labor organization was appointed as its director in 1977 (Stephens and Stephens 1986:312). Beneath the surface of the conflict of interests issue was the claim of excessive PNP partisanship.

Since independence, the replacement of high-ranking British civil servants with Jamaicans having inadequate training and working in subordinate positions produced a decline in administrative quality (Kaplan et al. 1976:205). The bureaucracy is perceived as highly centralized, inefficient, and incapable of the kind of innovation required for socioeconomic development (Hillman 1979b). The civil service "was infinitely better at shuffling papers and abdicating responsibility than at planning and managing the implementation of policies and programs" (Stephens and Stephens 1986:40). Another explanation for the decline in the status of the Jamaican civil service derives from middle-class opposition to use of the civil service as an agent of change (Nunes 1974). Consequently, the problems associated with bureaucracy in Jamaica have discouraged foreign investors, adding yet another obstacle to economic development. Edie (1991) concludes that a state-centered patronage system based on "dual clientelism" requiring external resources has impeded the ability of public policies to meet the needs of Jamaican citizens.

Clearly, the cultural and socioeconomic contexts in which Dominican and Jamaican public administrations operate have produced similarities despite the divergent bureaucratic models. Both systems are fueled by politics and steered by executive guidance. Therefore, the comparison of formal institutions should incorporate analysis of the overall regime types.

PRESIDENTIAL VERSUS PARLIAMENTARY SYSTEMS

The major purposes of governmental institutions include the provision of security, welfare, and justice. Because significant aspects of a country's political life are influenced by the formal structures of government, the ways in which these structures enhance or inhibit the provision of these goals is of significant analytical concern. Presidential and parliamentarian systems each exhibit major differences in the theory and practice of executive power, in their relationships with other branches and levels of government, and even in their patterns of democracy and stability.

Despite the paucity of research on these aspects of comparative politics, there have been several assessments suggesting that presidential systems may be inimical to democratic consolidation, especially in multiparty systems (Mainwaring 1990:158). Moreover, the purported advantages of the parliamentary system as compared to the presidential system have been the subject of much discussion (Diamond, Linz, and Lipset 1989:24). For some analysts the parliamentary system is "preferable to the other two models currently available to sovereign Caribbean states: the executive system and the Cuban one-party state" (Sutton 1986:135).

According to one Dominican political analyst, the presidential system in his country has been a failure as a form of government. Julio Brea Franco asserts that

There has been much discussion throughout Latin America, given the way things are now, of the possibility of shifting from the presidential to the parliamentary system. While a complete change is simply not possible, many Dominicans believe that the introduction of a series of partial reforms could somehow *parliamentize* our presidentialism (D'Agostino interview 1990).

The idea of structural reform rests on dual premises. The first premise is that executive policy can be immobilized by strong congressional checks. The second premise is that a strong, charismatic president can manipulate, dominate, or ignore a weak legislature. Thus, either the central authority required for development is compromised by democratic institutions or the development of legitimate institutional structures is stultified by authoritarianism. This is a fundamental dilemma throughout the Third World. On the one hand, centralized authority and state planning are perceived as vehicles that can formulate policies designed to treat endemic developmental problems. On the other hand, such centralization has failed to assure the implementation of policies that would serve the entire nation in the long-term but may negatively impact elite interests in the short-term. The formation of decentralized participatory institutions through which emerging interest groups (that are difficult to co-opt into vertically integrated structures) and the masses could make demands would similarly render long-term planning a very difficult challenge.

This dilemma is reflected in Michael Manley's assessment of executive authority in the United States when he states that

American government is not designed so much to create the conditions for the effective exercise of authority as to make the exercise of authority subject to constant checks and balances. It is both notorious and tragic that this objective, which is achieved by the separation of power under its constitution, often reduces the United States of America to the verge of paralysis in the face of the great problems of modern government (Manley 1974:29).

While Manley may be misrepresenting the efficacy of U.S. governmental dynamics, his understanding of the philosophical antithesis to tyranny (on which the checks and balances system is based) provides an interesting parallel in the Jamaican legacy of fear of slavery and colonial oppression. "To the Jamaican's historical distrust of authority must be added the fact that all institutions through which the newly freed slave, and indeed the entire society, began to attain social coherence, were designed in the shadow of the Westminster model of democracy" (Manley 1974:29).

Further analysis of the institutional structure limiting presidential mobility (occasioned by congressional checks) suggests a dramatic contrast with the wider range of options theoretically provided to a prime minister with legislative support. The reality, however, may be just the opposite. In the Dominican Republic, rather than presidential immobilism, we observe centralized executive power engendered by a formal constitutional tradition dominated by personalistic, authoritarian leaders. In Jamaica, we see charismatic prime ministers constrained by parliamentarian procedures and political structures. Michael Manley refers to structural constraints of the parliamentarian system that he considers an obstacle to the implementation of development programs. He emphasizes the need for greater flexibility in making appointments to what he considers an increasingly exclusive cabinet of ministers (Manley 1974; Hillman 1979a).

In these analyses, the presidential system is defined by two major features. First, the head of government is elected independently of the legislature. Second, the president is elected for a fixed period of time. It has been suggested that because the president cannot be subjected to a legislative vote of no confidence, the president is not formally accountable to Congress (Mainwaring 1990:159). This lack of accountability allows presidents to bypass Congress and thereby undermines democracy.

The practice of superseding the legislature may only be possible in those particular types of political culture that legitimate executive branch dominance. Clearly the Hispanic tradition is more supportive of authoritarian leadership than the British. The difficulty in attaining a viable separation of powers is exacerbated by the personalization of power that is inherent in Hispanic political culture. However, personalism appears to have characterized both presidential and parliamentary systems (Mainwaring 1990:173). Certainly Jamaican leadership has demonstrated this tendency, despite the fact that prime ministers are directly tied to their political parties and presidents are elected by popular vote.

If presidential democracies require more exclusionary politics than parliamentary democracies in order to attain stability in the Third World, then it is theoretically probable that there would be a higher degree of democratic consolidation in the Anglophone Caribbean than in the Hispanic Caribbean.[14] It would also follow that a greater concentration of power would be required for effective policy coordination and implementation in less stable systems. How, then, can Third World countries develop stable institutions?

One response to this dilemma is to strengthen congresses. Another is to create effective executives.[15] Some stability has been achieved in the short-term in the Dominican Republic through personalistic leadership at the expense of the institutionalization of democracy. Ironically, imitating the U.S. constitutional system allowed the Dominican Republic to use the presidential model as a vehicle for the expression of traditional power relationships perhaps more easily than a parliamentary system would have. The relative degree of stability achieved in Jamaica as a result of the incremental introduction of the Westminster model has not been without sacrifice. Domination of the political process by elitists and charismatic individuals has indeed hindered development programs. The problem of maintaining continuity in long-term programs that fail to show short-term gains has been attributed to the Jamaican parliamentary tradition in which there has been an alternation of governments after two terms in office.

Nevertheless, Jamaica has maintained a system where executive authority is circumscribed to an extent that preserves a degree of accountability to the legislature, and the Dominican Republic has generated some movement toward checking the president. These are positive advances. However, it is important to recognize the context in which these advances have been incorporated in the political systems. In both cases, power relationships and legitimate authority are derived from cultural patterns.[16] Therefore, the formal structure of the institutions cannot necessarily be considered the determining factor in the operation or modification of the political systems. More importantly, neither the Jamaican parliamentarian system nor the Dominican presidential system has been very effective in ameliorating the endemic problems facing the two countries.

NOTES

1. Constitution of the Dominican Republic, Section I, Article 4, reprinted in Brea Franco (1986a:142).

2. Accordingly, "the judicial branch is a weak political actor that receives very little respect from government officials" (Kearney 1985:14).

3. According to Vincho Castillo, "the lack of municipal autonomy in the Dominican Republic has been an impediment to democratic consolidation" (D'Agostino interview 1990).

4. References in this section are to the Constitution of the Dominican Republic, Title V, Section 1, Articles 49–60, reprinted in Brea Franco (1986a) and The Constitution of Jamaica, Chapter VI, Articles 68–96, published by the secretary general of the Organization of American States, Washington, D.C., 1971.

5. Jamaica is a member of the Commonwealth and is officially considered an independent constitutional monarchy. Attempts to change its status to that of an independent republic during the 1970s were unsuccessful.

6. The Constitution of Jamaica, Chapter VI, Article 69, Sections (1) and (2).

7. Constitution of the Dominican Republic, Title V, Section I, Article 55, clauses 7 and 8.

8. The cabinet consists of the prime minister (appointed by the governor general by virtue of leadership of the majority party) and approximately 15 members (of whom not less than 2 or more than 3 are appointed from the Senate). The cabinet members head the ministries of civil servants. The most important portfolios have been those of agriculture, finance, commerce and industry, external affairs, and national

security and justice. A cabinet member may resign or lose his position either by a decision of the prime minister or by an act of Parliament (Kaplan et al. 1976:203).

9. Kearney (1985:14) points out that the Dominican Congress "lacks the institutional resources to become a true partner, or initiator, in the policy-making process." Brea Franco expressed a similar view in an interview with the authors.

10. Dogan and Pelassy (1990) make this point throughout their analysis of the field of comparative politics. They also caution against ethnocentric approaches that fail to account for cultural relativity.

11. In reference to the Dominican Republic, "the needs of the people are not being met by a public sector lagging in its ability to provide a political and administrative environment conducive to further economic growth" (Kearney 1985:14).

12. See Geddes (1991:388–89) on the inability to professionalize public administration and its consequences.

13. Kearney (1985:14) states that "although the Dominican Republic has flirted with a career civil service on several occasions, and even had one on the books for several years during the early part of the century, the concept has never been implemented practically."

14. Riggs (1968:247) maintains that presidentialism hinders the emergence of stable democracy, except in the United States.

15. Mainwaring (1990:167) points out that in presidential systems it is difficult to attain concentration of powers while preserving democracy. Diamond, Linz, and Lipset (1989:26) show that a further weakness of democratic experiences in Latin America has been the lack of power and effectiveness of legislatures.

16. "Socioeconomic structural conditions shape the constellation of social forces and the emergence of political institutions, which in turn shape the arena for political actors and thus influence political outcomes. These results then have a feedback effect on institutional arrangements and even on socioeconomic structures" (Stephens 1990:168).

5

Political Parties and Elections

Broad-based support is essential for the legitimation of political leadership and institutions in societies that are becoming increasingly complex as they respond to the challenges of development and modernization. The generation of such support requires institutions that can channel the participation of newly emerging groups. Scholars agree that political parties are the most viable vehicles for the organization of the popular support that enables candidates to attain electoral office. Theoretically, parties facilitate the aggregation of interests among diverse groups and are, therefore, "an indispensable element of competitive electoral politics" (McDonald and Ruhl 1989:2) because they provide legitimation for control over public policy formation and implementation.

Parties are also idiosyncratic expressions of political culture. Their ideological orientations, particular goals, organizational characteristics, and the socioeconomic status of their party members and supporters are important aspects of the political dynamic. However, as McDonald and Ruhl (1989:1) caution, "although the importance of party politics has increased during the 1980s, the recent proliferation of elections should not lead us to exaggerate the role of political parties." Moreover, formal democratic institutions do not necessarily result in democratic practice. Edie (1991:48) convincingly argues that political parties, elections, and legislatures do not guarantee truly representative government. Bosch also strongly articulates this point (Hillman and D'Agostino interview 1990).

Party organizations are necessarily creatures of the political systems in which they operate. It is clear that "different kinds of parties have arisen in response to different societal needs and political opportunities" (Wynia 1978:91). Thus, important variables in understanding how party systems function include the degree to which formal political procedures have been institutionalized in different environments, legal traditions, varying patterns of partisanship, and modes of popular participation.

Political parties serve a variety of functions in different settings. For example, some contest elections in order to gain representation in the government; some seek to legitimize the regime in power; and others articulate a position with no real hope of gaining power. Yet others are conspiratorial in seeking to win and hold public office at any cost.[1]

The following overview of the roles of Dominican and Jamaican political parties reveals several common patterns that transcend profound historical and ideological differences. Since the early 1960s when parties began to emerge as relevant political forces in the Dominican Republic, an incipient multiparty system with two or three major power contenders in an evolving electoral process has emerged. Recently, several small parties have begun to raise issues that challenge the orientations of the major parties and other powerful groups, such as the military. With the rise of nationalism and the emergence of parties as political expressions of organized labor, Jamaican elections have been contested within a dominant two-party system since the early 1940s. Third parties have not been successful in Jamaica, but they have articulated radical alternatives to a power structure represented by the dominant parties.

Therefore, to some extent parties have helped to channel participation, avert potential instability, and heighten social mobility in both countries. Despite obvious contrasts, parties in both the Dominican Republic and Jamaica have accomplished these objectives and have used them as vehicles for the expression of personalistic leadership, for forming loose alliances for the provision of patronage in exchange for support, and for creating mechanisms for the perpetuation of elite dominance. Ideological images of alternative programs for the amelioration of social and economic problems have reinforced the dominance of strong leaders in both countries.

Social mobilization and participation patterns have had varying effects on party institutionalization and stability. In both the Dominican Republic and Jamaica, political leaders are chosen through electoral systems with universal adult suffrage and no literacy requirement. However, the direct election of the Dominican president by means of a simple plurality system contrasts with the selection of the Jamaican prime minister by virtue of being the leader of the party gaining the majority of seats in the House of Representatives. Nevertheless, the dominance of charismatic leaders in both countries has resulted in voting behavior characterized less by issue determination than by clientelistic voting, ritual, and inertia (McDonald and Ruhl 1989:14). Recently, leadership performance in providing solutions to endemic problems has begun to emerge as an additional significant support criteria. This reflects the view that "the stability of any regime depends on its performance, its ability to meet the needs of its population, or at least those members of the population who, by political action or inaction might endanger the regime" (Peeler 1989:3).

The single-member district plurality system, used to elect Dominican senators and Jamaican representatives, favors large political parties over small ones or independent candidates due to the winner-take-all character of the contests. Although election to the Dominican Chamber of Deputies is determined by a system of proportional representation, the strength of small opposition parties is constrained by the nature of the relationship between the executive department and the legislature. While local officials are directly elected in both the Dominican Republic and Jamaica, their very limited powers diminish the significance of these elections.

This chapter compares the major political parties in each country in terms of their origins, types, functions, bases of support, and performances. We also analyze general patterns of participation and outcomes of national elections. Clearly, in facing the challenges of transitional societies, political parties have tended to perpetuate significant aspects of the traditional structures of power. Nevertheless, changes are taking place that could allow the parties to aggregate more effectively their diverse interests and thereby to enhance the consolidation of democracy in both the Dominican Republic and Jamaica. An alternative could be a devolution to authoritarianism.

THE POLITICAL PARTIES

Competitive party politics is a recent phenomenon in the Dominican Republic because the contemporary political party system dates back only to the demise of the Trujillo dictatorship in 1961.[2] Over the past 30 years, the country has struggled to institutionalize an indigenous brand of party politics, one that is derived from its dual political traditions of authoritarianism and democracy. This process has yielded an emerging party system that, within Dominican society, exhibits a fundamental tension between a traditional political culture deeply rooted in the nation's colonial heritage and the pressures for change generated through modernization. The difficulties encountered in attempting to institutionalize party politics in a democratic framework attest to the persistence and resiliency of traditional patterns and values amidst profound socioeconomic change.

Throughout most of its independent history the Dominican Republic has been characterized by strong individual leadership and a persistently low level of institutionalization. At no point was the dearth of viable institutions more apparent than at the time of Trujillo's demise. Under Trujillo's guidance, the country experienced a protracted period of economic expansion during which Dominican society began to exhibit definitive signs of transforming itself from traditional to modern. The ranks of the middle class began to swell and a nascent urban working class emerged in what had been a predominantly rural, agrarian society.

Moreover, there occurred significant changes in the values, expectations, and loyalties maintained by the newly mobilized segments of the populace. Over time, this expanding participatory population, seeking access to the political arena, found itself at odds with a Trujillo regime that had become increasingly inflexible in the face of modernizing change.[3] The perceived threat to his power stemming from the emergence of the "modern" classes prompted Trujillo to intensify efforts to depoliticize Dominican society. The regime grew more and more bureaucratic and authoritarian, as evidenced by its increased reliance on the repressive capacity of the Partido Dominicano (PD), the armed forces, and the expansive state structure (Wiarda 1989:434). There were no independent channels for political expression because parties other than the PD and its state-mandated opposition were forbidden, because efforts to develop autonomous civic institutions were strictly controlled, and because the fledgling labor movement was co-opted and subordinated to regime control.

When Trujillo was assassinated in May 1961, the Dominican Republic was again faced with the task of filling the massive void created by the demise of a powerful authoritarian leader. Contrary to popular belief, Trujillo's death did not precipitate the immediate collapse of the regime. Joaquín Balaguer, who was serving as titular president at Trujillo's behest, remained in office while control of the military was passed on to the dictator's son, Ramfis. Both sought to preserve the existing power structure; yet it soon became apparent that this arrangement was no longer tenable given the widespread changes in Dominican society.

Under mounting pressure from the United States, which feared the potential rise of another Castro in the Caribbean, and from an increasingly vocal domestic opposition, a number of "democratic" reforms were initiated. While many of these measures were superficial and largely ineffectual, one of the most significant involved easing the long-standing restrictions on political activity. This step facilitated the establishment of a variety of political organizations and movements to accommodate rising demands for participation within the newly mobilized urban classes. The emergence of the first modern Dominican party, the Partido Revolucionario Dominicano (PRD), and other organizations including the Unión Cívica Nacional and the Fourteenth of June Movement reflected the degree to which political activity had been suppressed under Trujillo. It may be understood as a response to the impact of rapid socioeconomic modernization and the various crises it gives rise to in transitional societies.[4]

Bowing to internal and external pressures, the Trujillo family fled into exile in November 1961, leaving Balaguer in power. With the dramatic increase in political activity and the proliferation of political groups and organizations, pressures for democratization intensified within both the Dominican Republic itself and the United States. In response, a seven member Council of State, decidedly conservative in makeup, was established under Balaguer's leadership. Inaugurated on January 1, 1962, this body was intended to stabilize the country in preparation for an upcoming election and the subsequent transition to democratic rule. Balaguer was ousted and forced into exile by a military coup launched against the council shortly after its inception. However, the country continued to enjoy the "burgeoning of new political associations" under a reconstituted council that successfully guided the nation through the difficult period leading to the election on December 20, 1962.[5]

Both the structure of the party system and the nature of party politics in the Dominican Republic have evolved considerably in the post-Trujillo era. During its formative stages, the party system was essentially bipolar, consisting of two dominant parties and a multitude of smaller, ephemeral factions and groupings. With the emergence of Bosch's Partido de la Liberación Dominicana (PLD) as a viable electoral alternative and with the appearance of several well-organized minor parties, the trend has been toward multipolarity. Although the contemporary parties continue to rely on the appeal of charismatic leaders, increasing concern for organizational development has been unmistakable. Thus, a vibrant multiparty system has taken form over time, manifesting both the deeply rooted cultural preference for strong individual leadership and a growing recognition of the importance of an effective party apparatus.

At the present time, there are three major political parties in the Dominican Republic. The oldest of these, the PRD, was founded by Juan Bosch while in exile in 1939 and comprised the earliest organized opposition to the Trujillo regime. By virtue of its social-democratic orientation and its advocacy of social and economic reform within a democratic framework, the PRD has traditionally drawn the bulk of its support from the urban masses and, to a lesser extent, from segments of the middle class. Until recently, the party had been widely recognized as the nation's foremost democratic institution, characterized by a well-defined ideological foundation and programmatic emphasis and by a strong organizational structure. This reputation has been tarnished, however, by the dubious performance of the successive PRD governments (1978–86) and by the bitter infighting that has deeply divided the party.

This factionalism dates back to the late 1960s when a rift emerged within the party leadership concerning the viability of mounting an electoral challenge against the Balaguer regime in the face of mounting state-sponsored repression. The party's boycott of the 1968 municipal elections and the 1970 general elections reflected its transition to a more radical, antisystem ideology under Bosch's guidance. The intraparty debate eventually shifted from ideological and tactical concerns to organizational issues that focused on what some perceived as the excessive centralization of power at the expense of organizational diversity (Kryzanek 1977a:127–28). Bosch's efforts to consolidate his authority met with increasing resistance, particularly from moderates who opposed the decision to abandon electoral politics. These elements gained the upper hand in the party's internal struggle when Bosch resigned in November 1973 and announced the formation of the PLD.

Although Bosch had been the founder and driving force behind the PRD, his defection after nearly 35 years at the party's helm did not signal its impending demise. Led by Peña Gómez, a new generation of party leaders emerged that enabled the PRD to manage the succession crisis.[6] This shift served to revitalize the organization because Peña Gómez's push for a collegiate form of leadership facilitated a more decentralized and equitable distribution of power. Although this marked a significant stage in the party's internal evolution, it did not eliminate the deep divisions and may have reinforced existing cleavages.

Upon returning to power in 1978, the party entered a period of intense fragmentation and internal decline. With the gradual erosion of the charismatic leadership provided by Peña Gómez (a trend Oviedo associates with the transformation of the PRD from opposition to governing party), the PRD was deprived of a dominant, unifying figure (Oviedo 1987:226). As a result, the rift between the Guzmán and Jacobo Majluta and Peña Gómez and Jorge Blanco tendencias widened and became increasingly bitter. With the national economy continuing to falter and the government immobilized by the PRD's internal power struggle, the Guzmán and Jorge Blanco administrations enjoyed little success in implementing their desired programs. As discontent spread and its mass base began to erode, the PRD effectively abandoned its reformist agenda and resorted to clientelism and other nondemocratic means of maintaining support (Oviedo 1987:228).

Ironically, the decline of the PRD has coincided with the emergence and rapid development of the PLD. Following his defection from the PRD, Bosch established the PLD to serve as a vehicle for the advancement of his "dictatorship with popular support."[7] The PLD continues to be a highly centralized body under the strict control of its founder and leader. However, an extremely active, well-defined organizational apparatus has taken form which has enabled the party to substantially expand its support base. It is generally conceded that the PLD is the most disciplined and rigidly organized of the major parties.[8]

In spite of Bosch's earlier rejection of electoral politics, the PLD has made steady and impressive gains since its initial appearance in 1978. The party has taken advantage of the mounting dissatisfaction with the PRD to make inroads into that party's traditional urban constituency. The impact of this trend manifested itself in 1986, and Balaguer's victory over Majluta has been attributed to a sizable exodus of PRD supporters to Bosch (Hartlyn 1987:34). In fact, the PLD has effectively displaced the PRD as the nation's principal social-democratic alternative as evidenced by its strong showing in 1990.

A significant shift in ideological orientation and programmatic focus has accompanied the PLD's evolution from 1978, when it received 1 percent of the vote and lost its official status, to 1990, when it emerged as the frontrunner.[9] Bosch has moderated his rhetoric considerably, most notably in 1986 and again in 1990 (Hartlyn 1987:33).[10] This willingness to discuss foreign investment and privatization was a far cry from his traditional anti-imperialist stance. The party's evolution also underscores the growing importance of an effective party organization to supplement strong, personalistic leadership. Although some have raised questions about the party's future given the pervasiveness of Bosch's control, its sophisticated organization may provide for its continued development.

Since the demise of the PRD in 1986, the Dominican government has been under the control of Balaguer's Partido Reformista Social Cristiano (PRSC). This party was the product of a 1984 merger between the Partido Reformista (PR) and the small Partido Revolucionario Social Cristiano (also PRSC). Balaguer formed the PR prior to the 1966 election to act as a vehicle for his candidacy. Through the PR-PRSC, Balaguer has been elected on five separate occasions (1966, 1970, 1974, 1986, and 1990). His program of "order and progress" has remained virtually unchanged over the years, although he has been compelled to make certain modifications in leadership style and party structure. For example, while the party continues to be highly centralized and personalistic, the merger with the small but well-organized PRSC reflects Balaguer's realization of the need for enhancing the party's internal structure and cultivating linkages with international organizations.

Balaguer's popularity in the countryside has stemmed in large part from his inheritance of Trujillo's enormous rural support base. He has successfully maintained this support through an intricate network of clientelistic relations. The provision of highly visible public works projects and other forms of patronage has enabled Balaguer to cultivate the image of national patrón. He has also enjoyed the support of the Dominican elite and the United States, both of whom have sought a stable environment that would be conducive to business interests.

Balaguer's defeat at the hands of PRD, first in 1978 and later in 1982, underscored the need to make party modifications. In light of the significant demographic shifts the nation had experienced, it was apparent that the party would have to expand upon its rural support base. Like the PLD, Balaguer was able to play upon the discontent within the urban classes to draw support from the PRD. His ability to mobilize this support was certainly enhanced by the organizational apparatus gained through the merger. While in office, Balaguer has relied upon massive public expenditures for infrastructural development. For the masses, who saw in Balaguer an opportunity to return to the relative prosperity of earlier times, these projects constitute a visible testament to perceived progress and development.

In contrast to the Dominican experience, a two-party system was institutionalized in Jamaica during the period of political tutelage between 1944, when universal adult suffrage was granted to the colony, and 1962, when independence was achieved. The rules of the game were thus established as a consequence of forces that brought about the need for significant change in the political order.

Parties arose in Jamaica at a critical turning point in its history. After the global economic depression of 1929, Jamaican workers began to organize in order to express their grievances. At the same time, a movement toward self-government derived from increasing dissatisfaction with the ability of Britain to effectively respond to local Jamaican problems. These two mutually reinforcing tendencies combined to foster the emergence of the modern system. Jamaican parties began either as trade union-based populist movements or as national movements based on the demand for self-government.[11] This connection between unions and parties reflected the historically alienated position of Jamaican workers, their politicization as a result of the 1938 protests, and the new nationalism of the Jamaican middle class. Several scholars see the creation of parties by elites as a means of integrating the masses into the existing framework of power (Stone 1980; Edie 1991).

The People's National Party (PNP) was formed in 1938 by Norman Manley as a nation-building organization. The PNP was organized as an hierarchical structure through which the national movement could be coordinated and channeled.[12] The party was molded by Norman Manley's outstanding intellect, personality, and dedication until his retirement in 1969, when the party caucus chose his son, Michael, to succeed him.[13] Supported largely by middle-class professionals, the PNP initially cooperated with the Bustamante Industrial Trade Union (BITU). In 1943, the charismatic Alexander Bustamante used the BITU as a basis for the creation of the Jamaica Labor Party (JLP). Ten years later, the PNP created its own National Workers' Union (NWU), and the JLP-BITU became the sole effective rival of the PNP-NWU in the "most significant [political] polarization of Jamaica's population" (Kuper 1976:111).

The results of Jamaican elections since 1944 reflect the dominance of the PNP and the JLP in a system in which the two parties have attracted almost equal followings. This two-party system has become increasingly accepted, while third parties have been progressively eliminated as viable alternatives. Third parties have lacked charismatic leaders as well as trade union linkages. Thus a "passionate" (Kuper 1976) polarization between the PNP and the JLP has produced "staunch" party support (Hillman 1979a; 1979b), and the two-party system became firmly entrenched in Jamaica. This kind of support may derive from the need to find a focus for loyalty in a society largely devoid of indigenous institutions.

The PNP's intellectual appeal for self-government through a Federation of the West Indies during a time of accelerated decolonization drew the support of the educated middle class. However, Norman Manley recognized the need to generate working-class support as well. He did so through the NWU at the time of independence and "even penetrated the lumpen-proletariat of Kingston, through a canny decision to treat seriously with the Rastafarians" (Kuper 1976:114). Appearances in the presence of the lower classes and the Rastafarians, who personified rejection of British culture, symbolized an attempt to generate broad-based support.

An informal two-way influence between the NWU and the PNP has propelled trade unionists such as Michael Manley into political power.

This phenomenon is more a reflection of the "organic connection between labor and politics" (Kaplan et al. 1976:211) than of socialist theory.

PNP socialism as conceived by Norman Manley reflected egalitarian and humane principles modelled on the British Labor Party program and applied to a developing society. Despite conflicting interpretations and misperceptions of this ideological dimension, Norman Manley offered clear rationale for "commanding heights" theory, equal opportunity, and welfare programs in the Jamaican context (Nettleford 1971:49). The purge of left-wing radicals in 1952 provides evidence that the party was not based on doctrinaire Marxism. Thereafter, PNP socialism meant little more than national planning within a framework of private property and foreign capital (Kaplan et al. 1976:212).

As discussed in Chapter 2, Michael Manley's version of democratic socialism (originally designed to create a program that would appeal to the changing political and economic environments of the 1960s and 1970s) was compromised by his penchant for flamboyant rhetoric and was variously interpreted at home and abroad as a radical move to the left. Michael Manley tried to counteract an elitist image of "brown man's politics" through the use of Rastafarian symbols and reggae music, and he appealed to those wishing to challenge dependency through "the politics of change." However, the inability of his administration to promote visible socioeconomic development resulted in his loss of the government in the 1970s. The subsequent PNP government of the 1990s has returned to its typically social democratic roots as a reformist organization.

When it was founded, the JLP, like the BITU, was dominated by Bustamante whose conception of leadership was "demagogic and authoritarian" (Kaplan et al. 1976:214).[14] Bustamante's charismatic personification as a folk hero and patron of the "barefoot man" is legendary and continue to contribute to JLP campaign imagery. After emerging from the 1938 protests as a populist leader, Bustamante's negotiating skills and political acumen attracted support, not only from the workers and peasants, but also from a business sector uneasy with PNP socialism. Thus, the broadly-based JLP was pragmatic rather than ideological. Bustamante advocated self-government but opposed federation. However, the party was antisocialist only to the extent that it opposed the PNP (Hillman 1979a).

While Bustamante's messianic temperament precluded focus on organizational matters, other JLP organizers built a party machine structured around an activist cadre.[15] In the early 1970s Edward Seaga's leadership of the party was distinguished by his systematic constituency organization. However, his predecessor, Hugh Shearer, was known less for any programmatic or organizational contributions than for Bustamante's personal support of him.

Employing the image of a technocratic financial genius, Seaga promoted the JLP as a capitalist alternative to failed PNP socialism in the 1970s and 1980s. Support was drawn from the traditional (but paradoxical) coalition of populists and businessmen who were increasingly antagonized by the PNP's inability to deliver on its promises. Both the PNP and the JLP have won mass support through patronage and through the selective use of public funds in client constituencies and parishes. Despite ideological rhetoric and spurious images of a Christian JLP and an atheistic PNP, both parties seek to establish multiclass coalitions of the economically active members of Jamaican society.

Both parties have converged their focus on electoral competition, thus de-emphasizing the potential for true ideological divergence. Norman Manley's initial impulse to build on a middle-class foundation a nationalist movement designed to improve conditions in Jamaica needed working-class support. Bustamante's trade union-based populism required commercial allies. These tendencies became increasingly pronounced as Jamaican society continued to modernize and become more complex. Therefore, as the political system developed, the parties became more similar (Kuper 1976:114–15).

Beyond images and rhetoric, the only real difference in domestic policy making appears to be in the larger degree to which the PNP has increased public spending and taxation. Basic social and economic policies of the JLP have tended to emphasize private sector incentives but have included reformist initiatives as well. Political power in the main Jamaican parties is concentrated within a closed elite that exercises control over multiple class support. As Edie suggests, "the average Jamaican voter assumes the JLP and PNP are adversaries. The parties oppose each other in parliamentary debates and at general elections, and are expected to govern the country differently when each has its turn in office. But reality tells otherwise" (1991:49). In this regard, analysts have drawn from the conspiratorial explanation in defining the nature and effects of party competition in Jamaica. Stone, for example, finds that each party seeks to establish hegemony over defined political territory or areas.[16]

Both Jamaican parties have recruited through patronage and have provided a mediating function between elites and masses by issuing favorable policies and rhetorical responses to popular aspirations. Stone (1974) documents the low level of issue awareness in Jamaican political culture. He emphasizes the symbolic role of electoral mass mobilization and the manipulation of partisan loyalties by elites who thereby consolidate their preeminent position and control of public policy.[17] Accordingly, political elites "utilize rhetoric, patronage and personality appeals to maintain a minimal level of control over the poorer strata. This self-conscious manipulation and control of the masses is central to the past pattern of stability in Jamaican politics" (Stone 1974:89).

In the absence of real ideological differences or clear representation of special interests, political support has derived from emotional, party-generated images of charismatic leaders who promise to provide for their followers. Such mobilization in the past has ensured maintenance of the existing structure of power in Jamaica, but the forces of modernization have begun to exert pressure for innovative change.

ELECTIONS

Like political parties, elections in the Dominican Republic have been of genuine significance only in the post-Trujillo era. While elections were held on a more or less regular basis prior to 1930, they "did not directly affect many Dominicans" and were therefore of marginal relevance (McDonald and Ruhl 1989:329). Those held during the Trujillato were of even less consequence since they were blatantly fraudulent and were intended solely for the purpose of legitimizing the regime and providing a facade of democratic participation.

Since the demise of the Trujillo dictatorship, eight presidential elections have been held, some more competitive than others. While these contests (along with the party system) have facilitated the integration of the masses into the political process, they also have served to legitimize continued elite domination of the nation's political system. In spite of the unmistakable shift toward democratic values and principles that has occurred, elections continue to be characterized to a large extent by personalistic and patron-client voting. Nonetheless, recent experiences suggest that elections have been converted "into the mechanism par excellence for gaining power" and have therefore come to occupy "a position of centrality in the Dominican political process" (Brea Franco 1989:71).

Many scholars look to the 1978 election as a pivotal point in the evolution of the Dominican political system, contending that the reemergence of the PRD through a peaceful transfer of power initiated a true "democratic opening." While this and subsequent contests have not been without incident, certain patterns have taken form which have done much to lend an air of legitimacy to the electoral process. For example, recent elections have been contested within a relatively stable framework that are essentially free of coercion, intimidation, and political violence. Participation levels have been fairly high, notwithstanding a slight decrease in 1990. Finally, elections have grown increasingly competitive largely because of the emergence of new parties that challenge the more established organizations (see Table 5.1).

In contrast, of the four elections held prior to 1978, only the 1962 contest can be considered to have been genuinely competitive according to commonly accepted criteria (Weiner and Özbudun 1987). The victory by Bosch, which has been attributed as much to his charismatic appeal as to his party's platform, represented a clear repudiation of the excesses of the Trujillo regime and of those seeking to perpetuate the status quo.[18] Hailed at the time as a major step in the transition to democratic rule, the rise to power of the PRD transformed the masses into "a subject of political action" (Catrain 1987:269). Their preference for a more participatory, representative system was affirmed.

However, the subsequent coup, civil war, and U.S. intervention profoundly altered the terms of the 1966 election. The integrity of the entire electoral process was compromised by the U.S. government's extensive support of Balaguer and by the extreme levels of intimidation and terror endured by Bosch and his supporters. These factors certainly contributed to Balaguer's impressive victory. While allegations of massive fraud abound, they should not obscure the fact that Balaguer was a popular, well-respected leader and that his pledge to restore order and prosperity struck a responsive chord among voters weary of chronic instability.[19]

Over the next 12 years, Balaguer focused his efforts on restructuring Dominican society according to "a model of corporatist domination" (del Castillo 1984:59). During this period, party politics and elections were relegated to the periphery of the political system, a trend clearly illustrated by the high abstention levels characterizing the 1970 and 1974 contests. Under mounting pressure for reform toward the end of his third term, Balaguer eased restrictions on opposition groups. The ensuing resurgence of electoral activity culminated in 1978 with Guzmán's victory and the return to power of the PRD.

The renewal of the PRD's democratic experiment met with little success although it exemplified the party's resiliency and the broad support its reformist agenda enjoyed among the Dominican people. Nonetheless, the party remained in power in 1982 when Jorge Blanco managed to overcome the criticism levied against his predecessor and the

TABLE 5.1
Dominican Elections, 1962–1990

Year of Election	Number of Reg. Voters	% of Eligible Voters Partic.	Number of Valid Votes	Winner/Party and % of Votes	Main Opposition/Party and % of Votes	% of Votes for Others
1962	N/A	70 (est.)	1,054,944	Juan Bosch (PRD) 59.4	Viriato Fiallo (UCN) 30.1	10.5
1966	N/A	N/A	1,345,404	Joaquín Balaguer (PR) 57.2	Juan Bosch (PRD) 39.0	3.8
1970	N/A	56 (est.)	1,238,205	Joaquín Balaguer (PR) 57.1	Francisco Augusto Lora (MIDA) 20.4	22.5
1974	2,006,323	56	1,113,419	Joaquín Balaguer (PR) 84.7	Luis Homero Lajara Burgos (PDP) 15.3	0.0
1978	2,283,784	73	1,655,807	Antonio Guzmán (PRD) 51.7	Joaquín Balaguer (PR) 42.2	6.1
1982	2,601,684	74	1,830,730	Salvador Jorge Blanco (PRD) 46.7	Joaquín Balaguer (PR) 39.2	14.1
1986	3,039,347	72	2,111,745	Joaquín Balaguer (PRSC) 41.4	Jacobo Majluta (PRD) 39.5	19.1*
1990	N/A	N/A	1,934,214	Joaquín Balaguer (PRSC) 35.1	Juan Bosch (PLD) 33.8	31.0**

*The increasing vote totals for "others" from 1978–86 reflects the rise of the PLD as a viable third party. **Includes 23 percent for the PRD.

Sources: Julio G. Campillo Pérez, *Elecciones Dominicanas: Contribución a Su Estudio* (Santo Domingo: Relaciones Públicas); Julio Brea Franco, "Reforma Electoral y Representación Política en el Sistema Electoral Dominicano," *Ciencia y Sociedad* 12 (January-March, 1987); Junta Central Electoral, *Gaceta Oficial* (Nos. 9039, 9192, 9340, 9483, 9612) (Santo Domingo: Junta Central Electoral).

inherent burdens of incumbency to defeat Balaguer (Dix 1984). Of particular note during the 1982 election was the continued growth of the PLD. By increasing its vote total from 1 percent to nearly 10 percent (and gaining municipal and congressional representation in the process), the PLD served notice that it was a viable third party and an electoral force to be reckoned with.

This trend toward multipolarity was reinforced in 1986 when Bosch and the PLD gained nearly 20 percent of the vote. As expected, this increase came at the expense of the PRD, whose credibility as a democratic, reform-oriented organization was severely undermined after eight years in power. Ironically, Bosch's resurgence as an electoral alternative enabled Balaguer to win in what had been the closest election of the post-Trujillo era to that time. This victory may also be attributed to an aggressive and highly effective public relations campaign that focused attention on the PRD's lack of productivity while reinforcing Balaguer's image as a "nation-builder" (Bonnelly 1986).

Since the reemergence of Balaguer, the Dominican political system has experienced a period of realignment and recomposition, the implications of which were manifested during the 1990 election. The PLD has clearly supplanted the PRD as the principal opposition party, as evidenced by Bosch's near victory over Balaguer. Speculation that the PRD would suffer an irreparable split proved accurate when Majluta left to form the Partido Revolucionario Independiente. Neither he nor Peña Gómez, who remained as leader of the PRD, posed a serious challenge to the frontrunners. This period also saw the development of several smaller parties and organizations, including the Fuerza Nacional Progresista and the Partido Liberal La Estructura. Their emphasis on interest articulation, issue formulation, and public education significantly enhanced the democratic process.

As in 1986, questions were raised concerning the performance of the Junta Central Electoral during the 1990 election. A number of observers have attributed the organization's indecisiveness and low level of legitimacy to its lack of autonomy and inherent politicization (Hartlyn 1987). Another factor illustrating the low level of institutionalization in Dominican society has been the continued popularity of individual leaders, most notably Balaguer and Bosch. Their dominance, which may help to explain the surprisingly low turnout among younger Dominicans in 1990, reflects the perception among the general public that only strong individual leadership can resolve the nation's endemic problems.

The Dominican Republic has enjoyed a period of relative stability during which political parties and elections have gained credibility and become integral components of the political process. However, while it is clear that the country has achieved a certain degree of democratic growth and institutionalization (particularly since 1978), "economic problems are undermining the viability of its recently established and still-fragile democratic institutions" (Wiarda 1989:453). It seems apparent that the future of party politics and elections rests upon the ability of democratically elected leaders to provide visible amelioration of the current crisis. This situation is not unique in the Caribbean.

In the case of Jamaica, emotional attachments to particular leaders and their political parties are manifested in voting behavior and electoral outcomes. Patron-client and ritualistic voting in elections, characterized more by personality and image than by ideology, have been attributed to the imposition of an external political model that stultified the emergence of an indigenous focus for loyalty and social cohesiveness (Manley 1974). According to this explanation, the parties generated a form of tribalism.[20] Nevertheless, pragmatic political perspectives have cut across party ideologies (Hillman 1979b).

It is the perceived ability of political leaders to provide viable solutions to economic and social problems that defines their charisma and explains the basis of their support. In Jamaica, there has been an alternation between opposing forces such as free enterprise capitalism versus democratic socialism, "industrialization by invitation" versus promotion of a New International Economic Order, and strong ties with the West versus nonalignment. Each leader has received an opportunity to provide a solution and, in turn, has been repudiated by an electorate seeking visible results such as improvements in the living standard and increased opportunities.

The consequence has been a definitive pattern of power alternation in which the PNP and JLP have each served two consecutive terms in office followed by a period as the opposition party (see Table 5.2). The JLP was in power in 1944 and 1949, the PNP in 1955 and 1959, the JLP in 1962 and 1967, the PNP in 1972 and 1976, the JLP in 1980 and 1983, and the PNP in 1989. While this progression may not constitute a tradition and could be altered at any time, it appears to reaffirm the idea that Jamaicans elect leaders to fulfill their promises; then, after a second chance when the leaders have lost their appeal the voters turn to their opponents.[21]

This dialectical system of major party alternation may have gained a sense of legitimacy, albeit by default (Edie 1991). While the voter participation in national elections has grown fairly steadily from 52 percent in 1944 to 86 percent in 1980 (thus creating the impression of

TABLE 5.2
Jamaican Elections, 1944–1989

Year of Election	Number of Votes Cast	% of Eligible Voters Partic.	% of Votes for JLP	% of Votes for PNP	% of Votes for Others	Party Forming Government	Prime Minister
1944	389,101	58.78	41.4	23.5	35.1	JLP	Alexander Bustamante
1949	477,107	65.16	42.7	43.5	13.8	JLP	Alexander Bustamante
1955	495,680	65.12	39.0	50.5	10.5	PNP	Norman Manley
1959	564,071	66.09	44.3	54.8	0.9	PNP	Norman Manley
1962	580,517	72.88	50.0	48.6	1.4	JLP	Alexander Bustamante
1967	446,815	82.24	50.6	49.1	0.3	JLP*	Donald Sangster Hugh Shearer
1972	477,771	78.88	43.4	56.4	0.2	PNP	Michael Manley
1976	742,149	85.20	43	57	N/A	PNP	Michael Manley
1980	860,750	86.80	59	41	0.0006	JLP	Edward Seaga
1983	N/A	N/A	100**	0	N/A	JLP	Edward Seaga
1989	N/A	N/A	43	57	N/A	PNP	Michael Manley

*Sangster died in office.   **PNP boycotted this election.

Sources: Wendell Bell, "Democracy in Jamaica" (unpublished); William Jesse Biddle and John D. Stephens, "Dependent Development and Foreign Policy: The Case of Jamaica," International Studies Quarterly 33 (December 1989):411; Statistical Institute of Jamaica, Statistical Yearbook of Jamaica (Kingston: Statistical Institute of Jamaica, 1986).

increasing confidence), the cathartic or psychological role of this dialectical system may have begun to face challenges. The visible results sought by a more expectant electorate have not materialized.

As explained previously, third party attempts in Jamaica have resulted in failure. The Jamaican Democratic Party, formed to protect the colonial order, was dissolved in 1944. The Farmer's Party did not survive the 1955 election. The left-wing People's Progressive Party failed in its attempt to revive Garveyism in 1962. The United Party proposing the maintenance of free enterprise was able to gain only one seat in parliament in 1972. The Jamaica/America Party, founded in 1986 in order to advocate "state partnership," also dissolved. In spite of these precedents, the Worker's Party of Jamaica (WPJ), organized by the Marxist-oriented Worker's Liberation League, has continued to seek support from workers and intellectuals.[22] Edie maintains that the WPJ "has little chance of forming the government or official position, but [its] presence cannot be ignored" (1991:48). Significantly, the number of votes cast for candidates other than those supported by the PNP or the JLP dramatically decreased from 122,000 in 1944 to under 1,000 in 1980. This reinforced the interpretation that, without charismatic leaders and a strong union linkage, only the two major parties have been able to channel mass participation through elite tutelage (Statistical Yearbook 1986:53).

These patterns of major party power alternation, expanded voter participation, and declining third party viability can be more fully understood with reference to the Jamaican electoral system. These patterns also help explain the frequent challenges of election results in a country with a high degree of institutional formalism.

General elections, held at least every five years, may be called by the prime minister at any time there is a question of confidence in the House of Representatives or any time there is a need for a public mandate. Votes are counted under the supervision of civil servants in the presence of party agents in constituencies determined by a committee of parliament.[23] Party-nominated candidates make deposits that are forfeited if they receive less than one-eighth of the votes cast (Kaplan et al. 1976:217). As we have seen, third parties have been unable to salvage their electoral deposits. However, despite limitations on campaign expenses, loopholes allow for the use of registered voters as campaign assistants. In addition, gerrymandering is common, political gangs intimidate voters, and the number of votes cast may not determine the number of seats won.[24] In light of these and other factors, claims of electoral fraud are common.

In the first election in 1944, the PNP, advocating a form of self-government in which power would be decentralized from the governor, was defeated by the extremely popular and opportunistic Bustamante. Newly committed to self-government, the JLP was returned in 1949. By this time, the PNP, with new overtures to the labor movement, gained 13 seats in the House and emerged as a respectable opposition party.

In the early 1940s, PNP purges of the radical left accompanied by Norman Manley's cultivation of a liberal, nationalist image allowed the PNP to win the 1955 and 1959 elections. Manley's attempt to gain popular support through a referendum on the question of federation failed by a small margin. He was subsequently defeated, enabling Bustamante and the JLP to lead Jamaica into independence in 1962. The JLP was returned in 1967 at a time when industrialization by invitation policies appeared to be reaping positive results.

By the early 1970s, Michael Manley's PNP slogans "Power to the People" and "Better Must Come" fused the disappointments of the late 1960s with the optimism of the earlier years (Kaplan et al. 1976:209). The implications of Manley's victories in 1972 and 1976 and of Seaga's JLP governments of 1980 and 1983 are the subjects of extensive in-depth analysis.[25] Stephens and Stephens (1986) investigate the efficacy of an innovative path toward development through Manley's attempted democratic socialism. Stone's extensive work reveals the ways in which electoral mass mobilization and public opinion are manipulated by elites who project illusory images of social change. Edie (1991) offers compelling explanations for the failure of either liberal capitalism or democratic socialism to sustain economic development in a system characterized by state-centered patronage that has undermined the ability of public policies to meet the needs of Jamaican citizens. Thus, Manley's reelection in 1989 under a moderate platform (see Chapter 2) raises questions about a "resurgence of clientelism rather than a return to democratic socialism" (Edie 1991:143).

In an era characterized by democratization in the Third World, it is ironic that the efficacy, not only of alternative styles of government but also of competitive party politics and elections has been called into question. It is clear that the consolidation of democracy in Jamaica has neither directly correlated with rapid modernization and socioeconomic development, nor (according to Edie [1991]) necessarily provided true democratic choices for Jamaicans.

The party systems of the Dominican Republic and Jamaica have achieved different degrees of institutionalization for different historical reasons. Although Dominican parties could only be characterized as occasionally relevant by the early 1970s, they have since begun to occupy a more central position in the political process.[26] While Jamaican parties have contributed to a dialectical electoral process since the 1940s, recently their relevance has been questioned (Edie 1991). Overreliance on strong leaders in both political systems has inhibited a higher degree of party institutionalization. Nevertheless, the party systems and elections have helped to mitigate the destabilizing effects of increasing socioeconomic pressures.

The party systems have been stabilizing agents to the extent that their domination by elites has channeled popular participation as a means of co-opting the masses into a corporatist framework through patronage and clientelism. Therefore, party politics has been exclusionary and unrepresentative. Such elite control has been characterized as "the functional equivalence of colonialism" (Cammack, Pool, and Tordoff 1989:114). Rapid modernization, rising expectations, and the impending disappearance of charismatic leaders have begun to challenge the efficacy of traditional patterns.

These patterns have persisted in systems with a relatively high degree of party legitimacy. This suggests a potential for further hybridization of the systems. It is clear, however, that unless the parties are modified in some way, they could be supplanted by alternative organizations.

Can the parties in either country aggregate informal political forces in order to create a coalition with real policy options? Some scholars conclude that such moderation can occur only if "elites become persuaded that the use of state resources to perpetuate party dominance is counterproductive" to their own interests (Cammack, Pool, and Tordoff 1989:114). At that time, it is suggested, the elites will become more cooperative and allow for greater equity in the distribution of resources. Of course, this has not been the case to date.

The Dominican Republic's struggle to overcome an authoritarian tradition through the consolidation of democracy and Jamaica's struggle to avoid devolution into authoritarianism by maintaining the legitimacy of its democratic system imply a kind of systemic convergence. Both countries are confronted by very similar problems. Party linkages to labor and students, the de-emphasis of ideology, the tendency toward moderation of leaders (both Bosch and Michael Manley have moved to the center), the emergence of pragmatic performance critieria, and the difficulty in replacing popular leaders are themes that exemplify convergence as well.[27]

While most scholars agree that parties possess great potential for coping with complex changes caused by modernization, political parties have only been partially effective in the Dominican Republic and Jamaica. As long as basic political and socioeconomic aspirations are insufficiently fulfilled, the stability of these Caribbean countries will remain precarious.

NOTES

1. "Conspiritorial parties may be motivated by fear of being persecuted or destroyed by their opponents should the latter become the ruling party. Or they may only want to retain the spoils of politics for themselves. . . . Instead of concentrating on bargaining with their opponents over legislation, they devote their energies to undermining the opposition and reducing its ability to retaliate. Partisanship becomes intense and distrust common" (Wynia 1978:89).

2. According to Brea Franco, "one can begin to speak of more or less modern political parties in the Dominican Republic following the termination of the Trujillo dictatorship" (D'Agostino interview 1990). Wiarda makes a similar claim in many of his writings.

3. According to LaPalombara and Weiner, "authoritarian governments, by achieving large-scale economic growth while preventing any massive political participation, demonstrate that there is nothing inevitable about the expansion of political participation. But increased urbanization, the growth of mass communications, and the spread of education appear to be accompanied by an increased desire for some forms of political participation; and the amount of force needed by an authoritarian regime for maintaining control over its population is often in direct proportion to the development of this desire" (LaPalombara and Weiner 1966:400).

4. LaPalombara and Weiner (1966) argue that, in assessing the origins of political parties in developing societies, it is necessary to look beyond the Western-based institutional theories. Rather, it is more appropriate to focus on "historical crises" such as legitimacy, integration, and participation as factors contributing to the emergence of parties.

5. Wiarda (1985b:589) claims "thirty-one political parties, seven competing labor federations, and a variety of other new groups" appeared during the year prior to the election.

6. "The institutional strength of a political party is measured, in the first instance, by its ability to survive its founder or the charismatic leader who first brings it to power" (Huntington 1968:409). The capacity to generate new leadership is an indication of a party's adaptability, one of the four criteria Huntington uses in determining an organization's level of institutionalization. In the case of the PRD, the fact that Bosch was replaced by the younger Peña Gómez is even more significant because it also represented a generational shift.

7. This thesis is presented in Bosch's book *El Próximo Paso: Dictadura con Respaldo Popular* (1970).

8. This point was raised in separate interviews with Julio Brea Franco and Flavio Darío Espinal and by rival political leaders Marino "Vincho" Castillo and Andrés Van Der Horst.

9. By law, failure to achieve 5 percent of the vote results in a party's loss of official status.

10.   This trend was also apparent in an interview the authors conducted with Bosch prior to the 1990 election.

11.   Marcus Garvey's short-lived People's Political Party, based on black consciousness, was really the first attempt to form a modern political party in the early 1930s.

12.   The PNP is organized throughout the island in almost 2,000 groups that send delegates to an annual conference at which the officers of the party and its National Executive Council are elected. The council elects the party executive. Party programs and policies are debated by the delegates at the annual conference (*Statistical Yearbook* 1986:45).

13.   Norman Manley gained the reputation as a national hero in his lifetime. He was called "Man of Destiny," "Father of the Nation," and with regard to the failed West Indian Federation, the "Man with the Plan." His thinking was a critical influence in Jamaican national development (Nettleford 1971).

14.   The JLP and the BITU, like the PNP and the NWU, are formally affiliated but autonomous.

15.   The JLP is a democratic structure, not unlike that of the PNP, consisting of branches, constituency executives, and a central executive (*Statistical Yearbook* 1986:45).

16.   "Violence, intimidation, bribery, patronage, victimization, rehousing, and restrictive voter registration of known supporters of the competing party by the governing party are all used to establish party hegemony in areas of growing, established or potential voting strength" (Stone 1973:394).

17.   "The self-conscious pragmatism and seemingly non-ideological orientation to public policy adopted by recent and successive JLP and PNP governments rests on a clear consensus on various policy issues that maximize the political power of the organized vested interests such as foreign and local businessmen and financiers" (Stone 1974:88).

18.   "Personalism was an important factor in the 1962 campaign. A mystique of dynamic leadership enveloped the white-haired Bosch, whose daily radio broadcasts and occasional appearances on television and at political rallies attracted large audiences. Fiallo, on the other hand, suffered from a distinct lack of charisma. His mediocre talents as a public speaker, his inability to project warmth of personality, and his general ineptitude as a politician, undoubtedly contributed to the relatively poor showing of the UCN" (Wells and Wiarda 1966:45).

19.   Herman and Brodhead (1984) provide the most detailed discussion of the alleged fraud that took place during the election.

20.   According to Manley, "party loyalties in Jamaica are tangible things you can eat. You talk about bankable assurance" (Hillman 1979b:398).

21.   See note 9 in Chapter 2 for information on the question of Jamaica's electoral tradition. Explanations of the second term range from cyclical theories of power, to the advantages of incumbency, to mere coincidence.

22.   Professor Trevor Munroe, Director of the WLL, idealistically maintains "the future is ours" (Hillman 1979b:399).

23.   Nevertheless, both Manley and Seaga claimed bogus elections and fraud (Hillman 1979a), and, according to Kuper (1976:113), there has been gerrymandering of constituencies by the party in power. Until 1966, there were 45 constituencies; for the next 10 years there were 53, and since 1976 there have been 60.

24.   This may occur in single-member district plurality systems consisting of constituencies of varying sizes. For example, this occurred in 1949 when the PNP won the majority of popular votes but gained only 40 percent of the seats. This occurred in 1962 and in 1972 when the percentage of seats was larger than the electoral margins (*Statistical Yearbook* 1986:53).

25.   See especially Stephens and Stephens (1986), Edie (1991), and Stone's voluminous work.

26.   In one of the earliest and most comprehensive surveys of Latin American political parties, McDonald (1971:2) identifies the Dominican Republic as a country where parties are "occasionally relevant."

27.   As mentioned previously, the transfer of power within the PNP is perceived as problematic because, according to one informant, "no one believes P. J. Patterson has the stature to replace Michael." In that sense, Patterson, the PNP heir apparent, may become the Peña Gómez of Jamaica — qualified, but unelectable.

III

POLITICAL INFLUENCES
AND OUTCOMES

In the final analysis, politics is really a process through which a community influences its fate. The manner in which conflicts are resolved and values are allocated in society and the people responsible for those processes determine how people live. Therefore, the security of individuals and their psychological and physical well-being are consequences of the political processes within a particular environment.

We have seen the extent to which political institutions are subject to pressures and forces that operate within formal political cultures. We will now focus on informal political influences and the outcomes they help to produce. Chapter 6 will review major political forces and interest groups while Chapter 7 will analyze the general economic and foreign policies of the Dominican Republic and Jamaica. These chapters will provide evidence of how certain patterns appear to converge in the attempt by these states to develop effective responses to political, social, and economic problems. The way in which each country has approached these issues illuminates the plight of small, insular states in the Caribbean and shows how underlying similarities between an Hispanic country and an Anglophone country are manifested in functional reality.

6

Political Forces and
Interest Groups

When political institutions operate in a manner that is compatible with societal values, they are perceived as legitimate vehicles for serving individual and group interests. While the amenability of different political systems to informal pressures varies considerably, the capacity of noninstitutional actors to secure their interests is an important consideration for comparative analysis. This is especially relevant in societies characterized by a high degree of institutional formalism. The extent of the influence exerted by various political actors and groups on the formation and administration of public policy is determined by the effective scope and distribution of power within society.

This chapter surveys several of the most prominent interest groups and political forces operating in Jamaica and the Dominican Republic. There are striking similarities and differences in terms of the types of groups found in each country, the relative levels of power and influence, and the kinds of pressures that are brought to bear on political choices. Elite groups that play an important role through formal and informal government linkages include traditional oligarchies, the "new rich," and an array of commercial, industrial, and professional associations. Other relevant actors include the military, university students, organized labor, the peasantry, and religious organizations. This analysis of Caribbean politics would be incomplete without mention of external forces such as the U.S. diplomatic community, international business, and large expatriate populations.

It has been well established that the prospects for democratic consolidation and stability in transitional societies rest to a large extent on the presence of "a pluralistic, autonomously organized civil society" (Diamond, Linz, and Lipset 1989:35). Although political parties in Jamaica and, increasingly, in the Dominican Republic have clearly helped to institutionalize political competition within a relatively stable electoral framework, their credibility as aggregators and articulators of societal interests has been compromised to some extent by the continued dominance of party hierarchies and by the perpetuation of exclusionary politics. The quality of civil society in both nations has been enhanced by the emergence and maturation of a variety of organizations and informal groupings capable of performing similar functions. In terms of democratic evolution, this will represent a positive development only to the extent that it serves to further integrate and socialize the masses. Ultimately, of course, the response of the respective national elites will be the determining factor.

ELITES

Elite manipulation of the masses has been the historic reality in both Jamaican and Dominican society. In an effort to ameliorate the disproportionate representation of wealthy minorities' interests, certain observers have advocated populist democracy in order to facilitate mass influence on political decision-making processes. For example, Stone suggests that populism in Jamaica would enhance the possibility of radical policy changes that maximize welfare gains for the masses within the parliamentary framework of government (1974:86). The mechanisms for the creation of appropriate development programs, however, remain elite-dominated because of the marginal impact of the masses in the determination of public policy. The argument suggests that the conflict between multiple interests in pluralist society is dominated by particular social groupings that exercise "quiet power" through the occupation of key positions, extensive lobbying, and close personal relationships with governmental leaders.[1]

While powerful minorities have clearly dominated the historical and contemporary politics in both the Dominican Republic and Jamaica, in neither country is there a single, monolithic elite. Rather, there are landowners, businessmen, professionals, prominent families, student groups, and various other associations that profoundly impact government decisions. They often operate in concert with the military, the political parties, or the unions. At times they are in conflict with each other.

In both the Dominican Republic and Jamaica, race and class correlate closely with the distribution of political power. Although in the Dominican Republic some upward mobility is available to ambitious individuals of darker color, the white elite has traditionally dominated the nation's social, political, and economic life. This group constitutes around 6 percent of the population and receives 43 percent of the total income (Wiarda and Kryzanek 1982:52). The same is true in Jamaica where "new opportunities created by economic diversification eroded the dominant position enjoyed by the light-skinned Jamaican commercial classes but were taken advantage of more by other ethnic minorities and the brown middle class than by the blacks" (Kaplan et al. 1976:219). Moreover, a study of the Jamaican corporate economy reveals its domination by small ethnic familial elites and their "continued usurping of the political process and retention of a diffuse but nonetheless real political power" (Stone and Brown 1977:36).

The race and class correlation in both Caribbean countries is a legacy of the genetic and cultural impact of colonial societies based on plantation systems and slavery. Eurocentricity has left a deep-seated psychological disposition that continues to manifest itself in societies in which non-African immigrant groups have been able to attain status and mobility more easily than the indigenous masses. While the influx of Haitian workers has influenced Dominican life, they have suffered extreme prejudice as a consequence of historical animosities. The race and class theory is clearly substantiated by the configuration of controlling interests in the Dominican sugar industry and the significant role played by the Chinese, East Indians, Middle Easterners, and Europeans in Jamaica. Reid argues that, at one point, 21 families owned the majority of the resources in Jamaica and thereby exercised a disproportionate influence on political decision making (Stone and Brown 1977:15).

An informal network of families whose members occupy key positions in Dominican society has been able to influence the government and even initiate policy decisions on important issues.[2] Among them are those whose fortunes can be traced to the ownership of land and those whose wealth derives from industrialization during the Trujillo era. Moreover, several studies of Jamaican elites reveal a pattern of informal power distribution similar to that in the Dominican Republic.[3] The proverbial 21 families in Jamaica continue to maintain their wealth through diversification and through the sale of land parcels that were originally granted under the Crown Colony and subsequently passed down through the generations. A high concentration of ownership with interlocking directorates suggests that power positions are distributed among a very small number of actors who are connected by kinship ties and familial relationships.

The new rich in both the Dominican Republic and Jamaica appear to be less psychologically secure than traditional aristocrats whose sense of status is more definitive. While the upper classes in both countries express certain anxieties regarding the prospects of socioeconomic and political reforms, the concerns of the new rich have clearly exceeded those of the oligarchy. Many informants attribute the fear of the masses to historic patterns of minority dominance in societies that were based first on slavery and later on an extremely inequitable distribution of wealth.

There are several organizations through which elite interests are represented in both countries. These include chambers of commerce and industry, manufacturing associations, banking businesses, and financial and trade associations (Garrity and Picard 1991:377). The National Council of Businessmen has actively represented the economic and business elite in the Dominican Republic, and so has its counterpart in Jamaica, the Jamaica Manufacturers' Association. Both organizations have been influential in affecting taxes, subsidy and monetary policies, restrictions on labor unions, and reductions of export duties. They have supported candidates with economic programs that are perceived as serving their special interests. For example, the chambers of commerce, the Sugar Manufacturing Association in Jamaica and the Sugar Planters Federation in the Dominican Republic, and the professional associations lobby their own governments, U.S. diplomats, and even U.S. congressmen in the hope of influencing the formation of favorable policies. Their role, however, has not been institutionalized to the point where strong sectoral relationships between government and business associations have produced beneficial development through partnership.[4]

Despite multiple class support, the political parties are also controlled by a closed elite at the top of the party hierarchy. Their connections with business elites and the use of the party system as a channel for state patronage divides the masses and reinforces corporatist relationships (Edie 1991:49). Social bifurcation has resulted in an asymmetry of power that has had a profound impact on political outcomes.

STUDENTS

The ideological perspectives and relatively weaker power position of university students clearly distinguish them from the more conservative elements of the elite. Although their access to higher education and the potential for upward mobility that it provides have given them a certain prestige, Caribbean students have been respected as interest articulators for the masses. Students consciously accept "direct social responsibility . . . as actual or aspirant members of an expanding elite. . . . The exclusiveness of higher education in Latin America would seem to contribute importantly to the psychology of leadership" (Silvert 1966:112).

The University of the West Indies (UWI) in Kingston is a multinational institution administered by the states of the Commonwealth Caribbean. It serves around 6,000 students of whom approximately half are Jamaican. While only intermittently involved in political activities, such as the riots of 1968, there has been increasing political organization and ideological emphasis since the 1970s. Students at the UWI rioted in 1968 over the deportation of a popular Guyanese professor whose radical politics served to unite Marxists and Rastafarians in the Abeng movement. Lacey concludes that these "Rodney Riots" were neither revolutionary nor insurrectionist (Lacey 1977:98).

Trevor Munroe, a member of the UWI faculty, organized the Workers' Liberation League with support from young intellectuals. This organization formed the basis for the communist Workers' Party of Jamaica directed by Munroe.[5] Also, the Institute of Social and Economic Research at the UWI has consistently published studies based on Marxist theory. However, UWI students' interest in socioeconomic and political change along with their generally leftist perspectives should be understood in the context of their privileged position in West Indian society. For the vast majority, involvement in radical politics ends upon graduation and co-optation into the power structure. The authors have observed several student radicals become staunch defenders of the status quo when they take their place in their family business or profession.

Student political expressions in the Dominican Republic, like those in Jamaica, have been influenced by leftist ideologies and are critical of conservative governments and the role of the United States. Their more pervasive impact may be attributed to their larger numbers as well as to the relative weakness of social institutions that make more salient the power of any organized group.

The Universidad Autónoma de Santo Domingo, the largest of the Dominican universities, has been a center of political activity. Protests against the government have led to violent confrontations with the police on numerous occasions. In the early 1960s, a group known as the Fragua espoused revolutionary ideals and gained great popularity on campus. Other universities have remained more conservative. The Universidad Nacional Pedro Henríquez Ureña with 10,000 students, the newer Universidad Católica Madre y Maestra, and the Universidad Iberoamericana have fewer total students, but who appear to be interested mainly in their education and future employment. The students' campaign to refrain from voting in the 1990 presidential election indicates disaffection, rather than apathy. Many students told the authors that the election was an irrelevant exercise in which they refused to participate due to the dominance of elderly caudillos. However, their future potential as active participants may be a significant factor in the legitimation of the electoral process.

University-inspired violence and protests have occurred in response to government austerity measures in both countries during the 1980s. Along with these demonstrations, the ideological debates and ideas emanating from the universities have contributed to an ongoing political dialogue and, while less efficacious than the machinations of the economic elites, have had an impact on national politics.[6]

THE MILITARY

The Dominican armed forces have traditionally been highly politicized. A Dominican army officer's comment on the detention of an opposition candidate for president in 1974 is revealing: "The constitution is one thing; the military is another" (Lowenthal 1976:3). The Jamaica Constabulary Force (JCF) and the Jamaica Defense Force (JDF), although theoretically subordinated to civilian authority in a country that has never had a military government, are also politicized but to a lesser extent than the armed forces of the Dominican Republic (Lacey 1977:122). According to one Jamaican informant, "you should never underestimate the behind-the-scenes influence of the Defense Force."

On the one hand, there is a dramatic contrast between the history of Dominican caudillismo, which is punctuated with several significant foreign occupations and direct military control of the government, and the indirect influence of the Jamaican armed forces, which is based on the British military tradition.[7] On the other hand, the formation of internal police forces by dominant foreign nations (the British in Jamaica and the United States in the Dominican Republic) has created instruments for the protection of a particular set of interests in each country (Lacey 1977:102; Black 1986:102; Edie 1991:107).

As a political actor in the Dominican Republic, the armed forces have operated as an instrument of both the domestic economic elite and of U.S. policy. The influence exerted by the military in Balaguer's regime grew through representation in his administration. Military officers were appointed to one cabinet seat in his first administration, to two in his second, and to three in his third (Bell 1981:213). Moreover, the military share of government spending rose from 39.9 percent in 1970–74 to 46.7 percent in 1975–76.

In Jamaica, the armed forces have been relatively autonomous, operating politically in their own interests despite allegations to the contrary during the past two decades. To the extent that the Jamaican armed forces have been subordinated to the prevailing political order, they have been much less politicized than their Dominican counterparts. Experiences in these two countries confirms that "complete subordination of the armed forces to the state occurs rarely" (Rial 1990:277). It is axiomatic that the greater the military's political involvement through civilian regimes, the less intervention is necessary as a means of achieving their corporate interests.

In the context of democratic consolidation, the Dominican Republic has experienced a change in the pattern of direct military intervention in government. "The relation between the level of military institutionalization and the institutionalization of civilian political procedures may be a key determinant of the varying roles army officers play" (Lowenthal 1969:128). The professionalization of the military has been accompanied by a tendency to remain in the background, or to exercise influence through political positions within the government. Although other interest groups have gained legitimacy in Dominican society, expansion of the military's economic and institutional power has ensured that the military remains the most powerful single group. Its antidemocratic organization and antiliberal interests figure into the political system as an omnipresent influence that civilian leaders cannot ignore.

The potential role of the Jamaican armed forces as a powerful political actor was illustrated by a series of joint operations involving the JDF and JCF during the late 1960s.[8] Serious questions about the political role of the Jamaican armed forces emerged with the Jamaica Labor Party (JLP) charges in the late 1970s that the People's National Party (PNP) was "planning a military solution in the form of a State of Emergency, a terror campaign against JLP supporters" (Stephens and Stephens 1986:207). This plan would be supplemented by the creation of a powerful Home Guard, a local paramilitary operation run by the government. These allegations led to official inquiries and court proceedings. While the findings failed to support the charges, the PNP government's legitimacy was already damaged.

In June 1980, after a plot involving members of the JDF was terminated by the JDF command, the armed forces began to criticize vociferously the PNP government's relationship with Cuba. The threat of armed intervention caused the government to respond in ways that were perceived by the armed forces as interference "violating corporate autonomy" (Stephens and Stephens 1986:330). This change in the allegiance of the armed forces coincided with middle-class disaffection and thereby contributed to the downfall of the PNP government.

The Jamaican armed forces, unlike those of the Dominican Republic, are probably too limited in numbers and too insufficiently disciplined to actually conduct a successful coup. Their influence in politics, however, is unmistakable. For example, it has been shown that the security forces' middle-class perspective was influential in the JLP's defeat of the PNP in the 1980 election.[9]

While its role in the Dominican Republic and Jamaica is substantially different, the influence of the military in each political system has been an important calculus of the institutionalization of democracy. The scope and limitations of power, in the two societies, are defined by the interrelationships between the armed forces, the elites, and the governments and by the potential conditions in which the Dominican military would once again intervene or the Jamaican forces would play a more active political role.

RELIGIOUS ORGANIZATIONS

In the Dominican Republic, 93 percent of the citizens identify themselves as Roman Catholic and the great majority of Jamaicans say they are Christian. However, while upper- and middle-class affiliations and practices are similar to European patterns, the masses adhere to fundamentalist or syncretic forms of worship.

Politically active Jamaicans are associated with Anglican, Methodist, Baptist, Presbyterian, and Roman Catholic churches. There is also a small, but influential, number of Jews. The lower middle class and working poor generally subscribe to fundamentalist Christian sects that emphasize upward mobility through one or another variant of the work ethic. Afro-Christian cults combining spiritualism, ceremonialism, and revivalism include Pocomania, Zion Revival, Obeah, and Rastafarianism.

The Catholic church in the Dominican Republic, traditionally part of the power structure along with the military and the oligarchy, remains a conservative institution. However, the younger and more liberal clerics have begun to espouse interpretations of liberation theology and to work with labor and in peasant cooperatives. The political importance of the church has diminished due to a shortage of priests, a decline in church attendance, an increase in Protestant conversions, and the continued influence of syncretic Santería. Its political influence is either symbolic, as in its various pastoral letters advocating human rights and agrarian reform, or indirect, as in its ability to shape political values. The involvement of the archbishop of Santo Domingo, Monseñor Nicolás de Jesús López Rodríguez, in the 1986 presidential election "revealed the church's desire to influence the course of national governance" (Kryzanek and Wiarda 1988:93).

However, it is at the local level that both the performance of the church and the conflicts within it have been most visibly manifested. The influence of local deacons in molding attitudes has been as important an ingredient in the Jamaican political equation as has that of the parish priests who have organized "comunidades de base" (grass roots Christian communities) in the Dominican Republic. In both countries, the responsiveness of religious organizations to the needs of the poor is directly correlated to their newly emerging roles as indirect political actors.

ORGANIZED LABOR

The percentage of workers who are members of labor unions in the Dominican Republic and Jamaica is relatively small. An estimated 15 percent of the Dominican work force has been unionized compared to slightly over 20 percent in Jamaica. However, the impact of the labor movement on national politics in Jamaica has been much greater than it has been in the Dominican Republic.

Intensive efforts by the Partido Revolucionario Dominicano (PRD) to organize the nation's burgeoning working class in the early 1960s led to the emergence of the Dominican labor movement as an important political force. The mobilization of the urban workers resulted in a dramatic increase in the number of registered unions and elicited favorable legislation from the Bosch government.[10] However, deep divisions within the movement itself were exacerbated by the coup deposing Bosch and the subsequent civil war. Labor was brought under strict government control with the reemergence of Balaguer in 1966, ensuring that its political impact would be marginal at best.

Organized labor experienced a revitalization of sorts with the return to power of the PRD in 1978. The proliferation of labor unions that occurred under Guzmán and Jorge Blanco reflected the heightened mobilization of the urban workers and the emergence of a more open political system.[11] More recently, worker involvement in antigovernment strikes following the 1990 election attests to a growing militancy and politicization within the labor movement. Nonetheless, its influence has been constrained by constitutional and labor code restrictions, scarce financial resources, and a persistently high level of unemployment that undermines its negotiating leverage. As a result, organized labor has failed to provide an effective counterbalance to the power of the economic elite.

Dominican parties have historically maintained linkages to the labor movement in an effort to mobilize electoral support.[12] The nation's largest labor organization, the General Union of Dominican Workers, has been closely associated with the PRD while the Partido Reformista Social Cristiano is affiliated with the Autonomous Confederation of the Working Class. The rapid growth of the Partido de la Liberación Dominicana may be attributed, in part, to the significant inroads it has made in the labor movement. Through clientelism and the co-optation of union officials, the parties have been able to effectively control and manipulate the working class. However, while worker influence on the national level has been restricted, there have been indications of increased organizational activity at the grass roots level that could eventually lead to more substantial mass involvement in Dominican politics.

By virtue of their strong ties to political parties, Jamaican labor organizations have exerted a greater influence on national politics than have their Dominican counterparts. The Jamaican party system was an outgrowth of a labor movement that provided an initial vehicle for the expression of nationalism. When Jamaican workers returned to the island from countries affected by the worldwide economic depression of the 1930s, their newly acquired anti-imperialist ideological orientation gave expression to the view that only a local solution could succeed in their homeland.

Manley's argument that the labor movement in Jamaica was essentially a nationalist movement was fueled by the popular conclusion that, 100 years after emancipation (1838), the workers were no better off than the slaves. He maintains that "to understand the psychology of the labor movement one has to go back to the institution of slavery" (Manley 1975:46). The desire to organize public opinion coalesced with increasing sentiment for self-government. Thus, emergent nationalism and the movement toward the organization of labor were parallel and mutually reinforcing (Edie 1991:45). In fact, the labor disturbances of 1938 sparked the creation of trade union–political party linkages, the Moyne investigation, changes in the Crown colony system, attempted federation, and, ultimately, independence.

In the past two decades, trade unions have been relatively strong, growing to over 300,000 members. The largest and most important of these are the Bustamante Industrial Trade Union (BITU), affiliated with the JLP, and the National Workers' Union (NWU), affiliated with the

PNP. The BITU has approximately 100,000 members mainly in the sugar industry, but also in construction, commerce, and the public sector. The NWU's 102,000 members are drawn from the bauxite and alumina industry, tourism, communications, manufacturing, construction, commerce, and the public sector. Of lesser importance are the Trade Union Council, which is an off-shoot of the PNP, and several smaller unions, including Trevor Munroe's University and Allied Workers Union, which is affiliated with the Workers' Liberation League.

Experience in the major trade unions has provided a vehicle for political ascendancy. For example, Alexander Bustamante owed his political career to the fame engendered by his charismatic leadership of the BITU. Michael Manley's move from the NWU to leader of the PNP is another case in point.

The leadership of both the BITU and the NWU is recruited from the middle class rather than rank and file. This has resulted in an asymmetrical interdependence between party and union elites on one side and the general membership of parties and unions on the other. Union leaders generate workers' support for party leaders (delivering votes, manpower, and financial support in elections), but reliance on this support has not empowered labor.

The propensity toward the use of demonstrations and strikes on the part of union members may be attributed in large part to a lack of trust in union leaders. A survey conducted by Carl Stone in 1971 concludes "as much as 40 percent of unionized labor is convinced that the BITU and NWU leaderships do not adequately represent the interests of the working class" due to "ineffectiveness, corruption, and the alliance to the political parties" (Stephens and Stephens 1986:48). This lack of trust may be rooted in the nature of the relationship between workers and employers. Worker militancy and antagonisms between workers and employers are based on historical patterns of racial and class conflicts.[13]

In Jamaica, the awarding of jobs to union members through party patronage is accomplished either directly through government projects or indirectly through businesses run by party leaders. This practice has accentuated the asymmetry of the clientelistic relationship between elites and workers, whose interests are subordinated to those of the elite leaders. A similar pattern is obtained in the Dominican Republic where electoral support is mobilized for the party by labor unions in exchange for massive employment patronage.

In contrast to the very limited collective bargaining possible in the Dominican Republic where the state is predominant in industrial relations, the Jamaican state has played a relatively minor role in labor relations.

The British model of voluntary collective bargaining in the private sector has operated except in the area of essential services where the Ministry of Labor has used compulsory arbitration to resolve deadlocked negotiations.

Although there have been attempts in the past by small groups of radicals to internationalize the unions in both the Dominican Republic (through the General Confederation of Labor) and Jamaica (through the Caribbean Labor Congress), organized labor remains basically nonideological.[14]

THE PEASANTRY

The poor majority has been subject to oligarchic divide and conquer strategies in both the Dominican Republic, where campesino participation in politics has been sporadic, and Jamaica, where the incorporation of the peasant population in a national movement has proven illusive. Peasants are "hard to organize due to their dispersion throughout the countryside and subordination" through patronage (Wynia 1978:82). Minimal distribution of scarce resources to the masses has the effect of neutralizing their potential politicization. The peasants, therefore, have been generally excluded from the mainstream of national political life, despite their sheer numbers. Moreover, it is difficult to know what peasants want. Several scholars have suggested that an alliance between peasants, workers, and urban marginals could constitute a potent political force. However, these groups are each diverse in terms of ethnicity, region, and economic interest and their demands (for land, health care, markets, protection against exploitation, and so on) are expressed in nonideological terms. Thus, the potential for political action in the form of peasant revolt or lobbying for agrarian reform has been minimal (Wynia 1978; Stephens and Stephens 1986).

The peasantry in both countries work on commercial farms in the latifundia as wage laborers, share croppers, and tenant farmers, and as farmers on subsistence farms in the minifundia.[15] During the nonproductive seasons, most of the farmers operate small plots of land, work in other occupations, or are unemployed. As a result, the peasant communities are very poor. Annual income among the rural population remains far below the national per capita averages of both countries. Living conditions are substandard and deteriorating because access to health care, education, and other basic services is inadequate. Since urbanization has drawn increasing numbers of the peasantry from the land, there has been further erosion of rural political power. Despite some efforts at mobilization, the peasantry continues to be the least politically organized group in each society.

Aside from the short-lived Federation of Farmers' Brotherhoods, which was affiliated with the PRD in the early 1960s, most of the local federations and cooperatives that formed to assist Dominican campesinos are primarily economic and social. One exception has been the Independent Peasant Movement, which has grown to include around 75,000 members in the 1980s and has become more vocal politically. According to one source, expectations have been raised and "Balaguer can no longer count on passive farmers willing to listen to the local patrón or obey the local comandante" (Kryzanek and Wiarda 1988:107). The protests and disturbances following the May 1990 election and continuing through 1991 appear to confirm this assertion. In response to criticism of his economic policies, Balaguer stated in October 1990 that he would resign "if that is what the people want." Although it is not clear who initiated these disturbances, apparently both urban and rural workers have participated.

In Jamaica, slightly over half of the agricultural labor force consists of farmers, sharecroppers, and tenants. The rest are wage laborers, including around 5 percent unpaid family workers. Declines in the sugar industry have significantly reduced seasonal employment in sectors in which the "relations of the local elite with the poorer masses are based on authoritarian paternalism" (Kaplan et al. 1976:207). Moreover, the various agricultural associations that represent the interests of small peasants have "devoted their efforts mainly to extension work, the improvement of marketing facilities and the distribution of state subsidies" (Payne 1988:61). As in the case of the Dominican Republic, the relative degree of political influence of the Jamaican peasantry remains very low, despite occasional manifestations of potential power.

EXTERNAL FORCES

Foreign involvement in the domestic affairs of Caribbean nations began with colonialism. Independence and industrialization introduced new forms of involvement by foreign governments, multinational corporations (MNCs), and expatriot populations. Although these new relationships represent a change in form, countries in the Caribbean remain subordinated to external interests that continue to constitute a powerful force in their internal politics. Black's characterization of the Dominican Republic as an "unsovereign state" reinforces the assertion that foreigners "often determine the direction, the speed, and the quality of Dominican development" (Kryzanek and Wiarda 1988:124). Similarly, problems of internal security in Jamaica have been attributed to "the United States presence" (Lacey 1977:153). In addition, there has been much discussion of how alternate development strategies may have been constrained by economic dependence on the United States and by Jamaica's critical geopolitical position (Stephens and Stephens 1986:339).

Dominican history is replete with foreign military interventions and occupations by Spain, France, Haiti, and the United States. In contrast, Jamaica has not been subjected to foreign occupation since the withdrawal of British troops. From an economic perspective, however, both countries have been heavily influenced by external actors. Among the most important are U.S. MNCs and a variety of international organizations, including the International Monetary Fund (IMF).

The United States is the principal trading partner of both countries. Dominican imports from the United States total about one-half billion dollars, roughly the same value as its exports to the United States. Jamaican imports from the United States account for close to $3 billion and exports to the United States just over $1 billion (*The Europa World Year Book* 1990:892, 1454).

U.S. businessmen and their diplomatic supporters have constituted an important presence in domestic politics. U.S. ambassadors, for example, have exerted great influence. John Bartlow Martin's advice to President Johnson in the early 1960s helped lead to a military intervention in the Dominican Republic. Prior to his expulsion from Jamaica, Vincent de Roulet tried to influence the outcome of the 1972 election in favor of the candidate that would promise not to nationalize the bauxite industry. Loren Lawrence's critical reporting in 1979 of democratic socialist policies in Jamaica contributed to a level of increased pressure that Manley labeled "destabilization."[16]

U.S. embassy personnel have lobbied fairly successfully to maintain a trading system that allows for access to Jamaican natural resources, markets, cheap labor, low taxes, a favorable investment climate, and political stability. They have often operated in concert with MNCs such as Gulf and Western in the Dominican Republic and Kaiser, Reynolds, and Alcoa in Jamaica. The outcome of elections in both countries has been influenced, if not determined, by those representing U.S. and MNC interests.

The IMF has provided loans and credit on the condition of fiscal restraint and the reduction of public spending; those restrictions resulted in violent demonstrations in both countries in the 1970s and 1980s.

Analysis of the role of the IMF reveals a fundamental problem faced by Third World political leaders: short-term austerity measures designed for long-term economic rejuvenation diminished their capacity to distribute patronage and thus eroded their political support. An example of this is Balaguer's fear that adherence to IMF guidelines could destabilize a regime that has been based on its willingness to dole out support-building public works projects. In Jamaica, austerity measures mandated by the IMF failed to create short-term economic gains and resulted in negative political repercussions. Obviously, the political implications of the IMF have been important in both countries and throughout the developing world.

Many Dominicans have left their country to seek upward mobility. Located primarily in New York City, this emigrant community has provided financial assistance in the form of remittances to their families on the island and contributions to political aspirants who actively campaign outside the country. The same is true with regard to the large Jamaican contingent in New York City who have migrated for similar reasons and also maintain economic and political ties to their island.[17]

The emergence and evolution of vibrant civil societies in Jamaica and the Dominican Republic may be attributed, in large part, to the socioeconomic changes engendered through modernization.[18] Urbanization, industrialization, and the growth of the electronic media have contributed to heightened levels of social mobilization in each country. This impact has been particularly profound in the middle and upper classes as evidenced by the proliferation of business, financial, and professional associations. While the masses remain largely unintegrated in both political systems, there have been indications that pressures for change are mounting from the lower classes. Future democratic consolidation and stability will require national elites to accommodate these demands for economic and political reform.

It is clear that a variety of actors, both formal and informal, have exerted some degree of influence over the domestic politics of Jamaica and the Dominican Republic. While certain groups have been more influential than others, none has been able to singularly commandeer the respective systems. Rather, a network of powerful influences has generally prevailed. Political parties, for example, have attained a fairly high degree of legitimacy in both societies by virtue of the longevity and the dominance of popular, charismatic leaders. However, the inability of the respective party systems to effectively ameliorate pressing national problems has helped to expand the influence of informal interest groups and political actors. This trend has been manifested in the processes of issue determination and policy formulation in both countries.

NOTES

1. Quiet power is defined as "the ability of some groups to affect national life in ways not as visible or controversial as others" (Kryzanek and Wiarda 1988:109).

2. Generalizations are drawn from the work of Kryzanek and Wiarda (1988), Black (1986), and Weil et al. (1982) and from a series of interviews with political leaders and analysts in the Dominican Republic (see the Appendix).

3. Here we refer to Philips and Reid in the work by Stone and Brown (1977:1, 15). We also draw from interviews with Jamaican leaders (see the Appendix).

4. According to Garrity and Picard, in Jamaica "the government, although committed to working with the private sector, has failed to recognize the potential of business associations to make a substantive contribution to the policy process. On the other side, business associations, while generally pleased and optimistic about the degree of access they currently have to top government officials, have been unwilling to concede that some independence might have to be foregone in order to obtain a greater participatory role in the policy process" (1991:387).

5. Munroe's elaborate intellectual defense of theoretical Marxism during an interview with Richard Hillman in 1978 revealed an extremely idealistic approach to the amelioration of development problems in Jamaica.

6. The relationship between university political activism and public opinion is discussed in Hillman (1990).

7. The JCF and its various auxiliary forces number fewer than 8,000 troops, and the JDF had fewer than 2,000. The Dominican armed forces number around 30,000 and the police number around 10,000. The number of military troops comprises approximately 4.1 per thousand of the population in the Dominican Republic and approximately 0.9 per thousand of the population in Jamaica.

8. These operations took place during the 1966 state of emergency in West Kingston, during the 1967 elections, and during the Rodney Riots.

9. Stephens and Stephens conclude that "the importance of having a security establishment of limited size is certainly one factor in explaining the survival of political democracy in most of the English-speaking Caribbean" (1986:338).

10. Catrain (1987:269) notes that the number of officially registered unions jumped from 13 in 1961 to 145 the following year.

11. According to Rosario Espinal (1987b:312), 881 unions were registered from 1978–85, compared to only 313 during Balaguer's 12 years in office.

12. Kryzanek and Wiarda (1988:102–3) maintain that "labor confederations . . . are often affiliated with political parties and use their organizational strength as a means of furthering the ends of the party organization."

13. Accordingly, in the past "many employers regarded their workers as lazy, cheating, stupid, etc., and believed that only a strong hand could enforce discipline and ensure adequate work performance. . . . This tense and antagonistic relationship was frequently aggravated by racial overtones, as employers and managers were predominantly white or light-skinned and the workers black" (Stephens and Stephens 1986:51). Such patterns persist to this day.

14. Because national political relationships were highly clientelistic in both the Dominican Republic and Jamaica, in neither country did the unions function primarily as aggregators and articulators of workers' interests.

15. Of the approximately 45 percent of the Dominican population that lives in rural areas, only 10 percent owns 62.7 percent of the land. Thus, "most of the campesinos are forced to live on unused private land or on land controlled by the state" (Kryzanek and Wiarda 1988:105). In Jamaica, of the estimated 55 percent of the population living in the countryside, "on the average over 70% of the farmers with farms under 5 acres of land occupied only 11–16% of total farm acreage; while on the other hand between 300 and 350 large latifundia representing between 0.15% and 0.2% of all farmers monopolized between 38–45% of all the farm land" (Stone and Brown 1977:45).

16. "The U.S. hostility led to actions to undermine the Manley government and help its opponents in the form of reduced aid, negative reports damaging to tourism, and, in all probability, covert funding of the opposition" (Stephens and Stephens 1986:128).

17. The major Dominican and Jamaican parties maintain offices in New York City. Many emigrants from these countries return to vote in important elections.

18. Stephens (1990) provides a more detailed discussion of the linkage between socioeconomic development, civil society, and redemocratization.

7

Public Policies

Public policies are based on authoritative decisions regarding the allocation of values and resources that directly affect the quality of national life in the short and long terms. They are produced as a consequence of political forces operating through institutions grounded in political culture.

Regardless of regime ideology, the role of the state has been increasing in both the Dominican Republic and Jamaica and in the rest of the Third World. The fundamental objectives of securing national sovereignty and achieving political stability have been augmented by economic goals. New demands that are of little interest to private entrepreneurs (such as low-cost housing, mass transportation, education, and heath care) and widespread problems of productivity, unemployment, monetary inflation, and indebtedness have increasingly required government intervention.

How effectively the government responds to these demands is a clear measure of political performance.[1] Policies that are perceived as effective through the conceptual lenses of political values contribute to the sense of legitimacy required for systemic stability and continuity. Alternatively, the inability of political regimes to satisfy public demands through policy outputs that are perceived to deliver beneficial outcomes has often contributed to their downfall.

Our comparison of Dominican and Jamaican political cultures, institutions, groups, and forces reveals similarities in power configurations that influence the choice of the leaders who determine public policies. Given the nature of the endemic problems confronting the governments of both the Dominican Republic and Jamaica and the different institutions through which governing strategies are formed, several questions may be raised about the resulting public policies. For example, what are their major objectives? Who are their principal beneficiaries? How effective are they? What are the major constraints to their successful implementation?

GENERAL ECONOMIC POLICY

Although the primary objective of political leaders is to maintain power, achieving this goal in the Caribbean, as in most of the Third World, has been increasingly contingent on the performance of development policies and economic strategies that respond to people's evolving needs and aspirations. For example, leaders can no longer address the demands of the military and the elite while ignoring those of urban workers and peasants. The democratizing effects of newly emergent groups and forces became apparent in Latin America and the Caribbean after the global depression in the 1930s, and the effects have accelerated through the "revolution of rising expectations" of the 1960s and into the contemporary era.[2]

Both the Dominican Republic and Jamaica have been working to break the cycle of dependency and to achieve greater independence from external influences in order to be able to respond to the challenge of socioeconomic democratization. In this context, "economic performance — in terms of steady, broadly distributed growth — is probably more important for democracy than a high level of socioeconomic development" (Diamond, Linz, and Lipset 1989:43). Since the 1960s, the need to allow for expanded access to political power and economic rewards for newly mobilized social groups has contributed to an alternation between contending policy orientations in both the Dominican Republic and Jamaica. This is due, in part, to the requirement that new groups demonstrate their ability to coexist with more entrenched groups within the power structure. Hence, "a new group entering into the accepted circle of power groups must tacitly demonstrate that it will not do anything to harm already existent groups" (Wiarda 1985b:100). Both countries have experienced difficulties in accommodating modernization policies to this requirement. Therefore, even when economic growth is achieved, there are serious obstacles to development. The low levels of economic growth and high foreign debts are shown in Table 7.1.

One of the most frustrating of these obstacles has been rapid population growth. Although Jamaica and the Dominican Republic have experienced increases in agricultural and industrial production, these gains have been offset by the population growth. Rapid urbanization has compelled the respective governments to expend a large amount of capital

TABLE 7.1
Economic Growth

	GDP–GNP/Per Capita (average annual rate)			External Debt (US $ millions)
	1965–80	1980–86	1965–86	1986
Dominican Republic	7.3	1.1	2.5	3301
Jamaica	1.3	0.0	–1.4	3882

Source: World Bank, *World Development Report 1988* (Washington, D.C.: World Bank, 1988).

in subsidizing basic commodity prices. This strain on already limited resources has prevented the governments from providing essential services for their people and has compromised long-term development.

In the Dominican Republic, conservative modernization under the Partido Reformista Social Cristiano (PRSC) has encouraged entrepreneurial activity, rapid industrialization, expansion of exports, and receptivity to foreign investors and multinational corporations (MNCs). The progressive modernization of the Partido Revolucionario Dominicano (PRD) relied on policies of social and agrarian reform, based in part on state intervention, import substitution, and capital borrowing. The inability of either approach to satisfy the interests of the middle classes and the masses simultaneously through the production of visible short-term benefits has tended to discredit the regime in power. The attempt to maintain clientelistic control while initiating long-term distributed growth has resulted in policy options that elicit problematical social and political reactions. Not only does long-term economic development require short-term sacrifice, but it is often shaped by external forces over which the government has no control.[3]

While both the People's National Party (PNP) and the Jamaica Labor Party (JLP) have experimented with policies of progressive modernization, the PNP program of democratic socialism is much more reformist than JLP programs that favor reliance on the marketplace, foreign investment, and reduced public spending. The political ramifications and perceptions of the ideological bases and the performance of each of these governmental orientations has led to alternations in power. Thus far, no Jamaican administration has succeeded itself after two terms in office. The negative short-term impact of austerity programs has precluded the continuity needed for more comprehensive development programs to evolve over the long term.[4]

Like other developing countries, the Dominican Republic and Jamaica have tried to increase economic productivity through manufacturing, industrialization, and tourism. Further, they have implemented trade policies designed to enhance internationalism and regionalism. Neither country, however, has been able to break the debilitating pattern of cyclical alternation between policies of social reform and redistribution and those that have protected patterns of concentrated wealth. Leaders contend for authority to formulate public policies and allocate resources that would serve competing sets of economic and political interests. Obviously, no single model has prevailed, and countervailing liberal and conservative approaches continue to characterize political systems challenged by both internal and external constraints on their development.

The PRD during the administrations of Antonio Guzmán and Jorge Blanco and the PNP under Michael Manley's leadership both broadly represent progressive liberal approaches to economic policy. The PRSC under Joaquín Balaguer and the JLP under Edward Seaga broadly represent more conservative approaches within the classical liberal theories of development. Although there are obvious differences in the individual programs and styles of each of these leaders, their general directions and positions relative to their political opposition can be understood in terms of economic policy.

Several factors have contributed to Balaguer's political survival. In addition to cultivating strong ties to the military, the elites, and the United States, he has built an expansive base of popular support through patronage. His advocacy of free trade and foreign investment is in some respects closer to Seaga's general economic approach to dependent development than to that of the PRD, which under Jorge Blanco tried to revitalize the economy through austerity measures. This imposition of austerity through short-term sacrifice is reminiscent of Manley's invocation of suffering in order to achieve his more elaborate and far-reaching goals of economic reform, equitable distribution of wealth, and international economic independence.

There are strong tendencies on the part of these regimes to adhere to their general policy orientations. However, the failure of policies to ameliorate socioeconomic problems has caused occasional experimentation by leaders seeking to retain power. For example, statist regimes have expanded private sector development and advocates of privatization have allowed for state intervention.

However, the inextricable linkage of the domestic policies of small Caribbean states to international economics ultimately subjects a regime's performance to forces beyond its capacity to control. For this reason, as well as for the other obstacles and pressures discussed in this section, the implementation of successful economic programs constitutes one of the most difficult challenges for Caribbean leaders.

AGRICULTURAL POLICY

By virtue of their extensive agricultural sectors, the Dominican and Jamaican economies have been subject to fluctuations in world prices of primary products. With varying degrees of success political leaders have attempted to increase productivity and diversify marketable products through a variety of programs. When foreign sales decline, the cost of fertilizers, pesticides, irrigation and, consequently, food imports has required borrowing at levels that have contributed to the mounting foreign debt.

Economic activity in the Dominican Republic traditionally has been dominated by the production of sugar and several other cash crops. During the 1960s, agriculture contributed as much as 24 percent of the gross domestic product (GDP) annually, and sugar processing accounted for nearly 19 percent of GDP. Agricultural products accounted for 80 percent to 90 percent of total exports. Agriculture accounted for 60 percent of the labor force, while 93 percent of industrial laborers were engaged in processing agricultural products (Weil et al. 1985:179). Jamaica has also been traditionally dependent on agriculture, primarily sugar; but by the 1970s, it had reduced agricultural production to around 9 percent of the GDP. Although agriculture continues to provide employment for the largest number of Jamaicans, production has not kept pace with population growth.

By 1988, agriculture contributed 15.1 percent of the Dominican GDP and 6 percent of the Jamaican GDP. In that year, approximately 38 percent of Dominican and 25 percent of Jamaican laborers were employed in the agricultural sector. Slightly over half of the land in the Dominican Republic and slightly under half of the land in Jamaica was put to agricultural use in 1988, and sugar accounted for 15.2 percent of total export earnings in the Dominican Republic and 10.8 percent in Jamaica. In the 1980s, agricultural production increased by an annual average of 1 percent in the Dominican Republic and 1.3 percent in Jamaica. In absolute amounts, the Dominican Republic produced over 8 million and Jamaica 2.5 million metric tons of sugar.[5] This represents a large increase in the production of Dominican sugar from the 1970s and a decrease of sugar production in Jamaica.

The Dominican Republic has promoted diversification of agriculture through agroindustrial incentive programs designed to develop nontraditional exports such as fruits, cashews, and vegetables. Similarly, Jamaica has encouraged the production of fruits, vegetables, coffee, and rice in order to diversify and decrease dependence on food imports.

In order to decrease Dominican dependence on the importation of food, Guzmán designated 1980 as the "year of agriculture." His administration sought to expand access to irrigation and extended the program of rural credit to provide additional financing for small farmers. Moreover, the government purchased domestic agricultural products through the Price Stabilizing Institute and provided many landless peasants with a clear title to their land through resettlement programs administered by the Dominican Agrarian Institute (IAD).[6] As part of the policy of diversification into nontraditional agricultural exports, land was leased from the State Sugar Council and private owners and made available to small farmers. While the political right lobbied against these reforms, the left criticized them for being insufficient.

Food self-sufficiency was one of the primary goals of the 1972 PNP manifesto. One of the methods to accomplish this was to threaten large landholders with orders to bring idle land into production or to lease these tracts to the government under Project Land Lease. Through this program, privately held lands were leased to small farmers. Much more successful than the cooperative farming projects (Food Farms and Pioneer Farms), by the end of 1980 "37,661 farmers had been placed on 74,568 acres of land" in the various phases of the land lease program (Stephens and Stephens 1986:74).

LAND REFORM

The linkage between general economic policy, agricultural policy, and land ownership and use is obvious in developing countries where oligarchic patterns have shaped the political and economic systems.

At one time, the Trujillo family owned 60 percent of all farmland in the Dominican Republic. Since 1961, the size, ownership, distribution, and use of farmland has been highly unequal. Large landowners and the state have held the largest percentages of farmland, and small farms have comprised very small percentages of the farmland.[7] Similarly, the persistence of what one author terms a "uniform pattern of land monopoly" has affected agrarian relations in Jamaica (Stone and Brown 1977:45–57).

The more progressive regimes in each country have attempted, with varying degrees of success, to implement policies of land reform. Manley's Project Land Lease program was perhaps the most ambitious example of these attempts to redistribute land.

Legislation permitting the free use of state-owned land by individuals for ten years prior to the payment of rent was in effect in the Dominican Republic at the beginning of the twentieth century. In the early 1930s, in response to the fear that Haitians would intrude on the sparsely settled border region, an Agricultural Colonization Law required that small groups establish settlements for land grants of at least 250 acres. The IAD aimed at locating landless farm families and squatters in new settlements and cooperatives. However, land redistribution by the IAD has been minimal. In fact, a 1970 Autonomous University of Santo Domingo report concluded that only 2 percent of the rural population had received any benefits from agrarian reform.

Bureaucratic and legal problems have been exacerbated by political resistance to change, by campesino ignorance about these programs, and by general mistrust of the government. Legislation enacted in 1972 was designed to facilitate IAD redistribution of privately owned ricelands of over 80 acres, to purchase idle or exhausted farmland by the government, to prohibit certain sharecropping arrangements to make absentee landownership unprofitable, and to recover state lands being used illegally. Nevertheless, agrarian reforms in the Dominican Republic have not had much impact. As a result, large numbers of the rural landless continue to migrate to Santo Domingo where they join the ranks of the urban marginalized (unskilled and illiterate people who cannot find employment and must live in miserable slums and shantytowns).

Despite governmental efforts at land reform, the legacy of the Jamaican plantocracy is still prevalent. Although there is now a greater distribution of small farms throughout the countryside, a very few large landowners continue to control immense tracts of the most desirable farmland, and the rural poor continue to pour into Kingston only to find a place in the squalid shantytown life of Trenchtown, West Kingston, and the "Boulevard."[8]

Under the Land Settlement Program of 1929, the government subdivided land it owned or acquired, developed some infrastructure such as pipelines, electrical lines, and roads, and resold (under very liberal terms) or rented the plots to small farmers. Also, Jamaicans returning from the world wars received government land under special programs. The Land Settlement Program was superseded by a 1966 land reform program, but projects that it had initiated were completed. The goals of the Land Settlement Program were only partially achieved. In 40 years, only around 1,000 new settlers per year received small acreage farms, and agricultural production was not significantly increased. The 1966 Land Development and Utilization Act (also called the Idle Lands Law) allowed the government to purchase or lease lands lying fallow unless the owner submitted plans for the full development of the land within a certain time frame. However, only 50 percent of the affected lands were brought under compliance with this law.

In 1973, land reform was given a high priority as part of the PNP's democratic socialist program to overcome dependency. The government started Project Land Lease in order to lease land from private owners and re-rent to farmers living within a two-mile radius of the land. The new tenants were provided with fertilizer and easy terms of credit. In 1975, long-term leasing arrangements were included, with annual rentals equal to 2 percent of the land value, and a Facilities of Title Law permitted squatters who had been cultivating land for at least seven years to claim title to it.

Agrarian reform and increased agricultural productivity are fundamental for socioeconomic development in the Caribbean and the Third World. However, neither the Dominican Republic nor Jamaica has been able to accomplish a sufficient level of land redistribution to radically change historical patterns of land tenure and use, although some inroads have been made. One alternative to agricultural development and land reform is industrial development. However, that also has been highly problematical.

INDUSTRIAL POLICY

Both the Dominican Republic and Jamaica produce primary materials and agricultural products for export. The need to import machinery, finished products, food, and fuel is a great economic disadvantage that has led to dramatic increases in trade deficits and balance of payment deficits. In 1988, the Dominican Republic recorded a visible trade deficit of US $714.5 million and Jamaica had a deficit of US $395.0 million. The Dominican balance of payments deficit stood at US $127.5 million and the Jamaican at US $81.9 million.

Despite differing approaches, political leaders have each attempted to decrease dependency on foreign imports through policies ranging from import substitution to the creation of the New International Economic Order (NIEO). These industrialization policies have something in common. In seeking foreign investment to compensate for the lack of available domestic capital, they attract MNCs. Unfortunately, MNCs interested in low wage labor, favorable tax structures, and weak labor movements form alliances with local elites that reduce the potential for far-reaching spin-off effects on the Dominican and Jamaican economies. In fact, the elites have been able to maintain their wealth, privilege, and power at the expense of the masses.

In the 1980s, industry employed around 18 percent of the labor force and contributed 32 percent of the GDP in the Dominican Republic. During this period, Jamaica employed 22 percent of the labor force in industry contributing roughly 37 percent of the GDP. In both countries, policies have been designed to increase production of consumer and industrial goods in order to decrease excessive reliance on the processing of agricultural products. Nevertheless, during the 1980s there was almost no growth in industrial production in either country.

While mining contributed 4 percent of the Dominican GDP in 1988 and 6.4 percent of the Jamaican GDP in 1986, this activity employed less than 1 percent of the labor force in each country. However, ferro-nickel production provided 34.7 percent of total Dominican export earnings in 1988, and doré, a gold-silver alloy, provided 11.0 percent. Similarly, bauxite and alumina, of which Jamaica is the world's second leading producer, accounted for almost 50 percent of its export earnings in 1988. Ferro-nickel mining was the largest single investment project in the Dominican Republic, and was undertaken in the early 1970s by the Falconbridge Dominicana company in a joint venture with the United States and Canada. Six MNCs owned and operated the bauxite mines and five alumina-processing plants in Jamaica until 1974, when Manley announced a policy of recovering the land from the MNCs and leasing it to them. Manley negotiated an agreement with Kaiser Aluminum, and later with several of the other companies, to sell back to the Jamaican government all of the bauxite land and 51 percent of company assets.

Manufacturing in the Dominican Republic, including food products, petroleum refineries, beverages, and chemicals contributed 16.5 percent of GDP and employed 12.6 percent of the labor force in the 1980s. In order to augment the several thousand who were employed in the textile and clothing industries during the 1970s, the Dominican government created free trade zones in which clothing assembly plants were encouraged to hire the local laborers. These duty-free zones, modeled on the assembly and light industrial economies of the Pacific Basin, have been supported by conservative and liberal governments alike. The zones provide strong incentives for MNCs including favorable tax laws, low import duties, profit exemptions, cheap space rental, no strong unions or government regulations, and extremely low costs of labor. The companies, however, must pay in local currency exchanged at the Central Bank. This is an important source of foreign exchange for the Dominican Republic.

In Jamaica, manufacturing contributed 20.9 percent of the GDP in 1986 and employed 12.8 percent of the labor force in 1987. Processing agricultural products and bauxite (to produce alumina) accounts for much of this activity. However, food, beverages, and tobacco comprised 70 percent of industrial output, and nontraditional manufactured exports such as garments represented 30 percent of total commodity exports in 1988.

The services sector (including commerce, tourism, communications, transportation, financial services, business, government, social services, and personal services) accounted for over 50 percent of the GDP of each country. Within this sector, the tourist trade has emerged as a principal source of foreign exchange earnings.[9]

TOURISM

Both the Dominican Republic and Jamaica have attempted to develop their tourist industries as a means of improving their economies. Their excellent geographic and climatic conditions have attracted increasing numbers of vacationers, primarily from North America, but also from South America and Europe. Theoretically, tourism would generate foreign investment and exchange earnings, create employment opportunities, and stimulate the construction of infrastructure and related businesses. However, the importance of tourism to the economies of these and other Caribbean countries makes them particularly vulnerable to international perceptions of, and reactions to, their domestic politics and cultural penetration (destabilizing influences of foreign attitudes, beliefs, and values). A strong case can be made that attempts by Dominican and Jamaican administrations to promote this industry are constrained by U.S. perceptions of the acceptability of their overall ideological perspectives. Stephens and Stephens (1986:396) cite the precipitous decline in tourist arrivals in the late 1970s as evidence that U.S. destabilization of the Manley regime included the orchestration of negative, sensationalist press in order to frighten potential visitors. Weil et al. (1985:200) argue that tourism in the Dominican Republic was "virtually nonexistent until after World War II, and an unattractive political image abroad has kept the country's full tourist potential from being achieved."

Ownership of tourist facilities was under virtually exclusive foreign control until recent policies provided for acquisitions by the state or assisted in leveraged domestic participation. Moreover, the servile nature of tourist-related jobs and support services, the relatively low numbers of new jobs created in this sector, and the invidious cultural comparisons engendered by tourist activities have been very controversial. Many informants in both the Dominican Republic and Jamaica argue that these costs are not worth the small benefits that accrue in "prostituting" themselves. Many others, however, strongly support government efforts to increase tourism in countries that they "are very proud of and want visitors to appreciate." It is clear that the effects of this rapidly expanding sector are much more complex than they at first appear to be.

Governmental efforts that were initiated in both the Dominican Republic and Jamaica in the 1970s to promote tourism resulted in dramatic increases in the number of tourists visiting annually and in the amount of earnings generated from this activity. In the early 1970s, approximately 150,000 tourists visited the Dominican Republic each year. By 1980 there were over 500,000, and in 1988 the figure rose to 1,221,735. Over 530,000 people visited Jamaica in 1974 and by 1988, the number reached 1,016,605. The largest proportion of visitors in both countries are from the United States, accounting for 45 percent of the Jamaican market in 1988. In 1989, receipts from tourism were estimated at US $650 million in the Dominican Republic and US $550 million in Jamaica. These figures are equivalent to 70 percent of the value of total Dominican commodity exports and 66 percent of Jamaica's exports. Thus, tourism has become the principal earner of foreign exchange in both countries.

Accordingly, Dominican government programs have focused on the country's physical attributes, such as its beaches, and on its place in history as the island on which Columbus initiated European settlement. For example, the construction of El Faro is designed as an attraction to enhance tourism and thereby increase foreign exchange earnings to a level that would justify the initial investments.

These efforts have their counterparts in the expanded role that the Jamaican government has played over the past several decades. The Jamaican Tourist Board, created in the 1950s, and a cabinet-level Ministry of Tourism, created in the 1970s, assure direct inputs into this increasingly important aspect of the economy. The government has offered fiscal incentives for hotel construction and has expanded airline and airport facilities, improved roads and infrastructure related to tourism, and sponsored advertising campaigns.

Similarly, in 1971 the Dominican government established an agency (INFRATUR) to monitor "tourism-related infrastructure projects" (Wiarda and Kryzanek 1982:85). Also, a tourist incentive law was passed under Balaguer, and Guzmán later established a cabinet position for the director of tourism. Tourist-related legislation provides tax breaks, exemptions for investments, and fees for the governments of both the Dominican Republic and Jamaica. The promotion of tourism has become a high priority consideration in these Caribbean countries.

Perceptions of political stability are crucial to tourism. Reports of rioting or violence caused by protests against election outcomes or International Monetary Fund (IMF) austerity measures can have devastating consequences for the tourist industry. Similarly, crimes committed against visitors are particularly damaging to the reputation of resort areas. Because of these considerations, the governments of both countries have been sensitive to national images. The emergence of Third World nationalism, anticolonialism, and the black pride movement in the late 1960s and early 1970s prompted a Jamaican government survey that concluded that animosity toward white American tourists was not very widespread and therefore was insufficient to damage the industry (Kaplan et al. 1976:268). However, the data are conclusive in demonstrating correlations between declining numbers of visitors and periods of political or social unrest. There is steady growth in the annual number of visitors to Jamaica except for the mid-1970s, when democratic socialism was under assault in the international press. A slight decline was also registered in 1980, a year in which some preelection violence accompanied rumors that the PNP would not transfer power if it lost the election (*Statistical Yearbook of Jamaica* 1986:319).

Reliance on the tourist industry as a means to earn foreign exchange, predicated on projecting an image of hospitality and stability, carries important political implications that reinforce external dependency and internal clientelistic patterns.

FISCAL POLICY

The success of virtually every aspect of public policy making in the Third World resides in the ability to manage financial affairs that, paradoxically, require political solutions. Wiarda argues that because the debt cannot be paid back, it must be managed in such a way as to defuse its potential political damage (1990:411–18).

Among the most significant aspects of public financial programs in developing countries are trade, investment, aid, tax, and debt strategies and patterns. A brief overview of the economies of the Dominican Republic and Jamaica reveals increasing indebtedness, budgetary deficits, negative trade balances, high inflation, fluctuating exchange rates, and declining production. This general economic decline has had a devastating impact on agricultural and industrial policies and has resulted in far-reaching political consequences. The following summary draws from data compiled for the 1988 fiscal year.

Measured at average 1986–88 prices, the Dominican gross national product (GNP) of US $4,690 million resulted in a per capita amount of US $680. The Jamaican GNP of U.S. $2,610 million averaged US $1,080 per capita. While both GNPs increased very slightly (0.8 percent in the Dominican Republic and 0.7 percent in Jamaica annually), the per capita figures declined by an annual rate of 1.6 percent in the Dominican Republic and 2.1 percent in Jamaica. This trend can be attributed to high population growth rates.

The Dominican and Jamaican trade deficits were US $714.5 million and US $395 million and their balance of payment deficits were US $127.5 million and US $81.9 million, respectively. It should be noted that the payment of insurance claims resulting from damage during hurricane Gilbert had a positive effect on the Jamaican account balance in 1989.

The United States is the principal trading partner of both countries. The Dominican Republic sends two-thirds of its exports — mainly ferro-nickel and raw sugar — to the United States, and 35.2 percent of Dominican imports — mainly petroleum, food, and machinery — are from the United States. Jamaica sends 45.5 percent of its exports — mainly bauxite and alumina — to the United States. The United States provides 52 percent of Jamaican imports — primarily machinery, transport equipment, and mineral fuels.

In 1987, the budgetary deficits of both countries were equal to 1 percent of their respective GDPs. The Dominican foreign debt of approximately US $4 billion was serviced at a rate of 4.1 percent of the GNP. Jamaica's public debt of US $4.5 billion is one of the highest per capita figures in the Third World. The total Jamaican public debt was equivalent to US $1,900 per person in 1988. The debt-service ratio was 38.8 percent.

In 1989, the average annual rates of inflation were estimated at 60 percent in the Dominican Republic and 16 percent in Jamaica. Unemployment was around 30 percent in the Dominican Republic and 20 percent in Jamaica. Underemployment, a very serious problem in both countries, is difficult to measure but may exceed 40 percent.

Continuing declines in economic growth and private investment are compounded by widening trade deficits, a shortage of foreign exchange and investment capital, and debt. In Jamaica, there was a shortage of dollars even on the black market due to government measures to reduce the cultivation of ganja (marijuana) in 1989. As a mainstay of the illicit "parallel economy," ganja exportation earned over US $560 million in 1988.

Governments have experimented with various fiscal policies in order to respond to these challenges. The performance of public policies attempting to redress inequities that stem from economic decline is under constant evaluation by those who are most directly affected. Regimes unable to demonstrate tangible economic improvements lose legitimacy and are either subjected to serious challenges or driven from office.[10] This phenomenon has been exemplified by recent history in both the Dominican Republic and Jamaica, where governments perceived to be insufficiently responsive to economic problems have been replaced by ones that have adopted an alternative economic policy. This pattern may reflect a kind of political vitality; yet such vacillation has impeded economic development.

At one time or another, the Dominican Republic and Jamaica have each developed fiscal policies in conjunction with major multilateral agencies like the IMF and the World Bank. In light of the pattern of political oscillation, their parallel experiences raise questions about the potential contribution of these agencies to long-term solutions in the face of short-term requirements. Stephens and Stephens argue that "it is important to understand the IMF program not as a purely technical matter but as an inherently political one" (1986:201). For example, governments negotiating IMF austerity programs and strict monetary policies have had difficulty surviving the protests and demonstrations that have invariably accompanied their implementation.

Balaguer's attempts to control inflation in the 1970s included the imposition of austerity measures such as the prohibition against wage increases, removal of price subsidies for food, freezing of pensions, and welfare program cutbacks. Guzmán allowed gasoline prices to rise in 1979 and focused some attention on an inequitable tax system. In the early 1980s, Jorge Blanco banned the importation of automobiles and luxury items; raised taxes on imports, capital gains, and real estate; restricted capital flight; and cut the salaries of high-level public servants.[11]

These measures had little impact on growing government deficits and public debt that were viewed as "largely the result of payments made to the corrupt, patronage-bloated, ailing and inefficient public enterprises" (Kryzanek and Wiarda 1988:132).[12] Therefore, loans amounting to several hundred million dollars were sought from the IMF beginning in 1982. The impact of the IMF conditions included frozen wages, higher prices and interest rates, and recession. Trade restrictions had to be abandoned and the peso was devalued. In 1984, when the government began to implement another set of adjustments demanded by the IMF, strikes and demonstrations protesting the resulting price increases escalated into widespread rioting and looting throughout the country. The same outcome occurred in 1985 when the Dominican government unified the exchange system at free market rates. While some believed that this was a key reform that would produce long-term economic benefits, others concluded that the only Dominicans who benefitted were either PRD loyalists or bankers (Kryzanek and Wiarda 1988; Black 1986). In 1986, Balaguer returned to a more traditionally statist approach, shifting the rewards of patronage politics to PRSC supporters, de-emphasizing the strict monetarist programs, and thus leaving some uncertainty regarding the continuation of IMF measures.

Since Balaguer's reelection in 1990, the economic crisis has deepened. A series of strikes and protests has attributed the economic ills to a PRSC administration that remained in office in a questionable election. Washington de Peña, speaking on behalf of the PRSC, declared the third national strike (held on November 19–21, 1990) against Balaguer's regime to be illegal.[13] While Balaguer continues to finance public works projects and the costly Columbus monument, domestic sacrifice and suffering continue to destabilize the internal political climate. The country has become increasingly indebted to and dependent on the multilateral financial institutions and the United States.

Economic pressures have caused similar political responses in contemporary Jamaica. After Manley's 1976 electoral victory, the IMF came to the forefront of political debate. Between 1977–80, the left wing of the PNP began to oppose the provisional economic measures designed prior to the election. They rejected the monetarist approach that made an appeal to the IMF for financial assistance in favor of "careful rationing of earnings, supplemented by loans and other kinds of material support from socialist bloc and progressive OPEC countries" (Payne 1988:73). Manley articulated this position in his famous "we are not for sale" speech at the 38th Annual Conference of the PNP in 1976. Accordingly, the Jamaican dollar was not devalued, national planning was strengthened Radio Jamaica was purchased by the government, and negotiations commenced for the nationalization of three foreign banks and the cement factory owned by the Ashenheim family. These measures contradicted IMF directions. However, despite his flamboyant rhetoric, Manley was not prepared to commit the government to the radical program of populist anti-imperialism championed by a faction within the PNP. Many observers believe that Manley's repudiation of the left wing of the PNP demonstrated his middle-class loyalties.[14]

Manley was attempting to modify Jamaica's past pattern of state patronage. His reform policies were designed to overcome dependency in a way that would be more responsive to the needs of the majority. Manley realized that his goals of a more egalitarian society required restructuring of global economic relationships and the formation of an international bauxite cartel (Hillman 1979a). His resumption of negotiations with the IMF in 1977 was welcomed by most Jamaicans and the United States. In fact, "it was probably the readiness of the Carter administration to lean on the IMF on Jamaica's behalf that forced the Fund to settle largely on Jamaica's terms." The agreement was subject, of course, to IMF performance tests (Payne 1988:76). When the economy failed the first performance test in 1977 (domestic assets in the Bank of Jamaica exceeded the required ceiling), the IMF suspended its loan and asked for new terms. Manley (1982:160) characterized the subsequent agreement as "one of the most savage packages ever imposed on any client government by the IMF." Its main conditions were reunification of the exchange rate combined with currency devaluation, reduction of the public sector, a limit on wage increases, a cutback in the operations of the State Trading Corporation, tax increases, and guaranteed returns on private capital investments.

Manley, who continued to champion the NIEO, lost the support of the Carter administration and, despite compliance with the IMF's new terms, the economy showed no signs of recovery. After the economy failed a second performance test in 1979, the PNP began to consider a non-IMF path that led to a break with the fund in 1980. However, this path was highly problematical because Manley was unable to find an alternative source of funding at the level available through the classical IMF formula (Stephens and Stephens 1986:282).

The failure of Manley's policies, as manifested in declining economic indicators, allowed Seaga to cultivate an image of technocratic financial competence in his campaign against PNP mismanagement.[15] Faced with governmental bankruptcy soon after he was elected, Seaga initiated early talks with the IMF. By 1981, trade barriers were eased and his government was given increased U.S. aid and political support in dealing with the IMF. Significantly, Seaga was able to negotiate much more favorable terms with the fund than was Manley (Payne 1988:85). Seaga's approach has been characterized as a "test-case of the validity of the whole liberal development tradition when applied to conditions of dependency" (Payne 1988:127). However, expectations that the economy would grow with IMF support were deflated as bauxite production dropped, the currency was devalued, unemployment increased, and the debt grew. There were insufficient new employment opportunities in the capital-intensive industries attracted by the "industrialization by invitation" approach. By 1983, Seaga's technocratic image was undermined by another failure to pass an IMF performance test, and new austerity measures were initiated.

Reduction of the public sector, layoffs, currency devaluation, and increased prices led to the violent protests and riots of 1985. The PNP called for a price freeze, discontinuance of the devaluation, and abandonment of the reductions in the public sector required by the IMF. Manley further distanced himself from the party's left wing, broke ties with the Worker's Party of Jamaica, and projected the image of a democratic, rather than a socialist, alternative to the JLP's dependent capitalism. As the economic crisis deepened, IMF structural adjustment schemes were debated once again.

Throughout his administration, Seaga adhered to orthodox liberal development theory. The failure of the economy to grow under his leadership and the devastating effects of austerity and their social costs provide substance to the conclusion reached by many observers that the political price of exaggerated dependency and client status cannot be justified by theoretical appeals to long-term improvements.[16] The strong PNP victory at the polls in 1989 appears to reinforce this interpretation. Manley, whose earlier policies were regarded as mismanaged failures, replaced a financial "genius" who became associated with suffering and belt tightening.

As the experiences of the Dominican Republic and Jamaica illustrate, fiscal policies that are unable to produce visible benefits in the short term appear to be politically untenable in developing countries. Clearly, the need for material progress in the Caribbean and throughout the Third World has become a paramount consideration in public policy.

FOREIGN POLICY

In the absence of any serious external threat to national security, the international dimension of domestic development constitutes the primary component of Jamaican and Dominican foreign policy. Their status as micro-states with minimal internal capacity for development suggests vulnerability to dependent linkages. Further, the ability of Caribbean states to conduct autonomous foreign policy has been repeatedly questioned. Braveboy-Wagner (1989:7), however, argues that contemporary foreign policy raises more complex issues than previously because "small states have greater opportunities for regional and global cooperation and diversification of external ties; they have greater knowledge about the international environment, and more precedents for small-state influence from which to choose." Despite dependent status, then, a small state is "still capable of adopting strategies to project an individual presence abroad and even to develop penetrative linkages of its own" (Braveboy-Wagner 1989:7).

It is within this context that the Dominican Republic and Jamaica have sought to project a presence abroad. Although certain regimes have adopted divergent strategies in this pursuit, foreign policy in each nation has been influenced by several common factors. In addition to their comparable geopolitical positions in the Caribbean, the Dominican Republic and Jamaica are confronted by similar "intermestic" imperatives and have both experienced increased visibility and interdependence with other countries and multilateral institutions.[17]

The most obvious similarity between the two nations in the area of foreign policy has been the orientation each has maintained vis-à-vis domestic elites and the United States. Neither can successfully implement policies that are perceived to be in opposition to the interests of these groups. While the tendency has been toward the formulation of pragmatic foreign policies that would satisfy the mutual interests of elites and the United States, the Dominican Republic has been fairly consistent in maintaining a low-profile approach compared to the symbolic politics adopted intermittently by Jamaica. For example, the Dominican Republic has promoted strong measures to maintain a favorable foreign investment climate, has generally disassociated itself from global North/South disputes, and has supported the United States in international forums. Jamaica, on the other hand, has attempted to dramatize its national interests by promoting a more active international role that has included ties to Cuba and the Third World, confrontation with the United States, and reformulation of the requirements for foreign investment.

The success of a political regime in these small states is grounded in the inextricable interrelationship between domestic economic performance and external linkages. Due to the inherent difficulty in achieving demonstrable material progress, foreign policies have been reformulated from one government to another. This alternation is much more dramatic in Jamaica than in the Dominican Republic, where the goal of sustaining favorable economic and political relations with the United States has prevailed. Beneath the predominantly rhetorical and symbolic fluctuations lies a pragmatic recognition of the overriding influence external forces maintain in both countries.

Foreign policies have been moderated by "the perceived requirements of national or factional self-preservation" in the Dominican Republic (Black 1986:109). Trujillo's self-proclamation as the world's foremost anticommunist and the Dominican voting record in the United Nations (UN), which paralleled that of the United States more closely than did the record of any other Latin American government, illustrate this pragmatism. Thus, one author concludes that "no country in the Western Hemisphere has been more firmly locked into the U.S. sphere of influence than the Dominican Republic" (Black 1986:116).

Similarly, in 1962 Bustamante pledged Jamaican support of U.S. leadership in the West and promised his firm opposition to communism. However, Jamaica's anti-imperialist/anti-capitalist interim is explained as "a classic test case of the ability (or inability) of a regime in a small island state in the Western Hemisphere to sustain its self-declared challenge to the existing international economic order and the traditional hegemony" (Heine and Manigat 1988:144). The extent to which policy innovations are a function of either positive or negative relations with the United States suggests that such a challenge is untenable.

Both the Dominican Republic and Jamaica have sought and received large amounts of external assistance through the U.S. Agency for International Development (AID) and international agencies such as the World Bank, the International Finance Corporation, the Inter-American Development Bank, and the UN. Some assistance was either reduced or eliminated when policies appeared to challenge U.S. interests. For example, U.S. aid was withdrawn from Trujillo's government in 1960 and from the triumvirate that replaced Bosch in 1963. In contrast, combined U.S. economic and military assistance to the Dominican Republic reached an all-time high of US $111.6 million in fiscal year 1965/66, the fourth-highest sum extended to any Latin American country that year (Weil et al. 1985:156). U.S. loans and grants to Jamaica declined during the 1970s, and certain loans were frozen when Manley pursued a nonaligned foreign policy. A dramatic increase occurred in 1981 after Seaga pledged to return to closer relations with the United States, to renew IMF negotiations, and to repudiate ties to Cuba and the Third World. Economic assistance, for example, jumped from US $14.6 million in 1980 to US $73.5 million in 1981 and US $138.6 million in

1982. AID assistance went from US $2.7 million in 1980 to US $53.9 million in 1981 and US $119.4 million in 1982 (Stephens and Stephens 1986:397).

Although the minor border disputes and mutual distrust that have punctuated Dominican relations with neighboring Haiti have no counterpart in Jamaica, regional developments have generated an environment in which attention to Caribbean, hemispheric, and global interests are increasing in both countries. In 1962, the Dominican government took measures to obtain U.S. support for the removal of sanctions imposed against Trujillo by the Organization of American States (OAS). Also, in keeping with the principal theme of this book, Jamaica "attempted to overcome the tradition of mutual indifference between English-speaking Caribbean and Hispanic countries by joining the OAS in 1969" (Kaplan et al. 1976:227). In 1973, Jamaica joined the Caribbean Free Trade Association. While unreceptive to the idea of political integration, Jamaica saw an opportunity to promote a degree of economic cooperation. More recently, Jamaica facilitated the integration of the Dominican Republic in the Caribbean Common Market (CARICOM). The Dominicans were granted observer status in 1984 "at the urging of Prime Minister Edward Seaga of Jamaica, who has consistently sought wider ties with the Dominicans and the incorporation of the Dominican Republic and Haiti in CARICOM" (Kryzanek and Wiarda 1988:155).[18] Initiatives such as these underscore the mutual interests and objectives of the Dominican Republic, Jamaica, and, indeed, the entire Caribbean.

The main thrust of Dominican foreign policy has been the maintenance of a stable foreign investment climate and the sustenance of favorable economic and political relations with the United States. Despite the PRD's linkage to the Socialist International, Guzmán's foreign policy constituted no real departure from that of Balaguer. The country has sought to enhance its international profile, as evidenced by its participation in the Non-Aligned Nations Conferences of 1983 and 1985. Further, the Dominican Republic was the site of a series of meetings between representatives of the Sandinista government of Nicaragua and Contra groups in 1987. It has also participated, along with Jamaica, in the International Bauxite Association (IBA).

Like the Dominican Republic, foreign influences in Jamaica have far outweighed the impact the nation has exerted abroad. In response to this situation, Jamaica in the 1970s pursued a more active international role (Fauriol 1984). An appraisal of Jamaican domestic capabilities leads to the conclusion that foreign policy has been used to dramatize national interests. This has been accomplished in the 1960s through strong ties with the United Kingdom, the United States, and Canada; in the 1970s through innovative and controversial ties to Cuba and the Third World; and in the 1980s through repudiation of the previous decade's innovations. The beginning of the 1990s has witnessed a modified synthesis of these attempts to use largely symbolic foreign policies for domestic advantage.

Increased U.S. investment in bauxite and tourism in the 1960s shifted Jamaica's traditional linkages away from the United Kingdom. Even the Jamaica Defense Force, commanded by British officers until 1965, began to receive U.S. assistance. Hence, in the early 1970s, the trade deficit, decreasing foreign reserves, and general dependency caused by expanded external interests led to attempts to diversify the range of Jamaican foreign relationships. Prime Minister Hugh Shearer looked to the European Economic Community (EEC) for capital, technology, and new markets and established relations with six African states.[19] When Manley assumed power after 1972, African diplomacy and Third World solidarity were emphasized even more as a component of Jamaican foreign policy.

Manley's administration reveled in symbolic initiatives. In addition to his support for the NIEO, he offered rhetorical support for African liberation, discontinued relations with Taiwan, and held discussions of socialism with Julius Nyerere in Tanzania. He also made a point of traveling in Fidel Castro's personal jet to the Algiers summit of the Non-Aligned Movement. After the oil price crisis of 1974, Manley began to speak against free-market forces and the Western financial system. Beyond these symbolic initiatives, Manley negotiated a new bauxite production levy in which Jamaica gained 51 percent participation and joined the IBA.[20] In 1975, he championed preferential tariffs and export stabilization between the Caribbean, African, Pacific, and EEC countries at the Lomé Convention. He also attempted to generate joint ventures with Mexico and Venezuela and signed a technical assistance and cultural exchange agreement with Cuba. One observer argues that the Cuban connection "facilitated the rationalization of all that was a consequence of a 'revolutionary process' [preempting] any 'ordinary' criteria of performance measurement or comparison with 'nonrevolutionary' societies [that were at the time managing] a respectable pace of growth and development" (Maingot 1983:26).

Manley charged the United States with destabilization in 1976 when aid to Jamaica was terminated in response to Jamaica's official recognition of the Movimento Popular para a Liberação de Angola (MPLA) in Angola. A year later, he unsuccessfully approached the Soviet Union for assistance as an alternative to an IMF agreement that Jamaica could not fulfill. When the Manley regime became frustrated by mounting domestic problems, its increasing focus on the international scene produced a foreign policy "devoid of content or local implication and was merely political symbolism" (Heine and Manigat 1988:150).

Foreign policy was one of the JLP's main electoral issues in 1980. Seaga, contending that Manley's posturing was not consonant with Jamaican public opinion, intended to "revert Jamaica's foreign policy to the pre-1972 traditional role" (Heine and Manigat 1988:153). One of his first official acts called for the withdrawal of the Cuban ambassador as a symbolic countermeasure.[21] He further disassociated his regime from Manley's by tempering the call for the NIEO and by depoliticizing the anti-apartheid, African liberation theme by making it a moral issue. Merging anti-communism with attempts to initiate economic recovery, Seaga advocated the Caribbean Basin Initiative and sought to strengthen the U.S. connection. Attention was focused on Jamaica's strategic location in terms of U.S. security and hegemonic interests in order to obtain support for economic development.

In spite of Seaga's realignment with the West and the country's return to dependent capitalism, the flow of investment into Jamaica was disappointing, and economic development was not achieved. Upon returning to power in 1989, Manley moderated his rhetoric and assumed a more pragmatic approach. In contrast to his flamboyantly defiant posture of the 1970s, his softened position has included enhanced ties with the United States, accommodations with the MNCs, and working with the IMF. Discussions have been held and agreements reached with nations throughout the region because Manley has strived to revitalize the stagnant Jamaican economy.

Although Jamaica has attempted a wider range of approaches to foreign policy than has the Dominican Republic, basic requirements for external support of domestic programs and fundamental interests in projecting a presence abroad are very similar in both countries. As components of domestic development policies, the foreign policies of these Caribbean states reflect a basic dilemma in the Third World — socioeconomic pressures continue to increase the need for innovative political responses in countries with limited resources, numerous administrative constraints, and exclusive visions of their own sovereignty.

NOTES

1. Eckstein (1971) suggests four basic criteria for evaluating political performance: decisional efficacy, civil order, legitimacy, and durability. To these,

Macridis and Burg (1991) add the criterion of inclusiveness. While we draw from these criteria, our emphasis is on the perception of public policies.

2.   "The aspirations and expectations of the Dominican people are beginning to outstrip the institutional capacity of the government to respond" (Kearney 1985:13–14).

3.   As Kearney (1985:38) suggests, "within the temporal framework of the electoral cycle, no individual, or organization, can be relied upon to look to the long term. For that matter, few public organizations have the institutional memory to effectively plan for the future." This has been evident in both countries.

4.   Garrity and Picard (1991:369) point out that "after 12 years of IMF agreements and 8 years of structural adjustment measures in Jamaica, both the public and private sector continue to struggle with foreign debt payments that consume nearly half of export earnings, with shortages of foreign exchange, and with the difficult transition from a strategy of import substitution to one of export promotion."

5.   Data in this chapter is compiled from *The Europa World Year Book* 1990, vol. I, s.v. "Dominican Republic," 887–99 and s.v. "Jamaica," 1448–60; and *World Tables* 1988–89 (from the data files of the World Bank).

6.   The IAD, a semi-autonomous organization subordinate to the secretariat of agriculture, was created under the Agrarian Reform Law of 1962.

7.   See Weil et al. (1985:181) for data and a discussion of the State Sugar Council and Bienes Nacionales, a government agency that holds the idle property confiscated from the Trujillo family.

8.   The Boulevard consists of miles of shanties bordering the main highway in the northwestern area of Kingston. Trade from Kingston to the north coast via Spanish Town requires transit through this area.

9.   For the first quarter of 1989, total bauxite production was 26 percent higher than in the previous year, tourist arrivals increased by 17 percent, and overall exchange earnings increased by 21.7 percent, according to the Consulate General of Jamaica in the *Jamaica Letter* (1990).

10.   "What we may be seeing is a general, and perhaps too elegantly simple, process in which economic crises — whether their origins are primarily international, such as the oil and debt crises, or internal, such as the exhaustion of ISI (import substitution initiatives) — are destabilizing to the regime in power" (Klarén and Bossert 1986:327).

11.   Black (1986:139) observes that "the president even cut his own salary by 40 percent."

12.   These references are to the state companies in sugar, electricity, public works, and the food price stabilization institute.

13.   However, strike organizers (members of the PRD and the PLD) interviewed on Noticiero Univisión (November 20, 1990) emphasized the pervasiveness and peaceful nature of the protests. Their clearly stated goal was to change government economic policy that they maintain is crippling the country. While Balaguer has publicly expressed a willingness to hold an early election, most observers believe this to be merely a political ploy.

14.   Payne states that Manley is "anti-Marxist, and disavows either explicitly or by implication, all notions of class struggle and proletarian dictatorship as methods of political and social change" (1988:67).

15. From 1974–80, the Jamaican GDP fell 16 percent, unemployment rose from 24 percent to 31 percent, the cost of living skyrocketed, and there were food and goods shortages. Additionally, foreign exchange fell and Jamaican currency was devalued.

16. See Payne (1988), especially pages 111–30 for an in-depth discussion of each phase of the IMF-Jamaican agreements and their results.

17. Intermestic is defined as a combination of international and domestic policy (Spanier and Uslaner 1982).

18. Jamaica entered the CARICOM in 1973.

19. Ethiopia, Ghana, Sierra Leone, Tanzania, Zambia, and Nigeria began relations with Jamaica between 1967 and 1970.

20. The IBA includes Jamaica, Australia, Guinea, Surinam, Sierra Leone, Yugoslavia, Haiti, Ghana, and the Dominican Republic.

21. U.S. Ambassador Vincent deRoulet was declared persona non grata under the PNP, and Cuban Ambassador Ulyses Estrada was asked to leave Jamaica under the JLP

8

Comparative Perspectives

In examining cases of two apparently distinct Caribbean countries — one influenced by Hispanic political culture and the other by British political culture — we have attempted to enhance understanding of political change in transitional societies. It is our hope that extrapolation of general patterns and principles from the study of Dominican and Jamaican politics will provide the basis for analyses of other seemingly divergent cases.

The application of theory to reality raises questions about policy formulation and implementation as well as system effectiveness that are significant in the field of comparative politics. Our study is based on the assumption that the way systems operate, rather than their juridical and formal organization or professed ideology, is of paramount importance. It is in this approach that we have found underlying commonalities in the Dominican Republic and Jamaica that belie frequently identified differences between the two countries.

Knowledge about the evolution of institutions, political patterns, and their consequences reveals how and why distinct traditions have produced similar outcomes, types of leadership, and, most significantly, methods of governance. Despite historical, sociocultural, and political divergences, our selected cases illustrate how conflicting forces have coalesced in transitional societies.

We have arrived at this point of resolution by synthesizing elements of comparative theories and applying an eclectic approach to the analysis of historical legacies, political cultures, governing institutions and processes, informal influences, and policy outcomes in the Dominican Republic and Jamaica. At this point, we will turn our attention to the thoughts and general observations that derive from a review of our findings. The study concludes with a discussion of policy implications and suggestions for further research.

The Caribbean region provides a microcosm of a fragmented Third World in which linguistic, ethnic, and national divisions tenaciously obscure similarities and impede the evolution of common interests and aspirations. The absence of a single, holistic community may be attributed to the divisiveness of separate Caribbean societies "often fatally hostile to each other" (Moya Pons 1979:33).

This perception of the region reflects the divergent traditions and varying courses of political evolution assumed to be inherent in the Hispanic and British models. It also forms the basis for theoretical exclusion in the literature in the field of comparative politics. Hence the historical tendency toward military control and authoritarianism in the Dominican Republic is usually treated separately from the inclination toward gradual reformist political tutelage in Jamaica. The two countries are generally perceived as being much more dissimilar than they really are.

The exclusionary approach is based on several valid observations. However, a more penetrating analysis reveals underlying commonalities that derive, not from divergent starting points, but from similar patterns in the way in which these political systems have evolved in their attempts to cope with socioeconomic conditions that do not conform to Spanish-speaking or Anglophone jurisdictions.

Although national consciousness has indeed competed with the acceptance of a Caribbean identity, the idea of an integrated region is not new. Pére Labat observed as early as 1743 that the Caribbean peoples are "all together, in the same boat, sailing the same uncertain sea" (Knight 1990:307). We believe that academic and political navigation in this sea may be enhanced through a deeper understanding and appreciation of the forces that have shaped societies within the region.

GENERAL OBSERVATIONS

The analysis presented throughout this book is premised on a dynamic approach designed to provide a unifying vision of Caribbean politics. This approach has facilitated a rather unique comparison of Jamaica and the Dominican Republic — one that has led us to conclude that Caribbean societies are converging in a way that will have profound implications on the region as a whole.

In their attempts to cast off externally imposed developmental models and devise indigenous alternatives, both Jamaica and the Dominican Republic have experienced a process of hybridization through which conflicting traditional and modern forces have been at least partially reconciled. Regimes in both countries exhibit characteristics that are neither strictly authoritarian nor truly democratic. While Dominican leaders have struggled to realize democratic ideals within a history of anarchy and authoritarianism, Jamaican democracy has been challenged by inherent authoritarian impulses.

A high degree of formalism characterizes both societies. The lack of congruity between basic constitutional precepts and political reality reveals how divergent models have produced similar patterns. For example, the role of legislatures, judiciaries, and bureaucracies have been circumscribed by personalistic (rather than legalistic) authority. Moreover, informal power structures have gained prominence in light of the shortcomings of the formal systems.

Perhaps the most striking parallel between the Jamaican and Dominican political systems has been the manner in which people have come to evaluate political leaders and their regimes. The tendency to alternate competing developmental power orientations affirms that ideology has been subordinated to imagery, and that pragmatic economic concerns have prevailed in the minds of voters.

The emergence of more definitive performance criteria in both societies reflects the evolution of mass perceptions and aspirations. This trend poses major implications for the maintenance of stability, which requires a balance between people's expectations and the level of satisfaction derived from governmental policies. Political leaders in Jamaica and the Dominican Republic have found it extremely difficult to mollify increasingly mobilized populations that exhibit heightened expectations for resource distribution and for new conceptions of equity within the context of economic stagnation and decline. Regime legitimacy has been routinely questioned by those whose interests have been neglected. In fact, the very credibility of the respective systems has been undermined when alternative programs have been unable to satisfy expectations.

It has been widely surmised that a parliamentarian system such as that in Jamaica is more conducive to democratic stability than is the type of presidential system found in the Dominican Republic. Nevertheless, both countries have experienced difficulties that may be attributed to common obstacles they have faced.

One such obstacle has been the persistence of traditional institutions and patterns amidst profound socioeconomic change. While personalistic leadership and patron-client relations have clearly provided stability in the past, their legitimacy has been challenged by the emergence of new transitional forces More importantly, their durability has inhibited the formation of modern institutions. This has served to perpetuate elite dominance of the respective political processes and the exclusion of the masses.

Democratic consolidation in modernizing societies requires the promotion of sustained, equitably distributed economic growth. This type of growth, according to Peeler (1989:15), "is only likely to occur when pressure for a deepening of democracy emerges through popular organization and mobilization, and when competing political elites agree to cooperate." In the cases of the Dominican Republic and Jamaica, demands for greater participation and other reforms have already surfaced. However, elites in both countries thus far have been only partially receptive to these demands as evidenced by the manner in which the masses have been integrated into the respective party systems.

At present, the level of political incorporation provided through the respective party systems remains insufficient to ensure continued stability. If further democratic consolidation is to occur in these Caribbean states, it will be incumbent upon elites to recognize mounting pressures from the masses and to facilitate their further integration. This may be accomplished through the formation of concrete linkages between the party systems and community-level organizations that would serve to incorporate "popular participation into the structuring of the political debate on the national level" (Peeler 1989:11). It is envisioned that mass involvement in the decision-making process would generate policies responding to the interests of all.

Whatever the future holds, political change has become linked inextricably to popular perceptions of the quality of life provided by democratically elected governments. Ultimately, regime stability rests not on rhetoric and lavish promises but on the ability to meet demands and deliver results in substantive terms. In light of the pervasiveness and complexity of modern problems, many Dominicans and Jamaicans remain skeptical of the capacity of their governments to address even their most basic needs.

POLICY IMPLICATIONS

It has become painfully apparent that policymakers in the Dominican Republic and Jamaica, as well as in the United States, have overlooked regional similarities in the internal dynamics and limitations faced by Caribbean states. This tendency has served neither North American nor Caribbean interests since it has militated against the creation of mutually beneficial linkages.

Thus far, political leaders in the Dominican Republic and Jamaica have been unable to implement viable alternative policies for the provision of goods and services to satisfy the rising expectations of their citizens.

Bibliography

BOOKS AND ARTICLES

Almond, Gabriel A., and James S. Coleman, eds. *The Politics of the Developing Areas*. Princeton, N.J.: Princeton University Press, 1960.

Almond, Gabriel A., and Sidney Verba. *The Civic Culture*. Princeton, N.J.: Princeton University Press, 1963.

Ambursley, Fitzroy, and Robin Cohen, eds. *Crisis in the Caribbean*. New York: Monthly Review Press, 1983.

Ameringer, Charles D. "The Tradition of Democracy in the Caribbean." *Caribbean Review* 11 (Spring 1982):28–31, 55–56.

Apter, David E. *The Politics of Modernization*. Chicago: University of Chicago Press, 1965.

Arias, Luis. *Gobiernos del PRD y su Política Exterior: Período 1978–1986*. Santo Domingo: Editora Universitaria UASD, 1986.

Atkins, G. Pope. *Arms and Politics in the Dominican Republic*. Boulder, Colo.: Westview, 1981.

Atkins, G. Pope, and Larman C. Wilson. *The United States and the Trujillo Regime*. New Brunswick, N.J.: Rutgers University Press, 1972.

Beckford, George L. *Persistent Poverty: Underdevelopment in Plantation Regions of the Third World*. New York: Oxford University Press, 1972.

Bank of Jamaica. *The Central Bank and the Jamaican Economy*. Kingston: Bank of Jamaica, 1985.

Bell, Ian. *The Dominican Republic*. Boulder, Colo.: Westview, 1981.

Bell, Wendell. *Jamaican Leaders: Political Attitudes in a New Nation*. Berkeley: University of California Press, 1964.

____. "Remembrances of a Jamaican Past ... and Reflections on its Future." *Caribbean Review* 14 (Winter 1985):5–7, 34–36.

____, ed. *The Democratic Revolution in the West Indies*. Cambridge, Mass.: Schenkman Publishing, 1967.

Bell, Wendell, and J. William Gibson. "Independent Jamaica Faces the Outside World: Attitudes of Elites After Twelve Years of Nationhood." *International Studies Quarterly* 22 (March 1978):5–48.

Bell, Wendell, and Robert V. Robinson. "European Melody, African Rhythm, or West

Indian Harmony?: Changing Cultural Identity Among Leaders in a New State." *Social Forces* 58 (September 1979):249–79.

Bell, Wendell, and David L. Stevenson. "Attitudes Toward Social Equality in Independent Jamaica: Twelve Years After Nationhood." *Comparative Political Studies* 2 (January 1979):499–532.

Biddle, William Jesse, and John D. Stephens. "Dependent Development and Foreign Policy: The Case of Jamaica." *International Studies Quarterly* 33 (December 1989):411–34.

Black, Clinton V. *The Story of Jamaica.* London: Collins, 1965.

Black, Jan Knippers. *The Dominican Republic: Politics and Development in an Unsovereign State.* Boston, Mass.: Allen and Unwin, 1986.

Blasier, Cole. *The Giant's Rival.* Pittsburgh, Penna.: University of Pittsburgh Press, 1983.

Bonnelly Ricart, Rafael. "El Triunfo Reformista." *Listín Diario* (June 11, 1986):8.

Bohning, Don, Juan Tamayo, and Bernard Diederich. "The Springtime of Elections: The Status of Democracy in the Caribbean." *Caribbean Review* 11 (Summer 1982):4–7, 40–41.

Bosch, Juan. *El Próximo Paso: Dictadura con Respaldo Popular.* Santo Domingo: Arte y Cine, 1970.

____. *Clases Sociales en la República Dominicana.* Santo Domingo: Editora Corripio, 1983.

____. *Capitalismo, Democracia y Liberación Nacional.* Santo Domingo: Editora Alfa y Omega, 1987.

____. *El Partido: Concepción, Organización y Desarrollo.* Santo Domingo: Editora Alfa y Omega, 1988.

____. *El PLD: Colección Estudios Sociales.* Santo Domingo: Editora Alfa y Omega, 1990.

Braveboy-Wagner, Jacqueline Anne. *The Caribbean in World Affairs: The Foreign Policies of the English-Speaking States.* Boulder, Colo.: Westview, 1989.

Brea, Ramonina. "El Autoritarismo y el Proceso de Democratización en la República Dominicana." *Ciencia y Sociedad* 12 (April-June 1987):180–209.

Brea Franco, Julio. *Introducción al Proceso Electoral Dominicano.* Santo Domingo: Editora Taller, 1984.

____. *El Sistema Constitucional Dominicano* Vols. 1 and 2. Santo Domingo: Editorial CENAPEC, 1986a.

____. "Reforma Electoral e Ingeniera Política: Reflecciones en Torno al Caso Dominicano." In *El Régimen de Partidos y el Sistema Electoral en la República Dominicana*, FORUM 22, edited by Frank Moya Pons, pp. 103–48. Santo Domingo: Editora Amigo del Hogar, 1986b.

____. "Reforma Electoral y Representación Política en el Sistema Electoral Dominicano." *Revista de Ciencia y Cultura UNIBE* 1 (January-April 1989):67–80.

Brown, Aggrey. *Color, Class and Politics in Jamaica.* New Brunswick, N.J.: Transaction Books, 1979.

Bryan, Anthony T. "The Commonwealth Caribbean/Latin American Relationship: New Wine in Old Bottles?" *Caribbean Affairs* 1 (January-March 1988):29–44.

Calder, Bruce J. *The Impact of Intervention: The Dominican Republic During the U.S. Occupation of 1916–1924.* Austin: University of Texas Press, 1984.

Cammack, Paul, David Pool, and William Tordoff. *Third World Politics: A*

Comparative Introduction. Baltimore, Md.: The Johns Hopkins University Press, 1989.

Campillo Pérez, Julio G. *Elecciones Dominicanas: Contribución a su Estudio.* Santo Domingo: Relaciones Públicas, 1982.

____. *Origen y Evolución de la Junta Central Electoral.* Santo Domingo: Junta Central Electoral, 1982b.

Cardoso, Fernando Henrique, and Enzo Faletto. *Dependencia y Desarrollo en América Latina.* Mexico, D.F.: Siglo Veintiuno Editores, 1969.

Castillo, José del. "El Proceso Electoral Contemporáneo en la República Dominicana." In *Los Problemas de la Institucionalización y Preservación de la Democracia en la República Dominicana,* FORUM 2, pp. 79–94. Santo Domingo: Editora Amigo del Hogar, 1982.

____. *Ensayos de Sociología Dominicana.* Santo Domingo: Editora Taller, 1984.

____. "Partidos y Electores: Cambios y Constantes Entre dos Elecciones Nacionales." In *El Régimen de Partidos y el Sistema Electoral en la República Dominicana,* FORUM 22, edited by Frank Moya Pons, pp. 85–102. Santo Domingo: Editora Amigo del Hogar, 1986.

Catrain, Pedro. "Transición Democrática, Social Democracia y Clases Populares en la República Doinicana." *Ciencia y Sociedad* 12 (April-June 1987):262–84.

Cedeño, Víctor Livio. "Los Partidos Políticos en la República Dominicana." In *El Régimen de Partidos y el Sistema Electoral en la República Dominicana,* FORUM 22, edited by Frank Moya Pons, pp. 13–28. Santo Domingo: Editora Amigo del Hogar, 1986.

Cockcroft, James D. *Neighbors in Turmoil: Latin America.* New York: Harper & Row, 1989.

Collier, David. "New Perspectives on the Comparative Method." In *Comparative Political Dynamics: Global Research Perspectives,* edited by Dankwart A. Rustow and Kenneth Paul Erickson, pp. 7–31. New York: Harper Collins, 1991.

Consulate General of Jamaica (New York: Consulate General of Jamaica). *Jamaica Letter* 4 (March-April 1990).

Crassweller, Robert D. *Trujillo: The Life and Times of a Caribbean Dictator.* New York: Macmillan, 1966.

Dahl, Robert A. *Polyarchy: Participation and Opposition.* New Haven, Conn.: Yale University Press, 1971.

Davis, Stephen. "Jamaican Politics, Economics and Culture: An Interview with Edward Seaga." *Caribbean Review* 10 (Fall 1981):14–17.

Deere, Carmen Diana, Peggy Antrobus, Lynn Bolles, Edwin Melendez, Peter Phillips, Marcia Rivera, and Helen Safa. *In the Shadows of the Sun: Caribbean Development Alternatives and U.S. Policy.* Boulder, Colo.: Westview, 1990.

Dent, David W., ed. *Handbook of Political Science Research on Latin America: Trends from the 1960s to the 1990s.* New York: Greenwood Press, 1990.

Deutsch, Karl W. "Social Mobilization and Political Development." *American Political Science Review* 55 (September 1961):493–514.

Deutsch, Karl W., Jorge Domínguez, and Hugh Heclo, eds. *Comparative Government: Politics of Industrialized and Developing Nations.* Boston, Mass.: Houghton Mifflin, 1981.

Diamond, Larry, Juan J. Linz, and Seymour Martin Lipset, eds. *Democracy in Developing Countries.* Vol. 4, Latin America. Boulder, Colo.: Lynne Reinner

Publishers, 1989.

Diederich, Bernard. *Trujillo: The Death of the Goat.* Boston: Little, Brown, 1978.

Dix, Robert H. "Incumbency and Electoral Turnover in Latin America." *Journal of Interamerican Studies and World Affairs* 26 (November 1984):435–48.

Dogan, Mattei, and Dominique Pelassy. *How to Compare Nations: Strategies in Comparative Politics.* Chatham, N.J.: Chatham House, 1990.

Domínguez, Jorge. "Political Change: Central America, South America and the Caribbean." In *Understanding Political Development*, edited by Myron Weiner and Samuel Huntington. Boston, Mass.: Little, Brown, 1987.

Domínguez, Virginia, and Jorge Domínguez. *The Caribbean: Its Implications for the United States.* New York: Foreign Policy Association, 1981.

Duncan, Raymond W. "Caribbean Leftism." *Problems of Communism* 27 (May-June 1978):35–57.

Duverger, Maurice. *Political Parties: Their Organization and Activity in the Modern State.* London: Methuen and Co., 1959.

Easton, David. *Comparative Politics: A Developmental Approach.* Boston, Mass.: Little, Brown, 1966.

Eckstein, Harry. *The Evaluation of Political Performance: Problems and Dimensions.* Beverly Hills, Calif.: Sage, 1971.

Eckstein, Harry, and David E. Apter, eds. *Comparative Politics.* London: The Free Press of Glencoe, 1963.

Edie, Carlene J. *Democracy by Default: Dependency and Clientelism in Jamaica.* Boulder, Colo.: Lynne Rienner Publishers, 1991.

Eisenstadt, S. N. "Bureaucracy and Political Development." In *Bureaucracy and Political Development*, edited by Joseph LaPalombara, p. 96. Princeton, N.J.: Princeton University Press, 1963.

____. "The Civilizational Dimensions of Politics: Some Indications for Comparative Analysis." In *Comparative Political Dynamics: Global Research Perspectives*, edited by Dankwart A. Rustow and Kenneth Paul Erickson, p. 54. New York: Harper Collins, 1991.

Erisman, H. Michael, ed. *The Caribbean Challenge: U.S. Policy in a Volatile Region.* Boulder, Colo.: Westview, 1984.

Espinal, Flavio Darío. "Política, Constitución y Reforma: Avances y Obstrucciones de la Democratización Dominicana." *Ciencia y Sociedad* 12 (April-June 1987):232–45.

Espinal, Rosario. *Autoritarismo y Democracia en la Política Dominicana.* San José, Costa Rica: CAPEL, 1987a.

____. "Pactos y Participación, Élites y Pueblo: El PRD en el Poder o el Episodio de una Democracia Maltratada." *Ciencia y Sociedad* 12 (April-June 1987b):285–316.

____. "Crisis del Estatismo y el Desarrollismo: Dilemas del Liderazgo Político Dominicano." *Revista de Ciencia y Cultura UNIBE* 1 (January-April 1989):57–66.

____. "The 1990 Elections in the Dominican Republic." *Electoral Studies* 10 (February 1991):139–44.

The Europa World Year Book. London: Europa Publications Limited. Vol. I, Part 2. 1990:892, 1454.

Fauriol, Georges A. *Foreign Policy Behavior of Caribbean States: Guyana, Haiti, and Jamaica.* Lanham, Md.: University Press of America, 1984.

Feuer, Carl. *Jamaica and Sugar Workers' Cooperatives: The Politics of Reform.* Boulder, Colo.: Westview, 1984.

Fitzgibbon, Russell H., and Julio A. Fernandez. *Latin America: Political Culture and Development.* Englewood Cliffs, N.J.: Prentice-Hall, 1981.

Floyd, Barry. *Jamaica: An Island Microcosm.* New York: St. Martin's Press, 1979.

Foner, Nancy. "Party Politics in a Jamaican Community." *Caribbean Studies* 13 (July 1973):51–64.

Frank, Andre Gunder. *Capitalism and Underdevelopment in Latin America.* New York: Monthly Review Press, 1967.

———. *Latin America: Underdevelopment or Revolution.* New York: Monthly Review Press, 1969.

Galíndez, Jesús de. *The Era of Trujillo.* Tucson: The University of Arizona Press, 1973.

Garrity, Michele, and Louis A. Picard. "Organized Interests, the State, and the Public Policy Process: An Assessment of Jamaican Business Associations." *The Journal of Developing Areas* 25 (April 1991):369–94.

Geddes, Barbara. "A Game Theoretic Model of Reform in Latin American Democracies." *American Political Science Review* 85 (June 1991):371–92.

Gibson, Charles. *Spain in America.* New York: Harper & Row, 1966.

Girvan, Norman, and Richard Bernal. "The IMF and the Foreclosure of Development Options: The Case of Jamaica." *Monthly Review* 33 (February 1982):34–49.

Girvan, Norman, and Owen Jefferson. *Readings in the Political Economy of the Caribbean.* Kingston: New World, 1973.

Gleijeses, Piero. *The Dominican Crisis.* Baltimore, Md.: The Johns Hopkins University Press, 1978.

Gray, Obika. *Radicalism and Social Change in Jamaica, 1960–1972.* Knoxville: The University of Tennessee Press, 1991.

Guillén, Nicolás. *Jamaica Journal* 9 (1976):26.

Gutiérrez, Carlos María. *The Dominican Republic: Rebellion and Repression.* New York: Monthly Review Press, 1972.

Hamilton, B. L. St. John. *Problems of Administration in an Emergent Nation: A Case Study of Jamaica.* New York: Praeger, 1964.

Harris, Marvin, and Charles Wagley. *Minorities in the New World.* New York: Columbia University Press, 1958.

Hartlyn, Jonathan. "A Democratic Shoot-Out in the D.R.: An Analysis of the 1986 Election." *Caribbean Review* 15 (Winter 1987):14–16, 33–35.

Hayes, Margaret Daly. *Latin America and the U.S. National Interest.* Boulder, Colo.: Westview, 1984.

Hearne, John, ed. *The Search for Solutions: Selections from the Speeches and Writings of Michael Manley.* Toronto: Maple House Publishing, 1976.

Heine, Jorge, and Leslie Manigat, eds. *The Caribbean and World Politics: Cross Currents and Cleavages.* New York: Holmes and Meier, 1988.

Henry, Paget, and Carl Stone, eds. *The Newer Caribbean: Decolonization, Democracy and Development.* Philadelphia, Penna.: Institute for the Study of Human Issues, 1983.

Herman, Edward S., and Frank Brodhead. *Demonstration Elections: U.S.-Staged*

Elections in the Dominican Republic, Vietnam, and El Salvador. Boston, Mass.: South End Press, 1984.

Hill, George W., José A. Silva, and Ruth Oliver de Hill. "Patterns of Land Tenancy and Their Social Repercussions." In *Contemporary Cultures and Societies of Latin America*, edited by Dwight Heath and Richard Adams. New York: Random House, 1965.

Hillman, Richard S. "Interviewing Jamaica's Political Leaders: Michael Manley and Edward Seaga." *Caribbean Review* 8 (Summer 1979a):28–31, 53–55.

____. "Legitimacy and Change in Jamaica." *The Journal of Developing Areas* 13 (July 1979b):395–414.

____. "The Central University of Venezuela and the Government: Policy and Praxis." Presented at the New York State Political Science Association Annual Conference, State University of New York, Albany, April 22, 1990.

Hillman, Richard S., and Margaret V. Ekstrom. "Political Cynicism in Contemporary Caribbean Fiction." *SECOLAS Annals* 21 (March 1990):71–78.

Hintzen, Percy. *The Costs of Regime Survival: Racial Mobilization, Elite Domination, and Control of the State in Guyana and Trinidad.* Cambridge: Cambridge University Press, 1989.

Hippolyte-Manigat, Mirlande. "What Happened in Ocho Rios: Last Chance for CARICOM?" *Caribbean Review* 12 (Spring 1983):10–14.

Huntington, Samuel. *Political Order in Changing Societies.* New Haven, Conn.: Yale University Press, 1968.

Irvin, George, and Xabier Gorostiaga. *Towards an Alternative for Central America and the Caribbean.* London: George Allen and Unwin, 1985.

Janda, Kenneth. *A Conceptual Framework for the Comparative Analysis of Political Parties.* Beverly Hills, Calif.: Sage, 1970.

____. *Political Parties: A Cross-National Survey.* New York: Free Press, 1980.

Jimenes Grullón, Juan Isidro. *Sociología Política Dominicana, 1844–1966.* Santo Domingo: Editora Taller, Vols. I, II; Alfa y Omega, Vol. III, 1974–1980.

Johnson, Janis, and Robert A. Rankin. "Interviewing Michael Manley: The Role of the Opposition in Jamaica." *Caribbean Review* 11 (Summer 1982):26–29.

Kaplan, Irving, Howard I. Blutstein, Kathryn Therese Johnston, and David S. McMorris. *Area Handbook for Jamaica.* Washington, D.C.: U.S. Government Printing Office, 1976.

Kaufman, Michael. *Jamaica Under Manley: Dilemmas of Socialism and Democracy.* Westport, Conn.: Lawrence Hill and Co., 1985.

Kearney, Richard C. "Dominican Update: Can Politics Contain the Economic Crisis?" *Caribbean Review* 14 (Fall 1985):12–14, 18.

Keith, Sherry, and Robert Girling. "Caribbean Conflict: Jamaica and the U.S." *NACLA Report on the Americas* 12 (May-June 1978):3–36.

Klarén, Peter F., and Thomas J. Bossert. *Promise of Development: Theories of Change in Latin America.* Boulder, Colo.: Westview, 1986.

Knight, Franklin W. *The Caribbean: The Genesis of a Fragmented Nationalism.* New York: Oxford University Press, 1978.

____. *The Caribbean: The Genesis of a Fragmented Nationalism.* 2d ed. New York: Oxford University Press, 1990.

Kryzanek, Michael J. "Political Party Decline and the Failure of Liberal Democracy: The PRD in Dominican Politics." *Journal of Latin American Studies* 9 (May

1977a):115–43.

____. "Diversion, Subversion and Repression: The Strategies of Anti-Opposition Politics in Balaguer's Dominican Republic." *Caribbean Studies* 17 (April-July 1977b):83–103.

____. "The 1978 Election in the Dominican Republic: Opposition Politics, Intervention, and the Carter Administration." *Caribbean Studies* 19 (April-July 1979):51–73.

____. "The Dominican Republic: The Challenge of Preserving a Fragile Democracy." In *Latin American Politics and Development*, edited by Howard J. Wiarda and Harvey F. Kline, 3rd ed., pp. 535–50. Boulder, Colo.: Westview, 1990.

Kryzanek, Michael J., and Howard J. Wiarda. *The Politics of External Influence in the Dominican Republic*. New York: Praeger, 1988.

Kuper, Adam. *Changing Jamaica*. London: Routledge and Kegan Paul, 1976.

Lacey, Terry. *Violence and Politics in Jamaica 1960–1970: Internal Security in a Developing Country*. Manchester, England: Manchester University Press, 1977.

Lange, Peter. "Letter from the Chair." *APSA-CP* 1 (Summer 1990):1–3.

LaPalombara, Joseph. "Macrotheories and Microapplications in Comparative Politics." *Comparative Politics* 1 (October 1968):52–78.

LaPalombara, Joseph, and Myron Weiner, eds. *Political Parties and Political Development*. Princeton, N.J.: Princeton University Press, 1966.

Lawson, Kay. *The Comparative Study of Political Parties*. New York: St. Martin's Press, 1976.

____, ed. *Political Parties and Linkage: A Comparative Perspective*. New Haven, Conn.: Yale University Press, 1980.

Lehmann, David. *Democracy and Development in Latin America: Economics, Politics and Religion in the Postwar Period*. Philadelphia, Penna.: Temple University Press, 1990.

Levi, Darrell E. *Michael Manley: The Making of a Leader*. Athens: University of Georgia Press, 1989.

Levine, Barry B., ed. *The New Cuban Presence in the Caribbean*. Boulder, Colo.: Westview, 1983.

Lewin, Arthur. "The Fall of Michael Manley: A Case Study of the Failure of Reform Socialism." *Monthly Review* 33 (February 1982):49.

Lewis, Gordon K. "The Caribbean in the 1980s: What We Should Study." *Caribbean Review* 10 (Fall 1981):18–19, 46–48.

Lewis, Gordon. "The Contemporary Caribbean: A General Overview." In *Caribbean Contours*, edited by Sidney Mintz and Sally Price. Baltimore, Md.: The Johns Hopkins University Press, 1985.

Lijphart, Arend. "Comparative Politics and the Comparative Method." *American Political Science Review* 65 (September 1971):682–93.

Lindsay, Louis. *The Myth of Independence: Middle Class Politics and Non-Mobilization in Jamaica*. Kingston: Institute of Social and Economic Research, 1975.

Linz, Juan J., and Alfred Stepan, eds. *The Breakdown of Democratic Regimes*. Baltimore, Md.: The Johns Hopkins University Press, 1978.

Lipset, Seymour M., and Stein Rokkan, eds. *Party Systems and Voter Alignments: Cross-National Perspectives*. New York: The Free Press, 1967.

Lowenthal, Abraham F. "The Dominican Republic: The Politics of Chaos." In *Reform and Revolution: Readings in Latin American Politics*, edited by Arpad von Lazar and Robert F. Kaufman, pp. 34–58. Boston: Allyn and Bacon, 1969.

____. *The Dominican Intervention*. Cambridge, Mass.: Harvard University Press, 1971.

____. *West Indian Societies*. London: Oxford University Press, 1972.

____, ed. *Armies and Politics in Latin America*. New York: Holmes and Meier, 1976.

Macridis, Roy C. *The Study of Comparative Government*. New York: Random House, 1955.

Maingot, Anthony M. "The Role of the Opposition in the Caribbean: In Jamaica — Edward Seaga." *Caribbean Review* 7 (October-December 1978):27–30.

____. "Ideological Dependency and the Origins of Socialism in the Caribbean." In *The Continuing Struggle for Democracy in Latin America*, edited by Howard J. Wiarda. Boulder, Colo.: Westview, 1980.

____. "Cuba and the Commonwealth Caribbean: Playing the Cuban Card." In *The New Cuban Presence in the Caribbean*, edited by Barry B. Levine, pp. 19–42. Boulder, Colo.: Westview, 1983.

____. "The Commonwealth Caribbean." In *Dual Legacies in the Contemporary Caribbean: Continuing Aspects of British and French Dominion*, edited by Paul Sutton. London: Frank Cass, 1986.

Mainwaring, Scott. "Presidentialism in Latin America." *Latin American Research Review* 25 (1990):157–79.

Maisel, Louis, and Joseph Cooper. *Political Parties: Development and Decay*. Beverly Hills, Calif.: Sage, 1978.

Malloy, James M., and Mitchell A. Seligson, eds. *Authoritarians and Democrats: Regime Transition in Latin America*. Pittsburgh, Penna.: University of Pittsburgh Press, 1987.

Manley, Michael. "Overcoming Insularity in Jamaica." *Foreign Affairs* 49 (October 1970):100.

____. *The Politics of Change: A Jamaican Testament*. London: André Deutsch, 1974.

____. *A Voice at the Workplace: Reflections on Colonialism and the Jamaican Worker*. London: André Deutsch, 1975.

____. "Not for Sale: Address by Prime Minister Michael Manley at the 38th Annual Conference of the People's National Party." San Francisco, Calif.: Editorial Consultants, 1976.

____. *Jamaica: Struggle in the Periphery*. London: Third World Media, 1982.

____. "The Integration Movement." *Caribbean Affairs* 1 (January-March 1988):6–15.

Martin, John Bartlow. *Overtaken by Events: The Dominican Crisis — From the Fall of Trujillo to the Civil War*. Garden City, N.Y.: Doubleday, 1966.

Mayer, Lawrence. "Practicing What We Preach: Comparative Politics in the 1980s." *Comparative Political Studies*, July 1983, 173–91.

McDonald, Ronald H. *Party Systems and Elections in Latin America*. Chicago, Ill.: Markham, 1971.

McDonald, Ronald H., and J. Mark Ruhl. *Party Politics and Elections in Latin America*. Boulder, Colo.: Westview, 1989.

Millet, Richard, and W. Marvin Will. *The Restless Caribbean: Changing Patterns of International Relations*. New York: Praeger, 1979.

Milnor, Andrew J., ed. *Comparative Political Parties: Selected Readings*. New York: Thomas Crowell Company, 1969.

Mintz, Sidney W. *Caribbean Transformations*. Chicago: Aldine, 1974.

Mintz, Sidney W., and Sally Price, eds. *Caribbean Contours*. Baltimore, Md.: The Johns Hopkins University Press, 1985.

Moreno, José A. *Barrios in Arms*. Pittsburgh, Penna.: University of Pittsburgh Press, 1970.

Mörner, Magnus. *Race and Class in Latin America*. New York: Columbia University Press, 1970.

Moya Pons, Frank. *Historia Colonial de Santo Domingo*. Santiago: Universidad Católica Madre y Maestra, 1974.

____. "Is There a Caribbean Consciousness?" *Américas* 31 (August 1979):33.

Munroe, Trevor. *The Politics of Constitutional Decolonization*. Kingston: Institute of Social and Economic Studies, 1971.

Needler, Martin C. *An Introduction to Latin American Politics: The Structure of Conflict*. Englewood Cliffs, N.J.: Prentice-Hall, 1983.

Nettleford, Rex. *Mirror, Mirror: Identity, Race, and Protest in Jamaica*. Kingston: Collins and Sangster, 1970.

____. *Caribbean Cultural Identity: The Case of Jamaica*. Los Angeles: Center for Afro-American Studies and UCLA Latin American Center, 1978.

____. *Manley and the New Jamaica: Selected Speeches and Writings 1938–1968*. New York: African Publishing Corporation, 1971.

Nunes, Fred E. "The Declining Status of the Jamaican Civil Service." *Social and Economic Studies* 23 (June 1974):344–57.

____. "The Nonsense of Neutrality." *Social and Economic Studies* 25 (December 1976):347–66.

Neumann, Sigmund, ed. *Modern Political Parties: Approaches to Comparative Politics*. Chicago: University of Chicago Press, 1956.

O'Donnell, Guillermo. *Modernization and Bureaucratic-Authoritarianism: Studies in South American Politics*. Berkeley: Institute of International Studies, University of California, 1973.

O'Donnell, Guillermo, and Phillipe C. Schmitter. *Transitions from Authoritarian Rule: Conclusions About Uncertain Democracies*. Baltimore, Md.: The Johns Hopkins University Press, 1986.

Organization of American States. *The Jamaican Constitution of 1962*. Washington, D.C.: Organization of American States, 1971.

Ornes, Germán. *Trujillo: Little Caesar of the Caribbean*. New York: Nelson, 1958.

Oviedo, José. "El Partido Revolucionario y el Partido Reformista en la Dinámica del Cambio Político Dominicano." In *El Régimen de Partidos y el Sistema Electoral en la República Dominicana*, FORUM 22, edited by Frank Moya Pons, pp. 45–84. Santo Domingo: Editora Amigo del Hogar, 1986.

____. "La Tradición Autoritaria." *Ciencia y Sociedad* 12 (April-June 1987):210–31.

____. "Democracia en la Sociedad Contemporánea: la Cuestión de la Institucionalidad y la Formalización." *Revista de Ciencia y Cultura UNIBE* 1 (January-April 1989):49–56.

Patterson, Orlando. *The Sociology of Slavery*. London: MacGibbon and Kee, 1967.

Payne, Anthony J. *Politics in Jamaica*. New York: St. Martin's Press, 1988.

Peeler, John A. "Deepening Democracy and Democratic Consolidation in Latin

America." Presented at the Fifteenth International Congress, Latin American Studies Association, 1989.

Penn, Mark J. "Las Elecciones Dominicanas." *Listín Diario*, June 11, 1986, 8.

Planning Institute of Jamaica. *Economic and Social Survey — Jamaica 1984*. Kingston: Planning Institute of Jamaica, 1985.

____. "Quarterly Economic Reports." Kingston: Planning Institute of Jamaica, 1978.

Rial, Juan. "The Armed Forces and Democracy: The Interests of Latin American Military Corporations in Sustaining Democratic Regimes." In *The Military and Democracy: The Future of Civil-Military Relations in Latin America*, edited by Louis N. Goodman, Johanna S. R. Mendelsohn, and Juan Rial, pp. 277–95. Boston, Mass.: Lexington Books, 1990.

Riggs, Fred. "Comparative Politics and the Study of Political Parties: A Structural Approach." In *Approaches to the Study of Party Organization*, edited by William J. Crotty. Boston, Mass.: Allyn and Bacon, 1968.

Robinson, Robert V., and Wendell Bell. "Attitudes Towards Political Independence in Jamaica after Twelve Years of Nationhood." *The British Journal of Sociology* 29 (June 1978):208–33.

Rodman, Selden. *Quisqueya: A History of the Dominican Republic*. Seattle: University of Washington Press, 1964.

Rosenberg, Mark B. "Interviewing Peña Gómez: Leader of the Dominican Revolutionary Party." *Caribbean Review* 9 (Fall 1980):10–11, 44–46.

Rustow, Dankwart A., and Kenneth Paul Erickson, eds. *Comparative Political Dynamics: Global Research Perspectives*. New York: Harper & Collins, 1991.

Santos Theotonio dos. *Dependencia y Cambio Social*. Santiago: CESO, Universidad de Chile, 1970.

Sartori, Giovanni. *Parties and Party Systems: A Framework for Analysis*. Cambridge: Cambridge University Press, 1976.

Segal, Aaron. "Caribbean Realities." *Current History* 84 (March 1985): 127–30, 134–35.

Serbin, Andrés. "Race and Politics: Relations Between the English-Speaking Caribbean and Latin America." *Caribbean Affairs* 2 (October-December 1989):146–71.

Serbin, Andrés, ed. *Venezuela y Las Relaciones Internacionales en la Cuenca del Caribe*. Caracas: ILDIS/AVECA, 1987.

Shurz, William Lytle. *The New World: The Civilization of Latin America*. New York: E. P. Dutton, 1964.

Silvert, Kalman. *The Conflict Society: Reaction and Revolution in Latin America*. New York: Harper Colophon Books, 1966.

Slater, Jerome. *Intervention and Negotiation: The United States and the Dominican Republic*. New York: Harper & Row, 1970.

Spanier, John, and Robert Uslaner. *American Foreign Policy and the Democratic Dilemmas*. New York: CBS College Publishing, 1982.

Statistical Institute of Jamaica. "Statistical Abstract 1984." Kingston: The Statistical Institute of Jamaica, 1984.

____. *Statistical Yearbook of Jamaica*. Kingston: The Statistical Institute of Jamaica, 1976.

____. *Statistical Yearbook of Jamaica*. Kingston: The Statistical Institute of Jamaica, 1986.

Stephens, Evelyne Huber. "Democracy in Latin America: Recent Developments in Comparative Historical Perspective." *Latin American Research Review* 25 (1990):157–76.

Stephens, Evelyne Huber, and John D. Stephens. *Democratic Socialism in Jamaica: The Political Movement and Social Transformation in Dependent Capitalism.* Princeton, N.J.: Princeton University Press, 1986.

____. "Manley Prepares to Return: PNP Options in Today's Jamaica." *Caribbean Review* 16 (Winter 1988):16–19, 39–44.

Stone, Carl. *Class, Race and Political Behavior in Urban Jamaica.* Kingston: Institute of Social and Economic Research, University of the West Indies, 1973.

____. *Electoral Behavior and Public Opinion in Jamaica.* Kingston: Institute of Social and Economic Research, University of the West Indies, 1974.

____. *Democracy and Clientelism in Jamaica.* New Brunswick, N.J.: Transaction Books, 1980.

____. "Jamaica's 1980 Elections: What Manley Did Do: What Seaga Need Do." *Caribbean Review* 10 (Spring 1981):5–7, 40–43.

____. "Seaga is in Trouble: Polling the Jamaican Polity in Mid-Term." *Caribbean Review* 11 (Fall 1982):4–7, 28–29.

____. "Jamaica: From Manley to Seaga." In *Revolution and Counterrevolution in Central America and the Caribbean,* edited by Donald E. Schulz and Douglas H. Graham. Boulder, Colo.: Westview, 1984.

____. "A Political Profile of the Caribbean." In *Caribbean Contours,* edited by Sidney W. Mintz and Sally Price, pp. 13–54. Baltimore, Md.: The Johns Hopkins University Press, 1985.

____. *Power in the Caribbean Basin: A Comparative Study of Political Economy.* Philadelphia Penna.: Institute for the Study of Human Issues, 1986.

Stone, Carl, and Aggrey Brown, eds. *Essays on Power and Change in Jamaica.* Kingston: Jamaica Publishing House, 1977.

____. *Perspectives on Jamaica in the Seventies.* Kingston: Jamaica Publishing House, 1981.

Sutton, Paul, ed. *Dual Legacies in the Contemporary Caribbean: Continuing Aspects of British and French Dominion.* London: Frank Cass, 1986.

Tannenbaum, Frank. "The Hacienda." In *The Dynamics of Change in Latin American Politics,* edited by John D. Martz. Englewood Cliffs, N.J.: Prentice-Hall, 1965.

Verba, Sidney W. "Comparative Politics: Where Have We Been, Where Are We Going?" In *New Directions in Comparative Politics,* edited by Howard J. Wiarda. Boulder, Colo.: Westview, 1985.

Weber, Max. *Theory of Social and Economic Organization.* New York: Macmillan, 1947.

____. *On Charisma and Institution Building: Selected Papers,* edited by S. N. Eisenstadt. Chicago: University of Chicago Press, 1968.

Weil, Thomas E., Jan Knippers Black, Howard I. Blutstein, Kathryn T. Johnston, David S. McMorris, and Frederick T. Munson. *The Dominican Republic: A Country Study.* Washington, D.C.: U.S. Government Printing Office, 1985.

Weiner, Myron, and Samuel P. Huntington, eds. *Understanding Political Development.* Boston, Mass.: Little, Brown and Co., 1987.

Weiner, Myron, and Ergun Özbudun, eds. *Competitive Elections in Developing Countries*. Washington, D.C.: American Enterprise Institute, Duke University Press, 1987.

Welles, Sumner. *Naboth's Vineyard: The Dominican Republic, 1844–1924*. 2 vols. New York: Payson and Clarke, 1928.

Wells, Henry, and Howard Wiarda, eds. *Dominican Republic Election Factbook*. Washington, D.C.: Institute for the Comparative Study of Political Systems, 1966.

Wheaton, Philip, ed. *Jamaica: Caribbean Challenge*. Washington, D.C.: EPICA Task Force, 1979.

Wiarda, Howard J. *Dictatorship and Development: The Methods of Control in Trujillo's Dominican Republic*. Gainesville, University of Florida Press, 1970.

_____. *Dictatorship, Development, and Disintegration: Politics and Social Change in the Dominican Republic*. Ann Arbor, Mich.: University Microfilms Monograph Series, 1975.

_____. "The United States and the Dominican Republic: Intervention, Dependency, and Tyrannicide." *Journal of Inter-American Studies* 22 (May 1980):247–60.

_____. *Corporatism and National Development in Latin America*. Boulder, Colo.: Westview, 1981.

_____. *New Directions in Comparative Politics*. Boulder, Colo.: Westview, 1985a.

_____. "The Dominican Republic: The Politics of a Frustrated Revolution, II." In *Latin American Politics and Development*, edited by Howard J. Wiarda and Harvey F. Kline, 2d ed., pp. 581–98. Boulder, Colo.: Westview, 1985b.

_____. "Social Change, Political Development, and the Latin American Tradition." In *Promise of Development: Theories of Change in Latin America*, edited by Peter F. Klarén and Thomas J. Bossert, pp. 197–218. Boulder, Colo.: Westview, 1986.

_____. "The Dominican Republic: Mirror Legacies of Democracy and Authoritarianism." In *Democracy in Developing Countries*, edited by Larry Diamond, Juan J. Linz, and Seymour Martin Lipset, Vol. 4, pp. 423–58. Boulder, Colo.: Lynne Rienner Publishers, 1989.

_____. "The Politics of the Third World Debt." *PS: Political Science and Politics* 23 (September 1990):411–18.

_____. "Concepts and Models in Comparative Politics: Political Development Reconsidered — and Its Alternatives." In *Comparative Political Dynamics: Global Research Perspectives*, edited by Dankwart A. Rustow and Kenneth Paul Erickson, pp. 32–53. New York: Harper Collins, 1991.

Wiarda, Howard J., and Harvey F. Kline, eds. *Latin American Politics and Development*. 3rd ed. Boulder, Colo.: Westview, 1990.

_____. *Latin American Politics and Development*. 2d ed. Boulder, Colo.: Westview, 1985.

Wiarda, Howard J., and Michael J. Kryzanek. "Dominican Dictatorship Revisited: The Caudillo Tradition and the Regimes of Trujillo and Balaguer." *Revista/Review Interamericana* 7 (Fall 1977):417–35.

_____. *The Dominican Republic: A Caribbean Crucible*. Boulder, Colo.: Westview, 1982.

Will, Marvin W. "A Nation Divided: The Quest for Caribbean Integration." *Latin American Research Review* 26 (1991):3–37.

Williams, Mary W. *The People and Politics of Latin America*. Boston, Mass.: Ginn and Co., 1938.

Wynia, Gary W. *The Politics of Latin American Development*. Cambridge: Cambridge University Press, 1978.

Young, Alma, and Dion Phillips, eds. *Militarization in the Non-Hispanic Caribbean*. Boulder, Colo.: Lynne Rienner Publishers, 1986.

INTERVIEWS

This list includes formal interviews with political leaders and anaysts The authors also draw from informal and spontaneous interviews conducted in 1990 with approximately 50 Dominicans of all classes and from the reults of 61 informal and spontaneous interviews with Jamaicans of all classes (Hillman 1979b).

Juan Alsace, political officer, U.S. Department of State — March 12, 1990 at the U.S. Embassy, Santo Domingo (with Richard S. Hillman and Thomas D'Agostino)

Juan Bosch, president of the Partido de la Liberación Dominicana and former president of the Dominican Republic — March 15, 1990 at UNIBE (with Richard S. Hillman and Thomas D'Agostino)

Julio Brea Franco, political scientist — March 12, 1990 at UNIBE (with Richard S. Hillman and Thomas D'Agostino) and on March 15, 1990 at the offices of Brea Franco and Associates, Santo Domingo (with Thomas D'Agostino)

Marino Vinicio "Vincho" Castillo, leader of the Fuerza Nacional Progresista — March 14, 1990 at FNP headquarters, Santo Domingo (with Richard S. Hillman and Thomas D'Agostino)

José Israel Cuello, representative of Movimiento de Renovación — March 13, 1990 at MODERNO headquarters, Santo Domingo (with Richard S. Hillman and Thomas D'Agostino)

Rogelio Delgado, representative of the Partido Comunista Dominicano — March 16, 1990 at PCD headquarters, Santo Domingo (with Richard S. Hillman and Thomas D'Agostino)

Washington de Peña, representative of the Partido Reformista Social Cristiano — March 14, 1990 at UNIBE (with Richard S. Hillman and Thomas D'Agostino)

Flavio Darío Espinal, political analyst — March 12, 1990 at UNIBE (with Richard S. Hillman and Thomas D'Agostino) and March 16, 1990 at Universidad Católica Madre y Maestra, Santo Domingo (with Thomas D'Agostino)

Rodolfo Espinal, first vice-president of the Partido Liberal La Estructura — March 13, 1990 at Partido Liberal La Estructura headquarters, Santo Domingo (with Thomas D'Agostino)

Gerald Groves, former consul general of Jamaica — March 9, 1977 at the Jamaican consulate in New York (with Richard S. Hillman)

Sonia Jones, attorney-at-law and Jamaican radio personality — numerous occasions in Kingston, Jamaica (with Richard S. Hillman)

Jane Levinson, Office of Public Relations of the Jamaican Prime Minister — January 28, 1986 at Jamaica House (with Richard S. Hillman)

Michael Manley, prime minister of Jamaica — April 12, 1978 at Jamaica House (with Richard S. Hillman)

Tirso Mejía-Ricart, vice rector of the Autonomous University of Santo Domingo —
March 14, 1990 at UNIBE (with Thomas D'Agostino)

Trevor Munroe, professor of political science, University of the West Indies —
January 22, 1978 at the UWI, Kingston (with Richard S. Hillman)

Fred Nunes, professor of public administration, University of the West Indies — numerous occasions at UWI, Kingston and in New York (with Richard S. Hillman)

Fernando Periche Vidal, former governor of the Dominican Central Bank, minister of
the interior, and director of the State Electrical Corporation — numerous
occasions in Santo Domingo and Rochester, New York (with Richard S.
Hillman and Thomas D'Agostino)

Tony Raful, representative of the Partido Revolucionario Independiente — March 13,
1990 at UNIBE (with Thomas D'Agostino)

Claude Robinson, Office of Public Relations of the Prime Minister of Jamaica —
numerous occasions in 1978 at Jamaica House (with Richard S. Hillman)

Roberto Saladín, former governor of the Dominican Central Bank and candidate of a
coalition of the Partido Popular Cristiano, Partido Duartista, Partido
Constitucionalista, and Movimiento Solidaridad con Saladín — March 16,
1990 at UNIBE (with Richard S. Hillman and Thomas D'Agostino)

Miguel Sang Ben, political scientist and dean of graduate studies at UNIBE —
numerous occasions in Santo Domingo and Rochester, New York (with
Richard S. Hillman and Thomas D'Agostino)

Edward Seaga, leader of the opposition in Jamaica — February 7, 1978 at his New
Kingston office (with Richard S. Hillman)

Patricia Sharpe, U.S. Information Service, cultural affairs officer — March 12, 1990 at
the U.S. Embassy, Santo Domingo and March 16, 1990 at UNIBE (with
Richard S. Hillman and Thomas D'Agostino)

Thomas Smolik, economic officer, U.S. Department of State — March 12, 1990 at
the U.S. Embassy, Santo Domingo (with Richard S. Hillman and Thomas
D'Agostino)

Andrés Van Der Horst, representative of the Partido Liberal La Estructura and president
of the Federation of Liberal and Centrist Parties of Central America and the
Caribbean — March 13, 1990 at UNIBE (with Richard S. Hillman and Thomas
D'Agostino) and at Partido Liberal La Estructura headquarters, Santo Domingo
(with Thomas D'Agostino)

Index

ABOUT THE AUTHORS

RICHARD S. HILLMAN is Professor and Chair, Department of Political Science at St. John Fisher College in New York. He was a Fulbright scholar at the Central University of Venezuela; a lecturer at the Foreign Service Institute, U.S. Department of State; and a Latin American teaching fellow of the Fletcher School, Tufts University, assigned to the Getulio Vargas Foundation, São Paulo.

THOMAS J. D'AGOSTINO is Assistant Professor of Political Science at Siena College in New York.